Stalking Sociologists

Stalking Sociologists

J. Edgar Hoover's FBI Surveillance of American Sociology

Mike Forrest Keen

With a new introduction by the author

Transaction Publishers
New Brunswick (U.S.A.) and London (U.K.)

Second printing 2005

This book is printed on acid-free paper that meets the American National Standard for Permanence of Paper for Printed Library Materials.

Library of Congress Catalog Number: 2003065011
ISBN: 0-7658-0563-4
Printed in the United States of America

Library of Congress Cataloging-in-Publication Data

Keen, Mike Forrest.
Stalking sociologists : J. Edgar Hoover's FBI surveillance of American sociology / Mike Forrest Keen.
p. cm.
Rev. ed. of: Stalking the sociological imagination. 1999.
Includes bibliographical references and index.
ISBN 0-7658-0563-4 (alk. paper)
1. Sociology—United States—History—20th century. 2. United States. Federal Bureau of Investigation. I. Keen, Mike Forrest. Stalking the sociological imagination. II. Title.

HM477.U6K44 2003
301'.073'0904—dc22 2003065011

For Gabrielle

Where suspicion fills the air and holds scholars in line for fear of their jobs, there can be no exercise of the free intellect. Supineness and dogmatism take the place of inquiry. A "party line"—as dangerous as the "party line" of the Communists—lays hold. It is the "party line" of the orthodox view, of the conventional thought, of the accepted approach. . . . A deadening dogma takes the place of free inquiry. Instruction tends to become sterile; pursuit of knowledge is discouraged; discussion often leaves off where it should begin.

—Justice William O. Douglas
Adler v. Board of Education of New York, 1952

Contents

Introduction to the Transaction Edition

"It seems like deja-vu, all over again."
—Yogi Berra

"Preserving our freedom is one of the main reasons that we are now engaged in this new war on terrorism. We will lose that war without firing a shot if we sacrifice the liberties of the American people."
—Senator Russell Feingold, *lone vote against USA PATRIOT Act*

"The movement from one project to the other, from a schema of exceptional discipline to one of a generalized surveillance, rests on a historical transformation: the gradual extension of the mechanisms of discipline throughout the seventeenth and eighteenth centuries, their spread throughout the whole social body, the formation of what might be called in general the disciplinary society."
—Michel Foucault, *Discipline and Punish*

As I write this new introduction for the Transaction edition, it is tempting to join in the widespread chorus, "Since 9/11, everything has changed." Certainly we have a newly heightened sense of vulnerability in the wake of the most devastating attack to have occurred on our soil since Pearl Harbor. We think twice about a trip to Washington, D.C., and worry about living in New York City. As millions of us watched the streaming video of the space shuttle Columbia break apart in the clear blue sky over Texas, almost immediately a thought that wouldn't have occurred to us prior to 9/11, crossed the American mindscape, "Was this another terrorist attack?" As we move from a yellow to an orange alert, and back again, the homeland security warning system is teaching us the color of terrorism. The most recent mantra from our homeland security officials seems hauntingly familiar: duct and cover. In the face of this national insecurity, polls show many Americans increasingly willing to sacrifice civil rights and constitutional protections of privacy for promises of safety and security.

Recognizing opportunity amidst these fears, the secrecy and surveillance hawks within and circling around the current administration are attempting to capitalize on our fears in order to dismantle the few reforms and protections that were placed on our intelligence agencies in the aftermath of Watergate and revelations of J. Edgar Hoover and the FBI's secret, widespread, and often illegal surveillance of hundreds of thousands of Americans. In the name of national security, a new cloak of secrecy is being laid over the inner workings of our most powerful and pervasive government agencies even as new laws, executive directives, and technological advances provide them with unprecedented capabilities for domestic intelligence and nationwide surveillance.

When I originally wrote this book, fears of nationwide surveillance, domestic intelligence and FBI abuse appeared to be more the historic grist and analytic concern for a burgeoning body of FBI and FOIA scholarship, than the very real and pressing, if not threatening, issues they have once again become today. But has *everything* changed? FBI domestic intelligence and surveillance have been an integral component of the Bureau's activities since its very inception. So too, have been fears about abuse of its powers and potential to serve as a national secret police force.[1] In attempting to allay such concerns upon creating the Bureau in 1908, then Attorney General Charles Bonaparte assured Congress that the first federally centralized nation-wide law enforcement agency would be limited to investigating and prosecuting violation of the nation's antitrust and interstate commerce laws, and would not be monitoring political dissent, members of Congress, or critics of the executive branch and its incumbent administrations.[2]

Nonetheless, beginning with the white slavery scare between 1910 and 1914, and continuing during World War I and through the Red Scare that followed it from 1919–1921, the Bureau was engaged in a number of controversial domestic intelligence activities. These included the infamous Palmer Raids, as well as the monitoring of a wide spectrum of radical and liberal activists and organizations.[3] Not only were so-called communists and their sympathizers monitored, but also labor organizers and the American Civil Liberties Union and its members. During its birth, the Bureau laid the foundations for its national security bureaucracy and began the development of a nationwide surveillance network and sophisticated records and indexing system for collecting and managing its massive collection of information, the institutional infrastructure and basis for its power and legitimacy.[4]

Between 1917 and 1921, the Bureau compiled more than 200,000 dossiers on American organizations and residents.[5] In 1924, at the behest of President Calvin Coolidge and in response to the resulting furor, Attorney General Harlan Fiske Stone replaced its discredited Director, William J. Burns. As its new director, he chose then Assistant Director J. Edgar Hoover, even though, since 1919, Hoover had been head of the Bureau's General Intelligence Division, and the driving force behind its wide-ranging hunt for subversives.[6] Prophetically warning that, "A secret police may become a menace to free government . . . because it carries with it the possibility of abuses of power which are not always quickly apprehended," Stone also restricted the Bureau from wiretapping and limited its investigations to the prosecution of federal law violators only.[7]

However, all the resulting criticism and controversy notwithstanding, the Red Scare "made" the Bureau, insuring its early power and prestige.[8] From 1916 to 1919, fears of internal subversion and the threat to national security led to a quadrupling of the Bureau's budget from $510,000 to $2,350,000. In addition it enlisted the help of the American Protection League to develop a national network of nearly a quarter million volunteers to help it sift through the thousands of reports of subversion and disloyalty it was receiving on a daily basis, as well as to scrutinize the several hundred thousand alien enemies required to register with the Department of Justice and to help supervise the registration of potential draftees.[9] Perhaps most significantly, the budgetary and personnel gains made on the basis of the claim of national security and the necessity to combat the subversive threat during the war and the Red Scare were never retrenched. Under Hoover's direction during the next fifty years, this became a regular pattern and recurrent strategy that the Bureau would continue to employ as it became "the most secretive, free wheeling federally funded organization in the American government."[10]

In accepting his initial appointment to the helm of the Bureau, a wily and politically savvy Hoover appeared to support Attorney General Stone's strictures, writing "I could conceive of nothing more despicable nor demoralizing than to have public funds of this country used for the purpose of shadowing people who are engaged in legitimate practices in accordance with the constitution of this country and in accordance with the laws of this country."[11] Yet, from the very beginning of his long tenure, Hoover directed his agents to continue its surveillance of political and personal activities. A consummate bureaucrat as well as a master of deceit, Hoover drew upon his earlier employment at the Library of Congress to develop a special records system for the Bureau's surreptitious and sometimes outright illegal activities. Intended to insure that they were not serialized or recorded in the Bureau's central records, it also made use of fine semantic distinctions between "collecting information" and "conducting investigations" to hide the extent of the Bureau's surveillance activities from discovery and to provide its officials with deniability.[12] In the pre-World War II years between 1936 and 1940, President Roosevelt willingly and covertly authorized the FBI to expand its domestic intelligence activities, not only to encompass suspected fascists and Communists and their sympathizers, but also eagerly encouraged Hoover and the Bureau to provide him with political intelligence about his domestic critics.[13] Taking this as a broad licence to encompass any person or organization deemed to be "subversive," targets even included the president's own wife, Eleanor Roosevelt, as well as prominent politician and eventual Democratic presidential nominee Adlai Stevenson.[14] Activities used to gather such intelligence included illegal break-ins, "black bag jobs," and buggings.[15]

Capitalizing on the expanded authority it had obtained from the Roosevelt administration, in the 1940s and 1950s, during World War II and the Cold War that followed, the FBI once again used fears of threats to national security and anti-Communist sentiments to continue to increase its resources and to further develop its domestic intelligence capabilities. From 1936 to 1952, FBI appropriations expanded 1800 percent, and the number of its personnel increased from 609 agents and 971 support staff, to 6,451 agents and 8,206 support staff.[16] Yet, during the same period, it was unable to significantly uncover Soviet espionage activities or develop evidence for the prosecution of Soviet agents and their American contacts.[17] However, in a repetition of its role, and employing practices and procedures originally developed during the Red Scare of 1919–1921, the Bureau did manage to use its Crime Records Division as an anti-Communist publicity machine, and harnessed its national network of local authorities, American Legion chapters, and Red Squads to serve as the bureaucratic heart of McCarthyism.[18] While McCarthyism was at its height from 1946 to 1956, its political and intelligence machinery, including that within the FBI, was in place from the 1930s, and its ramifications continued long after the November 1954 censure of its namesake, Senator Joe McCarthy.[19]

In 1956, when the Supreme Court limited the government's ability to investigate and prosecute alleged subversives under the Smith Act of 1940, Hoover argued that this ruling would undermine the FBI's ability to investigate Communist subversion. On March 8, 1956, he approached President Eisenhower and the National Security Council with a request for authority to use "Every means possible to secure information and evidence." A few days later, the Bureau launched its COINTELPRO operation, a secret domestic counterintelligence program.[20]

Intended not only to investigate, but also aimed at "disrupting and neutralizing" domestic political groups, the COINTELPRO program simply formalized much of what the Bureau already had been doing on an ad hoc basis since the red scares.[21] Beginning with the Communist Party of the USA, COINTELPRO operations were eventually expanded to include the Socialist Worker's Party, white supremacist groups including the KKK and the American Nazi Party, African American organizations such as the Black Panthers and individuals such as Martin Luther King, Jr. and Malcolm X, the New Left, and a broad amalgam of anti-Vietnam war groups and other organizations deemed to be potentially "subversive."

In March of 1971, the veil of secrecy which had shrouded the activities of Hoover and the FBI was sensationally lifted when a group who identified themselves as the Citizen's Commission to Investigate the FBI burglarized one of its field offices, stole hundreds of documents that dealt with the COINTELPRO program, and released them to selected members of the media and Congress.[22] Eventually, the resulting investigations by the media, Congressional hearings such as those held by the Church Committee, and additional disclosures made possible by the Freedom of Information Act further unveiled the Bureau's abuse of civil liberties and the extent of its domestic surveillance and counterintelligence operations.[23] Between 1955 and 1978, the Bureau had conducted 930,000 surveillance cases. Between 1940 to 1970 it had employed 37,000 informants, conducted 13,500 illegal buggings, and carried out 7,500 illegal break-ins. From 1956 to 1971 it had implemented 2,340 COINTELPRO operations.[24]

The Bureau's COINTELPRO operations were officially shut down in 1971, and by 1976, the FBI's intelligence establishment had undergone much reform, resulting in a dramatic reduction in domestic intelligence activities.[25] However, in the end, there was little serious legislative action and reform resulting from the revelations of the early 1970s investigations of the U.S. intelligence community.[26] And, even though Attorney General Edward Levi imposed a new set of guidelines for domestic security investigations in 1976, much of the FBI's organizational culture and its infrastructure of secrecy and surveillance remained in place.[27] As a result, there remained a kind of institutional schizophrenia within the Bureau. On the one hand, perhaps less distracted by massive domestic counterintelligence operations, it experienced many high profile successes in investigating both organized and white collar crime.[28] On the other hand, beginning as early as 1973, in a haunting repetition reminiscent of the McCarthy era and the COINTELPRO operations which had followed, several disturbing cases of domestic surveillance and counterintelligence continued to be carried out by the Bureau.

From 1973 until the late 1980s, the FBI conducted its Library Awareness Program, a secret counterintelligence surveillance program carried out within America's libraries.[29] Under the program, the Bureau attempted to recruit librarians as informants, and to gain access to the confidential records of patrons, particularly those of Soviet and Eastern European foreign nationals and or anyone else with foreign sounding names or accents. Investigations were extended to include those librarians who resisted and criticized the program. The program was eventually shut down to avoid increasing embarrassment in the face of vociferous protest from librarians across the country spearheaded by the American Library Association.[30]

In the early to mid–1980s, the main targets were opponents of the Reagan administration's Central American policy. Justifying surveillance activities by labeling participants as potential supporters of "terrorism," FBI operations began with the Committee In Solidarity with the People of El Salvador (CISPES). However, they were eventually expanded and intensified to include 1,330 organizations and 2,375 individuals, even after an internal FBI memo indicated that the individuals and groups in question were engaged only in the legal exercise of constitutional rights protected under the first and fourth amendments to the Constitution.[31] In the end, though it involved fifty-nine field offices and generated thousands of pages of files, not a single conviction for illegal activity resulted.[32]

In the late 1980s and early 1990s, individuals and organizations associated with the environmental movement began to report several incidents of surveillance and suspicious break-ins, leading some to fear that "we may be entering an era in which government, industry, and the media substitute the Green Menace for the Red Menace."[33] During the 1990s, the FBI also began to include individuals and organizations from the Arab and Muslims communities in their domestic intelligence efforts.[34]

Much of the Bureau's history and abuse have been seen through the lens of its Director. However, recent scholarship has begun to suggest that while Hoover may well represent a personal incarnation of the FBI, and was undoubtedly a major figure in its development, its domestic intelligence and surveillance activities, as well as abuses, can only be fully and adequately understood with a more structural and institutional analysis. They cannot be discounted as an aberration born of the personal ambitions and ideological excesses of "The Boss."[35]

With its initial publication in 1999, this book joined a growing body of FBI and Freedom of Information Act scholarship that was made possible by the lifting of the veil of secrecy that had surrounded the Bureau until the early 1970s. While some of the early and leading scholars in the field, such as Athan Theoharis and Ellen Schrecker, have focused more broadly on the Bureau and its Director, and/or McCarthyism and its impact on American society and its social institutions such as academia, my work joined that of another group of scholars who were more narrowly examining FBI surveillance of particular groups of people, for example, America's authors, artists, and actors, the African-American community, the Central American solidarity movement.[36] My intent was to reveal the details of the FBI's surveillance of some of America's most prominent sociologists and to offer some speculation as to what impact this may have had upon the history of the discipline. In addition, I wanted to turn sociology's gaze back upon Hoover and the FBI by drawing upon concepts and analyses from the very sociologists they had investigated, to examine and explain the excesses of the Bureau. Finally, I hoped that it would provide a provocative and lively introduction to American sociology, as well as encourage further interest in its history.

However, my goals at the beginning of this project were nowhere nearly so clearly formulated as the preceding statements might suggest. In fact, I only got involved in the project by accident, through a totally unanticipated convergence of earlier interests I had developed in the sociology of knowledge, and a passing barroom conversation through which the Freedom of Information Act and FBI files were brought to my attention as potential sources of data for social historical research. Given the serendipitous nature of research, and exacerbated by the difficulties associated with FOIA scholarship, it took me over ten years to complete the book.

The cases that I present in the book mostly fall into the period between the late 1930s and early 1960s. FBI surveillance of these sociologists began as early as when Roosevelt was covertly authorizing the expansion of the domestic intelligence activities of the FBI prior to World War II, reached its apex during the height of the McCarthy period from 1946–56, and continued during the beginnings of the COINTELPRO program and the early developments of the Vietnam anti-war movement. However, some sociologists were caught in the FBI's net of surveillance as early as the 1920's, and no doubt continued to be systematically surveilled through the shutting down of the COINTELPRO program in 1971. One of the reasons I have no record of any sociologists beyond the early 1960s is that one can only request a file after someone has died, and therefore the records of the generation of sociologists who may have been subject to FBI surveillance during the 1960s was not available. I would also not be surprised to learn that a few sociologists were snared during the Central America operations and similar surveillance activities conducted by the FBI during the 1980s and 1990s, but there is currently no evidence that the massive efforts and abuses of the 1940s, 1950s, and 1960s were continued. It remains to be seen what will have transpired during the first decade of the twenty-first century, though the cloak of secrecy and newly imposed restrictions on FOIA releases may make this increasingly difficulty to determine.

I was pleased, that upon its initial publication, the book was well-received and positively reviewed. While the widespread domestic intelligence activities of J. Edgar Hoover and the FBI have become common knowledge, most readers were surprised to learn of the extent to which sociologists were targets. My sociological colleagues were particularly flabbergasted by the revelation that Talcott Parsons had come under investigation on suspicions of being the leader of a Communist cell at Harvard.

Reviewers gave the book high marks on substance for its detailed and documented presentation of the FBI's investigations of each of the sociologists included, as well as its placement of the investigations within the individual's biographies and the general context of the history of American sociology. However, they also agreed that the major weakness of the book was its failure to adequately place the FBI's investigations within the broader social, political, and economic context of the eras in question, and that I did not adequately establish a link or clearly demonstrate that FBI surveillance had indeed had an influence on either the individual sociologists targeted or American sociology as a whole.[37] Commented David Price, who offers the most detailed critique of the book as well as my earlier work leading up to it,

> As a fellow FOIA researcher, I understand that this work is complex and tedious under the best circumstances, and the actions of obstinate governmental censors add further difficulty to an already daunting task. Keen's summaries of these FOIA documents are quite good, but this work does not live up to its full potential to the degree that Keen did not expand upon either the non-FOIA archival sources consulted or the breadth of his analysis and critique of the FBI's role during the Cold War.[38]

The criticisms of Price and the other reviewers are accurate. However, Price's intimation that "Keen's . . . overall approach to the FBI is seen in his friendly acknowledgment of the assistance of the FBI's former FOIA Chief, J. Kevin O'Brien, telling the reader that O'Brien and his staff were, 'quite polite and cordial,' all but ignoring the extent to which O'Brien and staff successfully strove to keep significant portions of this story unknowable" appears to have missed the counterveiling though perhaps understated irony that I intended to impart with the remainder of the sentence Price neglected to quote, "and [I] only wish that they had been a little less enthusiastic with their exclusions and deletions."[39]

The shortcomings identified by Price and the other reviewers were largely the result of the limits of my own intellectual horizons and capabilities as a scholar. And, as all authors fear, I became aware of one of my biggest oversights barely three months after the book was released. I had begun work on an article based on Paul Lazarsfeld's file, and started by acquiring a finding guide from the archives where his papers are stored at Columbia University. In glancing through it I noticed a reference to a study he and Wagner Thielens had published in 1958, on the impact of McCarthyism on social scientists, entitled *The Academic Mind: Social Scientists in a Time of Crisis.*

While I had caught Stouffer's study on *Communism, Conformity and Civil Liberties*, I had missed this one completely, and I shouldn't have. I quickly went back and checked Ellen Schrecker's book, *No Ivory Tower: McCarthyism and the Universities*, which I had used as a reference, and sure enough it was mentioned. In a footnote, Schrecker laments the fact that unfortunately the original data for the study had been lost.[40] However, I have discovered that this was not the case after all. While working with Lazerfeld's papers in the archives at Columbia University, I came across the original interviews, as well as a code book that identifies each interviewee by both name and number. And, in an unexpected personal twist, while reading through the code book, I discovered that my grandfather, also a sociologist, had been one of the interviewees.

In their study, Lazarsfeld and Thielens found that two-thirds of the approximately 2,500 social science faculty members surveyed had been visited by the FBI at least once, and one-third had been visited three or more times.[41] In response to the question, "If a student had told you about some political indiscretion in his youth, but now you were convinced of his loyalty, and if the FBI came to you to check on that student, would you report this incident to the FBI?" 46 percent said they would reluctantly give the information.[42] Interestingly, Lazarsfeld and Thielens did not ask a similar question about informing on a colleague.

Lazarsfeld's and Thielens' study represents the most comprehensive empirical study done on the impact of FBI surveillance and the

McCarthy era. Based on the analysis of their data, they concluded that "a number of social scientists, for instance, have withdrawn from participation in community activities, and some have confined themselves to a narrower sphere of teaching and research. *In these respects, then, the effective scope of higher education in America was threatened.*"[43] Had I discovered their work earlier, I may have been able to use it to offer some additional evidence of the influence on individual sociologists and American sociology not present in the FBI files and missing in my book.[44]

Another shortcoming that I think the book reflects is an under-representation of female sociologists. During the course of the project, I was chagrined and embarrassed to have only belatedly recognized that my first request for the files of twenty "prominent American sociologists" was almost entirely limited to "dead white males." As soon as I recognized this oversight, I made another set of much more inclusive requests. However, by the time they arrived, the book had already been published.[45]

All of these shortcomings notwithstanding, as I have reread the book, I remain satisfied with what I accomplished. I am particularly pleased with the chapter on Sutherland, and I think that my application of his theory of white-collar crime to the excesses of J. Edgar Hoover and the FBI offers a fruitful line for further exploration. Finally, I could not agree more with reviewer Michael Frank that "A balanced assessment of the FBI's impact on sociology will require further research."[46] One of my hopes in publishing this book was that it would entice and encourage other scholars, particularly future sociologists who may still only be students in training, to do just that.

This republication through Transactions, even though the book is not even five years old, requires a re-examination in light of recent events and the current environment into which it enters. However, to put into context the increased concerns with safety and security on the one hand, and threats to civil rights and privacy on the other, we must look back beyond 9/11 to the passage of the Antiterrorism and Effective Death Penalty Act of 1996. The bill, put forth by the Clinton administration on February 10, 1995, was an amalgam of long sought and long rejected provisions. It appeared headed for defeat in the face of strong opposition from civil liberties and privacy rights groups and strong public resistance to giving the government additional powers. Then, little more than a month later, on April 19, 1995, the Oklahoma City bombing occurred. After a series of one-sided hearings in both the House and the Senate, the bill was passed, and then signed into law by the President just five days after the first anniversary of the bombing.[47]

Among the most disturbing provisions, the bill resurrected the McCarthyist principle of "guilt by association" by criminalizing humanitarian support to any group designated by the secretary of state as "terrorist." Such a designation may be made for groups that engage in lawful or unlawful activity if the secretary of state determines the group's activities threaten our foreign policy or economic interests.[48] It also revived the Cold War policy of "ideological exclusion" of foreign visitors legalized under the McCarran-Walter Act of 1952, but that had been rescinded in the Immigration Act of 1990.[49]

Just six weeks after the shocking attack of 9/11, Congress hastily passed another national security bill with wide-ranging implications, the Uniting and Strengthening America by Providing Appropriate Tools Required to Intercept and Obstruct Terrorist Act, i.e. the USA PATRIOT Act. And, while several provisions of the Act were long-overdue, i.e., increased coordination between and among law enforcement and intelligence agencies, the Act also gave the executive branch "broad new powers that go far beyond the fight on terrorism, and that infringe on fundamental liberties."[50] The USA Patriot Act further blurs the distinction between terrorism and ideology and strips non-citizens of constitutional protections.[51] Perhaps more important from a privacy and political perspective, the Act grants the executive branch unprecedented and virtually unchecked surveillance powers, including sneak and peak searches, secret access to personal records held by third parties (i.e., credit, employment, medical, financial, library, Internet, etc.), and nationwide roving wiretaps.[52] In addition, in a new directive not unsimilar to those of FDR in the late 1930s, on May 30, 2002, Attorney General Ashcroft and FBI Director Robert Mueller announced a major shift in the Bureau's mission from fighting crime to preventing terrorism, along with a new set of guidelines that even further loosen the controls placed on its domestic surveillance activities in the 1970s.[53]

Following 9/11, at the same time that the executive branch has been enhancing its surveillance powers, the Bush administration, which exhibited an early disdain and distrust of transparency in government, also has been accelerating efforts to draw ever tighter the cloak of secrecy around itself, including a direct assault on the Freedom of Information Act. On October 12, 2001, reversing the previous Clinton administration policy weighted in favor of disclosure, Attorney General Ashcroft instructed all federal agencies to withhold any information requested under the Freedom of Information Act if there was any possible legal basis to do so.[54] These actions have already begun to have a noticeable effect as the backlog of FOIA requests has been growing, and thousands of pages of information are being taken off government websites and removed from public library repositories.[55] Such restrictions left unaddressed will make the scholarly efforts of the FOIA research community, such as those of this book, even more difficult, if not impossible.

Most recently, concern has been raised about a leaked secret draft for a new "PATRIOT Act II," entitled the Domestic Security Enhancement Act of 2003. Allowing for the first time in American history for secret arrests and the potential to strip Americans of their citizenship, the Act "will give the government broad, sweeping new powers to increase domestic intelligence-gathering, surveillance, and law enforcement prerogatives, and simultaneously decrease judicial review and public access to information."[56] Some observers are concerned that in an attempt to repeat the success of PATRIOT I, the Justice Department was keeping the Act under wraps and waiting in the wings until war with Iraq begins or there is another terrorist attack. Several individuals and organizations from both the left and the right of the political spectrum have been raising concerns about the impact of the recent legislation and directives on civil liberties and privacy. However, in a post 9/11 broadside reminiscent of the red-baiting of the past, Attorney General John Ashcroft has ominously admonished any critics, "those who scare peace-loving people with the phantoms of lost liberty . . . your tactics only aid terrorists, for they erode our national unity and diminish our resolve," and [t]hey give ammunition to America's enemies and pause to America's friends."[57]

The events since 9/11, as well as continued reflection and scholarship in other areas before and after, have led to a broadening of my thinking and the beginnings of a redress to the analytic shortcomings identified by my reviewers. I have come firmly to agree with those scholars who embrace a more institutional analysis that sees the excesses and abuses of the FBI, such as those documented in my book, as historically built into its very structure and mission, organizational culture, and political function. But, even beyond this, I also have begun to view it as an element of a more general trend in the development of what Michel Foucault has termed a "disciplinary society."[58]

Foucault argues that as result of the growing need to organize and control, as well as to increase the efficiency and harvest the productivity of the growing concentration of masses of people which emerged with the beginnings of the industrial revolution in Europe, a great historical transformation in the nature and exercise of power occurred during the seventeenth and eighteenth centuries.[59] "Antiquity had been a civilization of the spectacle. 'To render accessible to a multitude of men the inspection of a small number of objects,'" that is, the personage and the accouterments of power and authority as incarnate in the figure of the king (or queen), and his or her entourage. "The modern age poses the opposite problem: 'To procure for a small number, or even for a single individual, the instantaneous view of a great multitude.'"[60] This was accomplished through the development of a new type of power, disciplinary power.

According to Foucault, disciplinary power is a type of power manifest in and exercised through the "disciplines," a series of techniques for separating, analyzing, and differentiating human beings and their activities in order to more effectively train and control them. He further argues, "The 'invention' of this new political anatomy must not be seen as a sudden discovery. It is rather a multiplicity of often minor processes, of different origin and scattered location, which overlap, repeat, or imitate one another, support one another, . . . and gradually produce the blueprint of a general method."[61] The disciplines first emerged in the military, on the factory floor, in the schools, and on the hospital ward. Through processes of hierarchical observation, normalizing judgement, and examination, they allow for the operation not of a spectacular power incarnate in the figure of the king or queen, but rather a much more dispersed power exercised through a generalized surveillance.[62]

Foucault sees Bentham's *Panopticon* as the architectural embodiment and paradigm for the creation and exercise of disciplinary power.[63] Through it, "The crowd, a compact mass, a locus of multiple exchanges, individualities merging together, a collective effect, is abolished and replaced by a collection of separated individualities . . . Hence the major effect of the Panopticon: to induce in the inmate a state of conscious and permanent visibility that assures the automatic functioning of power.[64] It is this pervasive yet at any given moment unverifiable surveillance and the potential visibility it makes possible that makes for the lightness and efficiency of the control of the individual caught within a panoptic schema:

> He who is subjected to a field of visibility, and who knows it, assumes responsibility for the constraints of power; he makes them play spontaneously upon himself; he inscribes in himself the power relation in which he simultaneously plays both roles; he becomes the principle of his own subjection. By this very fact, the external power may throw off its physical weight; it tends to the non-corporal; and, the more it approaches this limit, the more constant, profound and permanent are its effects. ...[65]

It is the crux of Foucault's argument, as well as Bentham's dream, that the "panoptic schema, without disappearing as such or losing any of its properties, was destined to spread through the social body; its vocation was to become a generalized function."[66] Furthermore, Foucault argues, "it is not that the beautiful totality of the individual is amputated, repressed, altered by our social order, it is rather that the individual is carefully fabricated in it. . . . [67] In other words, as an alternative to the liberalist story of the emergence of the individual as the foundation of freedom and democracy, Foucault offers a countervailing complication that argues that through the development and dispersion of the disciplines, the modern individual is socially constructed, and then serves as a mechanism of the social control of human activity through the ever more pervasive gaze of a growing network, though today we might want to say "web" of generalized surveillance of the disciplinary society.

Finally, Foucault argues we cannot ignore the symbiosis between the development of the society of surveillance and that of the social sciences. At the same time this new form of power was emerging, so too was a new form of knowledge, "there is no power relation without the correlative constitution of a field of knowledge, nor any knowledge that does not presuppose and constitute at the same time power relations.[68] Sociology was one of the new types of knowledge constituted as part of the disciplinary constellation, made possible by the fact that the panoptic schema functions not only as a mechanism of power, but also as an observatory and a laboratory. "It makes it possible to draw up differences . . . to observe performances . . . , to map attitudes, to assess characters, to draw up rigorous classifications . . . .[69] Hoover and the FBI were not the only inspectors in the American panopticon engaged in massive surveillance of American society during the 1940s, 1950s, and 1960s. So too were America's sociologists. As I only intimated in the conclusion to my book, but feel even more strongly today, we cannot ignore the eerie parallel between the two.[70]

The completion of the disciplinary project identified by Foucault, is being made possible by what Jean-François Lyotard recognized as yet another historical transformation, the computerization of society.[71] At the conclusion to his seminal work on the "postmodern condition," Lyotard observes:

> We are finally in a position to understand how the computerization of society affects this problematic. It could become the "dream" instrument for controlling and regulating the market system, extended to include knowledge itself and governed exclusively by the use of terror. But it could also aid groups discussing metaprescriptives by supplying them with the information they usually lack for making knowledgeable decisions. The line to follow for computerization to take the second of these two paths is, in principle, quite simple: give the public free access to the memory and data banks.[72]

Today, the elements of an extensive web of surveillance, often discounted as the stuff of Big Brother paranoia or trivialized in popular sci-fi films, are already in place and watching.[73] Nannycams are popping up in households across the nation. A growing number of workplaces regularly electronically monitor their employees with devices such as spycams and keystroke counters. Credit ratings companies have collected personal information on nearly every resident in the United States. Medical information is being collected and stored by insurance companies and HMOs, and even bought and sold without informing the patients. Car rental agencies are putting GPS tracking devices in their automobiles. Supermarkets offer customers special club cards which promise discounts but then also allow the surveillance of buying habits. Cities across the nation and around the world are installing city-wide video surveillance networks, and beginning to employ "biometric" face recognition systems in tandem with them. Super Bowl XXXVII was also the surveillance bowl, as fifty high-powered cameras swept the stands and offered live feed access to law enforcement agencies across the country.[74]

As Lyotard observed, the digitalization and commercialization of information, and the miniaturization and mass production of computers make all of this possible.[75] Now everyone of us has a digital dossier, albeit spread across hundreds of data bases, just waiting to be read. And, this is exactly what the Defense Department was proposing to do with its controversial Total Information Awareness Project (TIAP). Being developed by the Defense Advanced Research Projects Agency (DARPA), the group that originally created the Internet, TIAP uses third-generation Internet technology that allows computers to communicate with one another directly. Once employed, it would enable the linking and "data mining"of such different digital repositories as video feeds from airport cameras, credit card transactions, telephone calling cards, airline reservations, and so on.[76]

The information age is at the same time the invasive age; the information highway a snooper byway operating at the speed of light and driving us ever further into the age of surveillance. Growing recognition of this observation is reflected in a virtual explosion of books on the subject during the past few years.[77]

In response to these developments, and also drawing upon Foucault, political scientist Reg Whitaker has posed the possibility of the end of privacy. Making a series of observations similar to those of Lyotard, particularly the miniaturization, increasing affordability, and resulting "democratization of computing," Whitaker argues a new Panoptican is emerging, one that is decentered:

> The new information technologies offer the potential for real, rather than faked omniscience, while at the same time displacing *The* Inspector with multiple inspectors who may act sometimes in concert and sometimes in competition with one another. . . . There is less need for a central command

centre, a single, focused Eye, when the same effect can be achieved by multiple, dispersed, even competitive eyes that in their totality add up to a system of surveillance more pervasive than that imagined by Orwell.[78]

The new Panopticon has also become consensual and participatory, "The strength of the new Panopticon is that people tend to participate in it voluntarily because they see positive benefits from participation, and are less likely to perceive disadvantages or threats."[79]

Perhaps the most sobering evidence of how far the surveillance society has progressed sits on the shelves of our nation's toy stores. Children's play is a form of childhood socialization and early preparation for the culture they are about to enter. In the toyshops these days are "Night Mission Specialist" Barbie, and her friend, "Surveillance Specialist" Kenzie.[80] Toys "R" Us is marketing seventeen different surveillance and spy toys to children between the ages of five and eleven. Its special line, Under Cover Girl, includes a secret listener device, disguised as a fake CD player, that can pick up conversations up to thirty feet away.

In the face of the seemingly unstoppable growing pervasiveness of surveillance in the invasive age, some observers are beginning to entertain a radical shift in tactics. Rather than continue what appears to be an increasingly futile fight to limit the growing invasions of our privacy and to put up new barriers for protecting it, perhaps we should make a paradigm-shift and take the battle to a new terrain, to tear them down. This is the idea David Brin wants to "throw into the caldron," in his argument for the creation of a transparent society to counteract the potential abuses of the surveillance society. "In other words, we may not be able to eliminate the intrusive glare shining on citizens of the next century, but the glare just might be rendered harmless through the application of more light aimed in the other direction."[81] In the words of Lyotard, "give the public free access to the memory and data banks." From this perspective, the problem is not surveillance per se (it might even be the key to the solution), but rather the cloak of secrecy that all too often is draped around it.

Foucault anticipates the possibility of such a strategy which uses the Panopticon to monitor itself, "The Panopticon may even provide an apparatus for supervising its own mechanisms. . . . and it will even be possible to observe the Director himself.[82] Imagine, if a symmetrical transparency would have been in place and allowed for a reciprocal visibility of Hoover and the FBI's surveillance activities, could the same abuses have continued? No doubt it was recognition of the threat of such visibility that caused Hoover and the FBI to go to such elaborate efforts to make sure the details of the bureaucratic apparatus and often illegal sources of their information were never disclosed, and instead to use the public face of McCarthyism by covertly feeding information to sympathetic senators, congressmen, and journalists, to make its information available. It was only after the activities of the Bureau were made transparent that its COINTELPRO program was ordered shut down.

I find myself increasingly in agreement with Brin and others who have begun to entertain this strategy, but also share his recognition that this is by no means an unproblematic solution.[83] It would imply a major shift in our definitions of the situation, patterns of social interaction, and cultural norms and values concerning freedom and privacy. Do we see harbingers of such a transformation in the emergence of inside out architecture such as that of the Pompidou Center in Paris, the popularity of transparent technology such as see through telephones, CD players, and PCs, and the growing fascination with letting it all hang out on personal webcams and reality T.V.?

I am not naive as to the ability of government officials, corporate managers, and wealthy individuals to use their power and positions to shield themselves from the gaze of a transparent society. Nor am I sanguine as to the ability to actually create a transparent society, that is, to put the "cleansing effect of sunshine" into practice in real social, political, and institutional terms. However, such a social and historical transformation might be begun in the same manner as that chronicled by Foucault, that led to the development and dispersion of the techniques of the disciplinary society in the first place, that is, through a "multiplicity of often minor processes, of different origin and scattered location, which overlap, repeat, or imitate one another, support one another, . . . and gradually produce the blueprint of a general method."[84]

While much further thought is needed, in my estimation, the work of Foucault and Lyotard, and those who have begun to build upon it, offers a powerful, though by no means complete or exclusive platform for examining the contemporary development of the society of surveillance. It can also help us to locate such elements as the FBI's domestic and political intelligence bureaucracy and its abuses, and the widespread surveillance of sociologists and any others that might have been characterized as subversive or associated with political dissent. In addition, it allows for recognition of the decentering of the panoptic function as it permeates the entire social body, as well as our own participation within it. Finally, it offers the possibility of resistance by embracing this decentering as a means for creating a reciprocal or symmetric transparency, that is, a transparent society in which the watchers are also being watched.

Over and over again our history has demonstrated that one cannot maintain national security and protect the very values which America celebrates by trampling on civil liberties and unleashing our intelligence agencies under a cloak of secrecy. In the short run this strategy has proved ineffective. In the long run it has proven to do more damage to ourselves than to our enemies. If the legacy of 9/11 is to once and for all exempt the FBI, Department of Justice, and other agencies of the executive branch and its intelligence agencies from the requirements of transparency, accountability, and oversight requisite for a democratic society, Osama Bin Laden will have succeeded in causing us to succumb to our fears and insecurities and undermined our most basic values and freedoms.

Prior to 9/11, books on the FBI and its domestic surveillance and counterintelligence programs tended to end with some kind of speculation as to whether or not it could happen again.[85] In its aftermath, and particularly with the passage of the USA PATRIOT Act just a few weeks afterwards, the threat of the Domestic Security Act of 2003 waiting in the wings, the cloak of secrecy that is being drawn ever more tightly around the government and the national security and intelligence bureaucracies, and at least an initial willingness among the public to exchange some civil liberties and constitutional protections for promises of safety and security, that question has become: Is it happening again? And, perhaps more importantly, given all of the post–9/11 secrecy, will we be able to tell?

In these lights, this book, as do the many other accounts of similar ilk, more clearly takes on the character of a cautionary tale. It reminds us of the dangers of unbridled secrecy. It warns us of the silly excess, abuse of power, waste of resources, and fundamental threat to democratic values and freedoms that seem almost inevitably to result from succumbing to our national insecurities. It encourages us to resist the recurrent siren's song of trading our civil liberties and constitutional protections for promises of the safety and security of a surveillance society.

NOTES

1. Athan Theoharis, "Dissent and the State: Unleashing the FBI, 1917–1985," *The History Teacher* 24 (1990): 42.
2. Athan Theoharis, ed., *From the Secret Files of J. Edgar Hoover* (Chicago: Ivan R. Dee, 1991), 1.
3. John A. Noakes, "A 'New Breed of Detective': The Rise of the FBI Special Agent," *Studies in Law, Politics, and Society* 14 (1994), 25–26. See also, Robert K. Murray, *Red Scare: A Study of National Hysteria, 1919–1920* (New York: McGraw-Hill, 1964).

4. Gerald K. Haines and David A. Langbart, *Unlocking the Files of the FBI: A Guide to Its Records and Classification System* (Wilmington, Del.: Scholarly Resources, 1993), xi. See also Regin Schmidt, *Red Scare: FBI and the Origins of Anticommunism in the United States, 1919–1943* (Copenhagen: Museum Tusculanum Press, 2000), 18–19.

5. Theoharis, *From the Secret Files of J. Edgar Hoover*, 1.

6. Murray, *Red Scare*, 193–94. Hoover's role was so pivotal that a recent reappraisal of the Red Scare and the FBI's role in it suggests that the Palmer Raids would be more appropriately and accurately labeled the Hoover Raids. See Stanley Coben, "Review Essay: J. Edgar Hoover," *Journal of Social History* 34 (2001): 704.

7. Quote by Theoharis, *From the Secret Files of J. Edgar Hoover*, 2. See also Schmidt, *Red Scare*, 324–25.

8. Murray, *Red Scare*, 193.

9. Noakes, "A 'New Breed of Detective,'" 37–38.

10. Jay Robert Nash, *Citizen Hoover: A Critical Study of the Life and Times of J. Edgar Hoover and His FBI* (Chicago: Welson Hall, 1972), 2.

11. Quoted by Schmidt, *Red Scare*, 325.

12. Theoharis, "Dissent and the State," 48. For a brief history and detailed guide to the Bureau's record and indexing system, see Haines and Langbart, *Unlocking the Files of the FBI.* Athan Theoharis, Tony G. Poveda, Susan Rosenfeld, and Richard Gid Powers, *The FBI: A Comprehensive Reference* (New York: Checkmark Books, 2000) also provide scholars with a detailed overview and guide to the FBI's records system, organizational structure, key personalities, and culture.

13. Charles F. Croog, "FBI Political Surveillance and the Isolationist-Interventionist Debate," *Historian* 54 (1992); and Charles M. Douglas, "Franklin D. Roosevelt, J. Edgar Hoover, and FBI Political Surveillance," *USA Today Magazine* 128: 74–77.

14. Theoharis, "Dissent and the State," 43–48.

15. Athan G. Theoharis and John Stuart Cox, *The Boss: J. Edgar Hoover and the Great American Inquisition* (New York: Bantam, 1990), 8–15.

16. Athan Theoharis, *Chasing Spies: How the FBI Failed in Counterintelligence but Promoted the Politics of McCarthyism in the Cold War Years* (Chicago: Ivan R. Dee, 2002), 11–12.

17. Ibid., 12.

18. Ellen W. Schrecker, *No Ivory Tower: McCarthyism and the Universities*, (New York: Oxford University Press, 1986), 203; and Schmidt, *Red Scare*, 367. For a detailed history and analysis of McCarthyism, its origins and impact on American society, as well as the role played by Hoover and the FBI, see also Ellen W. Schrecker, *Many are the Crimes: McCarthyism in America* (New York: Little, Brown and Company, 1998); and Richard M. Fried, *Nightmare in Red: The McCarthy Era in Perspective* (New York: Oxford University Press, 1990), along with his *McCarthyism: The Great American Red Scare* (New York: Oxford University Press, 1997).

19. Schrecker, *Many are the Crimes*, xvi–xvii.

20. James Kirkpatrick Davis, *Spying on America: The FBI's Domestic Counterintelligence Program*, (Westport, Conn.: Praeger, 1997), 4–8.

21. Tony G. Poveda, *Lawlessness and Reform: The FBI in Transition* (Pacific Grove, Cal.: Brooks/Cole, 1990), 2; and Schmidt, *Red Scare*, 367. For more on COINTELPRO see also Nelson Blackstock, *COINTELPRO: The FBI's Secret War on Political Freedom* (New York: Pathfinder, 1988).

22. Davis, *Spying on America*, 8–18.

23. Patricia M. Holt, *Secret Intelligence and Public Policy: A Dilemma of Democracy* (Washington, D.C.: Congressional Quarterly Press, 1995), 130. See also Kathryn S. Olmstead, *Challenging the Secret Government: The Post-Watergate Investigations of the CIA and FBI* (Chapel Hill: University of North Carolina, 1996).

24. Schmidt, *Red Scare*, 367.

25. Davis, *Spying on America*, 176.

26. Olmstead, *Challenging the Secret Government*, 3–6.

27. The guidelines were relaxed under Ronald Reagan's Attorney General William French Smith, and further modified at the behest of FBI Director Louis Freeh following the Oklahoma City bombing. Following these reinterpretations, the number of domestic security investigations rose from 100 in 1995, to more than 800 in 1997. Jack X Dempsey and David Cole, *Terrorism and the Constitution: Sacrificing Civil Liberties in the Name of National Security* (Washington, D.C.: First Amendment Foundation, 2002), 79–83. For additional information on internal guidelines regulating domestic security investigations, see Nancy Chang, *Silencing Political Dissent: How Post-September 11 Anti-Terrorism Measures Threaten Our Civil Liberties* (New York: Seven Stories Press, 2002), 32–37.

28. Athan Theoharis, *J. Edgar Hoover, Sex, and Crime: An Historical Antidote* (Chicago: Ivan R. Dee, 1995) argues that it was the Bureau's obsession with anti-Communist and anti-subversive activities that distracted it from successful pursuit and prosecution of organized and white-collar crime. See also Tony G. Poveda, "The FBI and Domestic Intelligence: Technocratic or Public Relations Triumph," *Crime and Delinquency* 28 April (1982): 205.

29. Herbert N. Foerstel, *Surveillance in the Stacks: The FBI's Library Awareness Program* (Westport, Conn.: Greenwood, 1991). For an extensive bibliography see John O. Christensen, *The FBI, Libraries, and the Library Awareness Program Controversy: Selected References* (Monticello: Vance Bibliographies, 1990).

30. America's librarians have been among our most courageous and outspoken leaders in the struggle to protect privacy and civil liberties. They have continued to lead the way since 9/11, recently passing a Resolution on the USA Patriot Act and Related Measures That Infringe on the Rights of Library Users (http://www.ala.org/alaorg/oif/usapatriotresolution.html).

31. The FBI's activities were part of a massive campaign of surveillance, disruption, and character assassination also involving the CIA, the State Department, and the National Security Council along with several

private conservative groups and foreign intelligence services. Ross Gelbspan, *Break-ins, Death Threats and the FBI: The Covert War Against the Central American Movement* (Boston: South End Press, 1991) offers one of the most revealing reports on the Central American operations, including a detailed insider's account obtained from Frank Varelli, an FBI "operational asset" assigned to infiltrate the Dallas chapter of CISPES.

32. Ibid., 228.

33. Chip Berlet, "Hunting the 'Green Menace,'" *The Humanist* July/ August (1991), 27.

34. Jack X. Dempsey and David Cole, *Terrorism & the Constitution: Sacrificing Civil Liberties in the Name of National Security* (Washington, D.C.: First Amendment Foundation, 2002), 44–48.

35. Schrecker, *Many are the Crimes*, 203. For an excellent survey of a selection of the recent and most important literature on the FBI, including analysis of Hoover-centric versus institutional analyses of domestic counterintelligence and political spying abuses, see Schmidt, *Red Scare*,10–17. For a prescient and early critical analysis of Hoover, see Irving Louis Horowitz, "Reactionary Immortality: The Private Life in Public Testimony of John Edgar Hoover," *Catalyst* 5 Summer (1970).

36. For a selected list of works in this area, see note 6 in chapter 1, the original introduction to this book. The recent publication by Fred Jerome, *The Einstein Files: J. Edgar Hoover's Secret War Against the World's Most Famous Scientist* (New York: St. Martin's Press, 2002), is one the most recent contribution to this area of FOIA scholarship and reflects the continued interest in its revelations and findings.

37. See Athan Theoharis, "Stalking the Sociological Imagination: J. Edgar Hoover's FBI Surveillance of American Sociology," *CHOICE* 37 October (1999): 1205; Richard Bilsker, "Stalking . . . " *Humanity and Society* 24 (2000): 318–19; Michael Frank, "Stalking . . . " *Science & Society* 65 Fall (2001): 409–411; David Cunningham, "Stalking . . . " *Contemporary Sociology* 30 September (2001): 525–26; David H. Price, "Spying on Radical Scholars," *Radical History Review* 79 Winter (2001): 169–72.

38. Price has been doing some excellent FOIA research on impact of the Cold War, including McCarthyism and FBI surveillance, on American anthropologists. See for example, "Anthropological Research and the Freedom of Information Act," *CAM: Cultural Anthropology Methods* 9 (1997): 12–15; and "Anthropologists as Spies," *The Nation* 271(16) 20 November (2000): 24–27. A more complete listing of Price's work can be found at http://homepages.stmartin.edu/fac_staff/dprice/CW-PUB.htm

39. Price, "Spying on Scholars," 170; Keen, *Stalking the Sociological Imagination*, x.

40. Schrecker, *No Ivory Tower*, 416, n.4.

41. Paul F. Lazarsfeld and Wagner Thielens, Jr., *The Academic Mind: Social Scientists in a Time of Crisis* (Glencoe, Ill.: The Free Press, 1958), 401.

42. Ibid., 208–209.

43. Ibid., 264.

44. Presumably, someone with the interest and quantitative skills could recode and reanalyze Lazarsfeld and Thielens' data. An even more provocative possibility would be to connect the interviewee responses to their authors and use them to examine individually identifiable sociologists. However, before carrying out such a project, one would have to be able to satisfactorily resolve the ethical questions involved in revealing the sources of responses given under a guarantee of confidentiality. What kind of ethical strictures regulate such historical archival research? What status do guarantees of confidentiality have once respondents are no longer living? Is there a statute of limitations? In an ironic parallel, these issues reflect the same limitations and challenges posed by the FBI's rather liberal evocation of privacy rights to justify the deletion and/or refusal to release FOIA information.

45. I would like to acknowledge the pioneering work of Mary Jo Deegan and Michael Hill for sensitizing me to the importance of including our founding mothers as well as fathers in our efforts to investigate the history of our discipline.

46. Frank, "Stalking . . . ," 411.

47. Dempsey and Cole, *Terrorism and the Constitution*, 107–115.

48. Ibid., 118–23.

49. Ibid., 123–24.

50. Ibid., 148.

51. Chang, *Silencing Political Dissent*, 44–46; 62–66. For an additional detailed and careful analysis of the Act's impact on civil liberties and constitutional protections, see The Rutherford Institute, *Forfeiting "Enduring Freedom" for "Homeland Security": A Constitutional Analysis of the USA PATRIOT Act of 2001 and the Justice Department's Anti-Terrorism Initiatives* (Charlottesville, Va.: Rutherford Institute, 2003).

52. Chang, *Silencing Political Dissent*, 43–62.

53. American Civil Liberties Union, "Urge Congress to Protect Against Domestic Spying," October 3 (2002):http:www.aclu.org?Natonal Security/NatonalSecurity.cfm?ID=9950&c=110; and Michael Tackett, "Ashcroft's Directive on Domestic Spying Not Unlike FDR's," *Chicago Tribune* 2 June (2002).

54. Steven Aftergood, "Making Sense of Government Information Restrictions," *Issues in Science & Technology* 18 Summer (2002): 25–26; Jeffrey Benner, "Closing the Books," *Reason* 34 (2002): 33–35; and Martin E. Halstuk, "In Review: The Threat to Freedom of Information," *Columbia Journalism Review* 40 Jan/Feb (2002): 8.

55. Adam Clymer, "Government Openness at Issue as Bush Holds on to Records," *New York Times* 3 January (2003): A1, A16. For a more extensive report, see also Mary Graham, *Democracy by Disclosure: The Rise of Technopopulism*. (Washington, D.C.: Brookings Institution, 2002).

56. Charles Lewis and Adam Mayle, "Justice Dept. Drafts Sweeping Expansion of Anti-Terrorism Act," *Center for Public Integrity* 2002: http://www.publicintegrity.org/dtaweb/report.asp?ReportID=502&L1=10&L2=10&L3=0&L4=0&L5=0.

57. Quoted by Chang, *Silencing Political Dissent*, 94.

58. I have found some initial and suggestive support for this observation in Noakes argument, drawing upon Giddens' work on the nation-state

and violence, that "the early years of the Bureau were a critical period in the "internal pacification"of the American nation-state, during which legal and administrative means replaced direct coercion as the primary means of social control. See Noakes, "A "New Breed of Detective,"26, and "Using FBI Files for Historical Sociology," *Qualitative Sociology* 18 (1995): 284. Also Anthony A. Giddens, *The Nation-State and Violence* (Berkeley: University of California, 1987). It would also seem to resonate with Schmidt's, *Red Scare*, 18–20, argument that the creation of the FBI was part and parcel of the centralization of authority in the federal government during the Progressive Era.

59. Foucault, *Discipline and Punish* (New York: Vintage, 1995), 206–207.

60. Ibid., 216.

61. Ibid., 138.

62. Ibid., 170–71.

63. Ibid., 200.

64. Ibid., 201.

65. Ibid., 202–203.

66. Ibid., 207.

67. Ibid., 217.

68. Ibid., 27.

69. Ibid., 203.

70. Ironically, one might argue that this very observation itself reflects the postmodern penchant for reflexivity, which we might just as well read as self-surveillance, that is fostered by the contemporary social formation of the disciplinary society. This analysis might be further extended to help to explain the contemporary popularity of the so-called "reality-TV" shows and their earlier predecessors, the tell-all talk shows.

71. Jean-François Lyotard, *The Postmodern Condition: A Report on Knowledge* (Minneapolis: University of Minnesota, 1984), 67.

72. Ibid., 67.

73. See Jay Stanley and Barry Steinhardt, *Bigger Monster, Weaker Chains: the Growth of an American Surveillance Society* (New York: American Civil Liberties Union, 2003).

74. Patrick O'Driscoll, "Big-time Security to Accompany Big Game," *USA Today* 21 January (2003): 9C. For an up-to-date survey of surveillance technologies currently in place see David Brin, *The Transparent Society: Will Technology Force Us to Choose Between Privacy and Freedom?* (Reading: Perseus Books, 1998), 54–68; and Reg Whitaker, *The End of Privacy: How Total Surveillance is Becoming a Reality* (New York: The Free Press, 1999), 80–119.

75. Lyotard, *The Postmodern Condition*, 3–4.

76. John Markoff and John Swartz, "Many Tools of Big Brother Are Now Up and Running," *New York Times* 23 December (2002): C1, C4. On January 23, 2003, the Senate voted that the system could not be used in the U.S. until specifically authorized by the Congress.

77. Fred H. Cate, *Privacy in the Information Age* (Washington, D.C.:

The Brookings Institute, 1997); Bruce Schneier and David Banisar, eds., *The Electronic Privacy Papers: Documents on the Battle for Privacy in the Age of Surveillance* (New York: John Wiley & Sons, 1997); Jeffrey Rosen, *The Unwanted Gaze: The Destruction of Privacy in America* (New York: Vintage, 2001); Richard Hunter, 2002. *World Without Secrets: Business, Crime and Privacy in the Age of Ubiquitous Computing* (New York: John Wiley & Sons, 2002); Douglas Thomas and Brian Loader, eds., *Cybercrime: Law Enforcement, Security and Surveillance in the Information Age* (New York: Routledge, 2002). Earlier pioneering works in this area which anticipated many of the pressing concerns of today are Frank J. Donner, *The Age of Surveillance: The Aims and Methods of America's Political Intelligence System* (New York: Knopf, 1980); and Gary T. Marx, *Undercover Police Surveillance in America* (Berkeley: University of California, 1990).

78. Reg Whitaker, *The End of Privacy: How Total Surveillance is Becoming a Reality* (New York: The Free Press, 1999), 140–41.

79. Ibid., 141.

80. Laureen Fagan, "Toying With Spying," *South Bend Tribune* 21 January (2003): C1–2.

81. Brin, *The Transparent Society*, 23. Amitai Etzioni, *The Limits of Privacy* (New York: Basic Books, 1999) does not take the same tack a Brin, but does present a thought-provoking communitarian argument for recognizing the need for balance between privacy and the common good.

82. Foucault, *Discipline and Punish*, 204.

83. Mary Graham, *Democracy by Disclosure*, puts forth a similar argument. Perhaps one of the earliest advocates of the transparency strategy was Louis Dembitz Brandeis, *Other People's Money: And How the Bankers Use It*, (New York: F.A. Stokes Co., 1932), who argued that business should reveal basic financial information in order to reduce the risk to the public.

84. Foucault, *Discipline and Punish*, 138. There are already several examples of how to harness the communications powers of the information highway to increase the transparency of government surveillance activities on the world wide web. See http://www.aclu.org/NationalSecurity/NationalSecurityList.cfm?c=110

http://www.icdc.com/~paulwolf/cointelpro/cointel.htm http://caselaw.lp. findlaw.com/data/constitution/amendment04/

http://www.ombwatch.org/article/articleview/1307/1/160/

http://www.rutherford.org/about/

http://www.ala.org/alaorg/oif/

http://sfgate.com/news/special/pages/2002/campusfiles/

http://www.freedomforum.org/first/

85. Schrecker, *Many are the Crimes*, 415.

Acknowledgments

The books we write often begin in unlikely places. This one can be traced to an afternoon conversation which took place in a pub just off of Harvard Square during the summer of 1988. It was one of the hottest summers on record and the Widener Library had to close its doors for the first time in its history when brownouts and outages began threatening the city's power grid. Several colleagues and I, all whom were participating in Everett Mendelsohn's NEH Summer Seminar on the Social History of Modern Science, took refuge in the pub's cool, dark confines. We ordered a couple of pitchers of beer and began to talk about our work. As the conversation became increasingly voluble, quickly ranging from one topic to another, one member of the group, Rick Patterson, informed us that Albert Einstein had an FBI file which he had acquired through the Freedom of Information Act. I somewhat hazily remember being quite intrigued, and thinking at the time, what a great source of data.

Several people have provided me with invaluable assistance or information during the course of this project. Nan Evangea and Deb Rapuano, two of my students, served as research assistants. Kathi Piekarski, the departmental secretary, provided invaluable last-minute assistance in helping to complete the manuscript. Anthony Platt kindly informed me that he had donated his copy of E. Franklin Frazier's FBI files to the Moorland Spingarn Research Center at Howard University. With the friendly help of JoEllen El Bashir, Curator of Manuscripts at Howard, and her staff, I was able to obtain them without the normal one- to three-or-more-year wait it often takes to get a file through a Freedom of Information Act request.

I would like to acknowledge J. Kevin O'Brien, the FBI's Chief of the Freedom of Information–Privacy Acts Section, and the many members of his staff who have processed my numerous requests over the years. It is not many scholars who can claim the FBI among their research assistants. I found them to be quite polite and cordial, and only wish they had been a little less enthusiastic with their withholdings and deletions. In addition, I would like to thank the librarians at the Indiana University South Bend (IUSB) Shurz Library. While the work of our librarians is often taken for granted and goes unacknowledged, without them our work would not be possible. In addition, librarians more than any other profession have been at the forefront of the struggle to maintain freedom of information in the United States.

An Indiana University South Bend Research and Development grant helped to cover the copy charges for the several thousand pages of documents released to me by the FBI, and an IUSB Summer Faculty Fellowship supported the final completion of the manuscript. While I was on sabbatical, an Indiana University Intercampus Scholars Grant enabled me to spend time at the Institute for Advanced Study and to carry out important background research. I would like to thank Jim Patterson and Ivona Hedin for making my work there both enjoyable and profitable.

Finally, I would like to acknowledge my greatest debt and gratitude to Gabrielle Robinson. She knew I would write this book before I did. Throughout the entire process she has been a perceptive critic, a supportive sounding board, and a sharp-eyed editor. I feel privileged to share with her an intimate and intellectual partnership that has made this work and all that I do a joy.

— 1 —

Introduction

On April 1, 1952, J. Edgar Hoover received a personal letter with a newspaper clipping entitled, "Columbia Fights Reds on Faculty." In the letter, the author indicated, "I can also tell you of an inside professor at Harvard who feeds out these different indoctrinated Professors to different outside Universities."[1] Apparently impressed with the letter, Hoover responded a week later that he would dispatch an agent to interview its author. He then sent a copy of the letter to SAC (Special Agent in Charge), New York, noting, "In view of the position of the correspondent and since the identity of the subject of his information is not divulged, it is suggested an agent experienced in security matters receive this assignment."[2] During the interview, the informant claimed "Professor TALCOTT PARSONS, head of the Social Relations Department at Harvard was probably the leader of an inner group of these teachers who were in this field. . . . Anyone not a member of this group would have difficulty in getting teaching assignments on the faculties of other universities and colleges" (see Figure 1.1).[3]

Such was the beginning of a three-year investigation, carried out across the United States and in seven countries overseas, of accusations that Parsons was the hidden leader of a Communist cell at Harvard. For

Portions of this chapter are reprinted by permission of Transaction Publishers. "The Freedom of Information Act and Sociological Research" by Mike F. Keen, from *The American Sociologist* 23 (Summer, 1992), 43–51.

Figure 1.1

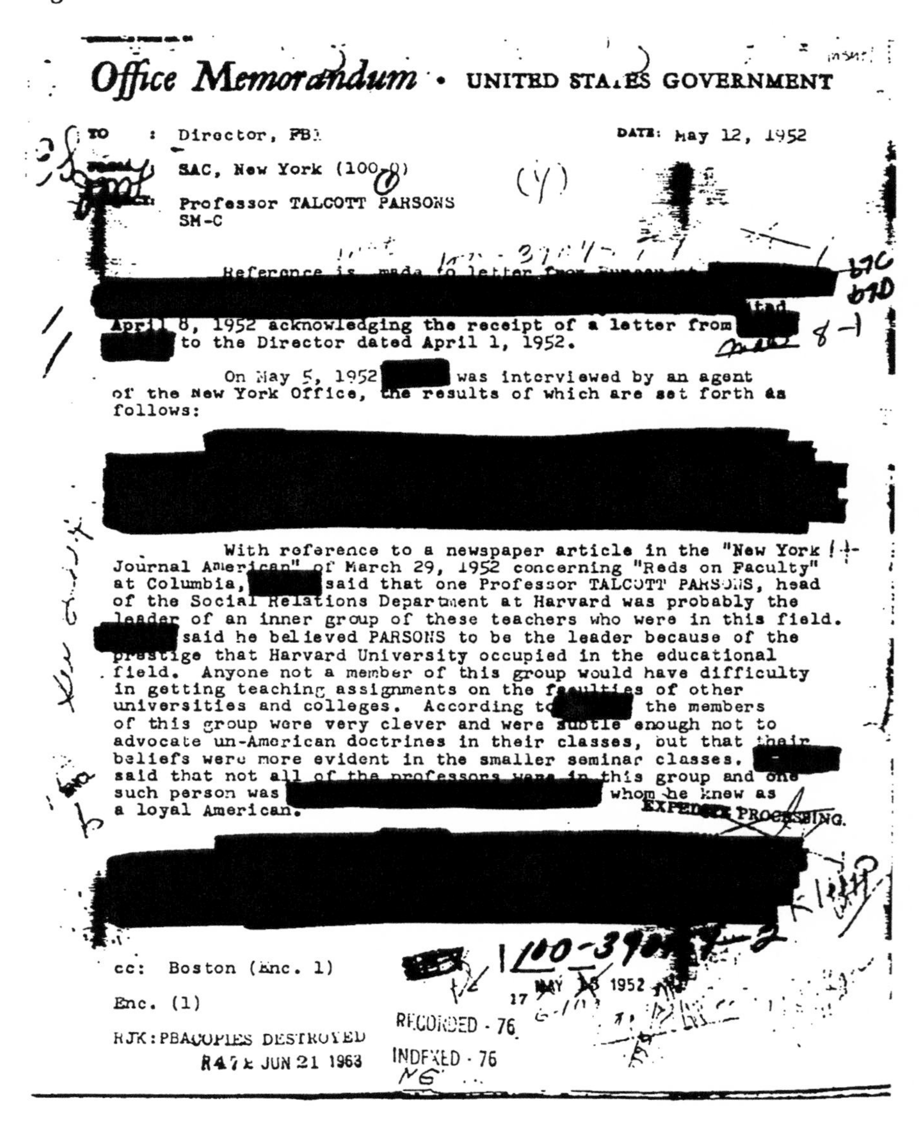
Office Memorandum • UNITED STATES GOVERNMENT

TO : Director, FBI DATE: May 12, 1952

FROM : SAC, New York (100-0)

SUBJECT: Professor TALCOTT PARSONS
SM-C

Reference is made to letter from Bureau [redacted] dated April 8, 1952 acknowledging the receipt of a letter from [redacted] to the Director dated April 1, 1952.

On May 5, 1952 [redacted] was interviewed by an agent of the New York Office, the results of which are set forth as follows:

[redacted]

With reference to a newspaper article in the "New York Journal American" of March 29, 1952 concerning "Reds on Faculty" at Columbia, [redacted] said that one Professor TALCOTT PARSONS, head of the Social Relations Department at Harvard was probably the leader of an inner group of these teachers who were in this field. [redacted] said he believed PARSONS to be the leader because of the prestige that Harvard University occupied in the educational field. Anyone not a member of this group would have difficulty in getting teaching assignments on the faculties of other universities and colleges. According to [redacted] the members of this group were very clever and were subtle enough not to advocate un-American doctrines in their classes, but that their beliefs were more evident in the smaller seminar classes. [redacted] said that not all of the professors were in this group and one such person was [redacted] whom he knew as a loyal American.

EXPEDITE PROCESSING.

[redacted]

cc: Boston (Enc. 1)

Enc. (1)

RJK:PBA COPIES DESTROYED
R47 JUN 21 1963

100-3904-2
17 MAY 1952
RECORDED - 76
INDEXED - 76

anyone familiar with Parsons's reputation and work, even to entertain the notion that he was the leader of a Communist cell is unimaginable. However, information obtained through the Freedom of Information Act (FOIA) reveals that he was just one of many of America's most prominent sociologists subject to surveillance by the FBI.

Throughout its history, the FBI has generally enjoyed an exalted reputation in the public consciousness as America's premier and most effective crime-fighting organization. Recent revelations and scholarship, however, suggest that much of this reputation was the result of a popular mythology carefully crafted and orchestrated by long-time director, J. Edgar Hoover.[4] Reconsideration beyond the mythology began in March 1971, when a self-appointed and covert citizen's commission to investigate the FBI burglarized its Media, Pennsylvania office, stole thousands of documents, and slowly released them to selected members of Congress and the press. The documents revealed the existence of the FBI's COINTELPRO (counterintelligence program), a massive domestic counterintelligence campaign begun in 1956, instituted not only to spy on thousands of Americans, but also to undermine and disrupt their political activities, activities legally protected under the Bill of Rights.[5]

The COINTELPRO papers primarily document the FBI's efforts against the Communist Party (CP), Socialist Workers Party, Puerto Rican Independence Movement, Black Liberation Movement (Panthers), the New Left, and the American Indian Movement. Investigations following on the heels of COINTELPRO, carried out through the legal procedures provided by the FOIA, show that the FBI's efforts extended far beyond these groups to encompass black America and its most prominent leaders (Martin Luther King Jr. and Malcolm X), America's most well-known authors, many churches and church leaders, academics, and virtually any others who might be construed as liberal, "un-American," or critical of the FBI.[6]

It is not surprising that sociologists were among the thousands investigated. Most sociologists in the United States have been vaguely aware that sociology, along with the rest of the academy, was not exempt from such surveillance. However, the scope and detail of these activities regarding the discipline and its practitioners have remained largely unknown. Using information obtained through the Freedom of Information Act, this book presents details of the FBI's investigations and attempts to place them within the general context of the history of American sociology as well as the more particular personal and intellectual biography of each sociologist in question. It will also investigate the impact the FBI's activities had on the discipline and its analysis of American society. None of this would have been possible, however, without a fundamental change in federal information policy which lead to the passage of the Freedom of Information Act.

Since its passage in 1966, the FOIA has been used by tens of thousands of citizens to obtain information from the government. It has also been at the center of controversy concerning U.S. government information policy, secrecy, and national security.[7] Not surprisingly, representatives of the news media comprise one of the largest group of users. In fact, the press's constitutionally sanctioned role as the eyes and ears of the people and safeguard of democracy would likely be impossible without it.[8] However, while scholars rely heavily on information provided by the government, they have made only limited use of the FOIA. The social scientific community relies primarily on current publications and is interested almost exclusively in statistical data such as economic indicators and census reports.[9] Historians appear to be the largest group of FOIA users, while sociologists seem to have virtually ignored it.

Several barriers might help to explain this lack of use by sociologists. The process of obtaining information is a tedious one and most sociologists lack familiarity with the governmental and information environment which must be traversed. To do so requires significant costs in time and sometimes money. In addition, no effective screening processes exist to eliminate duplication or unnecessary information, making the task unwieldy, imprecise, and uncertain.[10] Several hundred pages of information released may yield only one or two useful documents, if that.

Perhaps the biggest reason for lack of use is simply absence of an awareness of the act and the potential it offers for sociological research. While the mechanics of making an FOIA request are fairly straightforward, the uses for data obtained from such a request may not be as easily identified.[11] However, since the rise of the administrative state following the turn of the century, the government has become such a major and important institution that virtually no aspect of society has been left untouched by it. As a result, agency records available under the FOIA offer a broad range of data bearing on such diverse areas as public health, the environment, civil rights, business, labor, taxes, crime and law enforcement, education, consumer rights, communications, foreign policy, national defence, and the economy.[12] While it is unlikely that information obtained through an FOIA request will provide all the data needed for research, it may offer undiscovered details and unique insights otherwise unavailable. Given the breadth of information available, it could be employed as a source of data in virtually any area of sociology.

Using the FOIA, I have been able to obtain thousands of pages of documents which chronicle the FBI's extensive investigations of many of America's most prominent sociologists. In the process, I have experienced many pitfalls and obstacles. I submitted my first request, for information on the American Sociological Association (ASA), in November of 1988. In accordance with the law, I received a response within ten days. Unfortunately, as is generally the case with the larger and more visible agencies, I was given no direct information concerning my request, but only assigned a waiting number, 307,921. Six months later, I received notification that the FBI had located 305 pages of information concerning the ASA. Of the 305 pages identified, the FBI released 275. The thirty pages that were withheld were done so on the basis of exemptions in the interest of national security, for information related to internal personnel rules and practices of an agency, for unwarranted invasions of privacy, and for information that could reasonably be expected to disclose the identity of a confidential source.[13]

Many of the documents released were only partially complete, with significant portions being blacked out. This included virtually all the names and addresses of those providing the information, many of whom were clearly members of the ASA themselves. From a social-historical standpoint this is a serious problem, as individuals are the agents of intellectual history, and being able to locate them within their particular institutional constellation is crucial to determining the impact of social-historical factors on the conceptual development of a discipline. In addition, information received through the FOIA cannot always be treated at face value, particularly in the case of the FBI. Amitai Etzioni noted upon reviewing his own file several inaccuracies and misrepresentations that had been passed on to other agencies and resulted in his exclusion from a number of review panels at the Department of Health, Education, and Welfare (HEW).[14] Such qualifications notwithstanding, these documents remain a valuable source of information.

Records released under the FOIA reveal a history of FBI investigation directed at ASA activities. For example, in 1965, the sixtieth Annual Meeting of the ASA held in Chicago was the target of FBI interest. An article appearing in the *New York Times* indicated that T. B. Bottomore and Lewis Coser had addressed the opening general session of the meeting and discussed the work of Karl Marx. In a memo to Hoover, identified as a "section tickler," the Special Agent in Charge of the Chicago office noted that according to the *Times*, Bottomore and Coser had "stated that Marx's historical and political prophecies may have been untidy and exaggerated, but his theories of social conflicts and change have a contemporary relevance that deserves more attention."[15] The agent recommended that "Chicago should submit to the Bureau any reports on this convention which appeared in Chicago newspapers." In addition, Chicago was requested to contact established sources and discreetly obtain details of the discussion of Marxism at the convention. At the bottom of the memo was a final note: "It is felt that we should make an effort to obtain details of any effort to make Marxism respectable."[16]

Agents searched through local newspaper morgues and identified seventeen articles, including several with such provocative titles as "Totalitarianism Up Here, Down in USSR, Says Sociologist," and "Sociology Riot Tip: Read Marx." In response to a transcription of an article concerning a study presented at the meeting in which Stanley Lieberson and Arnold Silverman discounted traditional theories on why race rioting occurs and suggested that proper police training can prevent riots from developing, Hoover scribbled across the bottom of the page, "The sociologists at it again" (see Figure 1.2).[17]

In 1969, the FBI continued to be haunted by the specter of radical sociology, manifest this time at the annual meetings of the ASA being held in San Francisco, where the Western Union of Radical Sociologists and the Radical Caucus of the ASA sponsored a counterconvention. Using "confidential sources," FBI agents obtained a copy of the counter-convention call issued by *The Insurgent Sociologist.* Many of the names of counterconvention organizers and presenters listed in the program have been underlined. Investigations were conducted into several of the individuals and organizations listed in the call. Again, local newspapers were searched for articles pertaining to both the ASA meetings and the counterconvention. Summaries of all these activities were forwarded to FBI headquarters and to branch offices throughout the nation where the mentioned "subversive individuals" who had participated in the meetings lived.[18]

Were the activities of the of FBI limited to these few instances associated with the ASA, we might discount them as a silly excess. However, these examples represent just the tip of an iceberg of suspicion and surveillance directed at American sociology and sociologists. After receiving this initial packet of information, I submitted another set of FOIA requests, this time on twenty major American sociologists. In response to these requests, I was informed that another approximately 2,700 pages existed regarding Jane Addams, Herbert Blumer, Ernest Burgess, Erving Goffman, George Lundberg, Helen and Robert Lynd, C. Wright Mills, William Ogburn, Talcott Parsons, Pitirim Sorokin, Samuel Stouffer, Thorstein Veblen and Florian Znaniecki. Since then, I have made additional requests for files on W.E.B. Du Bois, E. Franklin Frazier, Paul Lazarsfeld, Alfred McClung Lee, Gunnar Myrdal, and Edwin Sutherland, as well as members of the Frankfurt School and several women, including Hanna Arendt, Frances Kellor, Florence Kelly, and Elsie Clews Parsons.

The picture which has emerged is a startling one. It would seem that throughout the history of American sociology, many of its prominent contributors have been under the surveillance of the FBI for suspected "radical" or otherwise "un-American" activities, such as disturbing accepted ideas or being critical of the policies of the Bu-

Figure 1.2

0-20 (Rev. 12-14-64)

Tolson
Belmont
Mohr
DeLoach
Casper
Callahan
Conrad
Felt
Gale
Rosen
Sullivan
Tavel
Trotter
Tele Room
Holmes
Gandy

UPI-44

(RIOTS)

CHICAGO--TWO SOCIAL SCIENTISTS, REPORTING ON A STUDY OF RACE RIOTS THAT SPANNED 50 YEARS, TODAY DISCOUNTED SOME TRADITIONAL THEORIES ON WHY SUCH RIOTING OCCURS AND SAID PROPER POLICE TRAINING CAN PREVENT RIOTS FROM DEVELOPING.

STANLEY LIEBERSON AND ARNOLD R. SILVERMAN OF THE UNIVERSITY OF WISCONSIN SOCIOLOGY DEPARTMENT PREPARED EXCERPTS OF THEIR STUDY FOR PRESENTATION TO THE 60TH ANNUAL MEETING OF THE AMERICAN SOCIOLOGICAL ASSOCIATION.

THE STUDY OF AMERICAN RACE RIOTS BETWEEN NEGROES AND WHITES FROM 1913 TO 1963 DISCOUNTED SUCH TRADITIONAL CAUSES AS HIGH NEGRO UNEMPLOYMENT, INADEQUATE NEGRO HOUSING AND THE INFLUENCE OF AGITATORS.

INSTEAD, THE STUDY INDICATES THE PRIME UNDERLYING CONDITIONS OF RACIAL RIOTING ARE THE ECONOMIC THREAT OF NEGROES TO WHITES AND THE POLICIES OF LOCAL GOVERNMENT AUTHORITIES, ESPECIALLY THE POLICE.

IN THEIR SURVEY OF 72 SEPARATE RACE RIOTS, LIEBERSON AND SILVERMAN FOUND THAT RIOTS WERE PRECIPITATED BY PROVOCATIVE CONTACTS BETWEEN MEMBERS OF THE TWO RACES, SPECIFICALLY CRIMES AGAINST PERSONS AND OFFENSES COMMITTED BY WHITE POLICE OFFICERS AGAINST NEGROES.

8/31--GE1121A

The sociologists at it again!

REC- 60 94-1-14

EX 105

16 SEP 14 1965

94-1-14852

70 SEP 1 1965

WASHINGTON CAPITAL NEWS SERVICE

reau and its director. Thousands of man hours and millions of dollars have been dedicated to this project. Faculty members of various departments of sociology, no doubt including members of the ASA, were recruited to inform on the activities of their colleagues. Unfortunately, since names of informants are deleted in accordance with the Privacy Act, it is difficult to trace who was involved. Nonetheless, there is little doubt that important social historical insight lies hidden within these documents. It should not be ignored. At stake is the collective memory of our society as well as an accurate history of our discipline.

NOTES

1. Federal Bureau of Investigation, *Talcott Parsons*, Bufile 100-390459-1 (Washington, D.C.: FBI Freedom of Information–Privacy Acts Section). The citation format used for all the documents obtained from the FBI through the Freedom of Information Act is based on the FBI's own classification system. Each file is identified through its office location and number. The designation Bureau refers to the FBI's central office in Washington, D.C. The separate documents within each file are further divided into batches and numbered accordingly. No page numbers are included because no consistent or chronological pagination exists within the files. If no batch number is cited, this is because one was not assigned by the FBI. The first set of numbers constitute a numerical prefix assigned according to the type of investigation. For example, 62 reflects a "Request for Information," 77 an "Employee Investigation," 100 an internal security or "Security Matter" investigation, and 121 a "Loyalty Investigation."

2. FBI, *Parsons*, Bufile 100-390459-1.

3. FBI, *Parsons*, Bufile 100-390459-2.

4. For an account of J. Edgar Hoover the man and his role in the development and direction of the FBI during his long tenure, see Curt Gentry, *J. Edgar Hoover: The Man and the Secrets* (New York: W. W. Norton, 1991); Mark North, *Act of Treason: The Role of J. Edgar Hoover in the Assassination of President Kennedy* (New York: Carroll and Graf, 1991); Anthony Summers, *Official and Confidential: The Secret Life of J. Edgar Hoover* (London: Gollancz, 1993); Athan G. Theoharis and John Stuart Cox, *The Boss: J. Edgar Hoover and the Great American Inquisition* (Philadelphia: Temple University Press, 1990).

5. Cathy Perkus, ed., *COINTELPRO: The FBI's Secret War on Political Freedom* (New York: Monad Press, 1975). For a more recent account, see James Kirkpatrick Davis, *Spying on America: The FBI's Domestic Counterintelligence Program* (New York: Praeger, 1992); and Ward Churchill and Jim Vander Wall, ed., *The COINTELPRO Papers: Documents from the FBI's Secret Wars against Domestic Dissent* (Boston: South End, 1990).

6. See Kenneth O'Reilly, *"Racial Matters": The FBI's Secret File on Black America, 1960–1972* (New York: Free Press, 1989); David J. Garrow, *The FBI and Martin Luther King, Jr.: From "Solo" to Memphis* (New York: W. W.

Norton, 1981); David Gallen, ed., *Malcolm X: The FBI Files* (New York: Carroll and Graf, 1991); Herbert Mitgang, *Dangerous Dossiers: Exposing the Secret War against America's Greatest Authors* (New York: Ballantine, 1989); Natalie S. Robins, *Alien Ink: The FBI's War on Freedom of Expression* (New York: William and Morrow, 1992); Sherry Sherod Dupree and Herbert C. Dupree, *EXPOSED! The FBI's Unclassified Reports on Churches and Church Leaders* (Washington, D.C.: Middle Atlantic Regional Press, 1993); Ellen W. Schrecker, *No Ivory Tower: McCarthyism and the Universities* (New York: Oxford University Press, 1986); Athan G. Theoharis, *Spying on Americans: Political Surveillance from Hoover to the Huston Plan* (Philadelphia: Temple University Press, 1978); Kenneth O'Reilly, *Hoover and the Un-Americans: The FBI, HUAC and the Red Menace* (Philadelphia: Temple University Press, 1983); William W. Keller, *The Liberals and J. Edgar Hoover: Rise and Fall of a Domestic Intelligence State* (Princeton: Princeton University Press, 1989); Richard Criley, *The FBI v. the First Amendment* (Los Angeles: First Amendment Foundation, 1990); and Ross Gelbspan, *Break-Ins, Death Threats and the FBI: The Covert War against the Central American Anti-War Movement* (Boston: South End, 1991).

7. For a detailed discussion of the history of federal information policy, the Freedom of Information Act, and its potential use in sociological research, see Mike Forrest Keen, "The Freedom of Information Act and Sociological Research," *American Sociologist* 23, no. 2 (1992): 43–51.

8. Lyle Denniston, "FOIA Ruling Helpful to Media," *Washington Journalism Review* 11 (October 1989): 61.

9. Peter Hernon, *Uses of Government Publications by Social Scientists* (Norwood, N.J.: Ablex, 1979), 14–15.

10. Peter Hernon and Charles R. McClure, *Federal Information Policies in the 1980's* (Norwood, N.J.: Ablex, 1987), 19.

11. Several guides exist which give detailed instructions on how to make a FOIA request. See Robert Allan Adler, *Using the Freedom of Information Act: A Step by Step Guide* (Washington, D.C.: American Civil Liberties Union, 1990); Rebecca Daugherty, *How to Use the Federal Freedom of Information Act* (Washington, D.C.: FOI Service Center, 1987); and David F. Trask, *User's Guide to the FOIA* (Bloomington, Id.: Organization of American Historians, 1984).

12. Adler, Using the Freedom of Information Act, 15; Daugherty, *How to Use the Federal Freedom of Information Act,* 28–29.

13. An agency may legally refuse disclosure of selected information if it can provide justification through at least one of nine exemptions. Information is exempt under the FOIA if it relates to (1) national security, (2) internal agency personnel rules, (3) information exempted by other statutes, (4) trade secrets and confidential commercial information, (5) internal agency communications, (6) personal privacy, (7) law enforcement investigations, (8) financial institutions, or (9) oil and gas wells. Even though some portion of a document may be exempt from release, the FOIA requires that the agency release the rest of the material after the exempted portion has been edited. Any complete or partial denial of a request may be appealed.

14. Amitai Etzioni, "FBI and the Scientific Community," *Science News*

114, no. 20 (1978): 334. Sociologists, or anyone else, who suspect or might have never suspected they have a file would be well advised to submit a request in their own names to be sure they are not subject to the same happenstance as Etzioni.

15. Federal Bureau of Investigation, *American Sociological Association*, Bureau File 94-1-14882-8 (Washington D.C.: FBI Freedom of Information–Privacy Acts Section).

16. Ibid.

17. FBI, *American Sociological Association*, Bufile 94-1-14882.

18. Federal Bureau of Investigation, *American Sociological Association*, Bureau File 100-455276 (Washington, D.C.: FBI Freedon of Information–Privacy Acts Section).

— 2 —

W.E.B. Du Bois: Sociologist beyond the Veil

William Edward Burghart Du Bois was born in 1868, five years after the Emancipation Proclamation, in the small town of Great Barrington, Massachusetts. An usually gifted child, Du Bois was the only Black student in his high school, and at age sixteen graduated among the top of his class. Though he wanted to go to Harvard, initially Du Bois was only able to attend the all-Black Fisk University, where, for the first time in his life, he entered what he described as "the land of the slaves . . . a region where the world was split into white and black halves, where the darker half was held back by race prejudice and legal bonds, as well as by deep ignorance and dire poverty."[1]

Even though five to ten years younger than most of his classmates, upon entering Fisk, Du Bois placed as a sophomore. At Fisk, he became an impassioned orator and belligerent opponent of the color bar: "I was determined to make a scientific conquest of my environment, which would render the emancipation of the Negro race easier and quicker."[2] Following his graduation from Fisk in 1888, Du Bois received a scholarship and was admitted to Harvard as a junior. However, he was isolated from his fellow white students, rejected by the all-white Glee Club, and found himself "in Harvard, but not of it."[3] No doubt the bitterness from such rejection contributed to his being always on the move with little time for small talk, bare acknowledgment of the minimal pleasantries, and a reputation for abruptness, aloofness, and short-patience.[4] Nevertheless, while there he became a devoted follower and friend of William James and upon graduating cum laude in 1890 was one of five students selected to speak at commencement. He spent the next two years as a Harvard fellow studying what would have been sociology had such a field been recognized at the time, but instead eventually received his Ph.D. in history in 1895. He was the first Black man to receive a doctorate degree from Harvard and went on to become the first Black sociologist in America.[5]

After initially suffering a racially tainted rejection by the Slater Fund and the head of its board, former President Rutherford B. Hayes, Du Bois vigorously remonstrated and received a grant to spend two years at the University of Berlin.[6] He studied under Gustav Schmoler and Adolf Wagner, and attended lectures by Max Weber, who would later recognize him as one of the most important sociologists in America.[7] While at Berlin, he also began to develop a sense of sociology as a science which might be employed in the settlement of the Negro problem in America. Traveling extensively throughout Europe, he was pleasantly surprised by its racial openness and felt himself "not standing against the world, but simply against American narrowness and color prejudice, with the greater, finer world at my back."[8] Nonetheless, at the end of the two years, as he remarked, he had to return to a "'nigger'-hating America."[9]

Du Bois returned to an American society and sociology permeated by racism and racist ideology. The Negro's position within the society was deteriorating as disenfranchisement, lynchings, and Jim Crow were quickly rolling back the gains made after the Civil War. Almost every social scientist except Franz Boas maintained that racial differences were innate. With the exception of W. I. Thomas, sociological theory stressed the biological superiority of the white race and the primitive inferiority of Negroes.[10] As E. Franklin Frazier later observed of early American sociology, "The sociological theories which were implicit in the writings on the Negro problem were merely rationalizations of the existing racial situation."[11]

Following a disappointing appointment at Wilberforce University (the institution would have no sociology), in 1896 Du Bois was given the opportunity to make a study of Negroes in Philadelphia under the auspices of the University of Pennsylvania, though not without the increasingly familiar accompanying insult. He was given an unorthodox appointment as an assistant instructor, but only for one year and with no real academic standing, not even an office at the university. Eventually, even his name was removed from the university catalogue. Nonetheless, he settled into the city's 7th Ward with his new bride, Nina Gomez, and during the next year personally interviewed over 5,000 people. The result was his classic study, *The Philadelphia Negro*, which established the framework for the scientific study of Negro life and the race problem in America, and which would serve as the model for Gunnar Myrdal's later classic, *An American Dilemma*. Even though it was one of the first empirical studies of social life in the United States, the *American Journal of Sociology* ignored Du Bois's work while publishing glowing reviews of other, racist books, and the American Sociological Society ignored his call to "put themselves on record as favoring a most thorough and unbiased scientific study of the race problem in America."[12]

Du Bois was galled by the fact that following the completion of the study he was not offered a professorship at one of the major universities, even though white classmates of lesser accomplishment were. Nonetheless, he remained committed to the development of a scientific sociology through the study of the conditions and problems of the Negro in America, and for the next thirteen years pursued his academic and sociological agenda at Atlanta University, where he was asked to take charge of an annual series of conferences on the Negro problem. Du Bois turned the Atlanta Conference into a systematic scientific study of the conditions of Negro life in America, produced eighteen major publications on a shoestring budget, and laid out an ambitious agenda for 100 years of longitudinal study of all areas of Negro social life.

In 1903, Du Bois published the work for which he is most well-known, his eloquent classic and landmark in the literature of Black protest, *The Souls of Black Folk*. In it, he argues that the color line divided American society into two social worlds, one black and one white, and placed a veil between the them, setting off one from the other and filtering the information which passed between the two.[13] He observed that "the Negro is a sort of seventh son, born with a veil, and gifted with second-sight in this American world—a world which yields him no true self-consciousness, but only lets him see himself through the revelation of the other world."[14] Negroes such as himself, born behind the veil, were shut out from the vast world beyond it, yet always forced to see themselves through it, leading to a double-consciousness: "It is a peculiar sensation, this double-consciousness, this sense of always looking at one's self through the eyes of others, of measuring one's soul by the tape of a world that looks on in amused contempt and pity. One ever feels his two-ness—an American, a Negro; two souls, two thoughts, two unreconciled strivings; two warring ideals in one dark body, whose dogged strength alone keeps it from being torn asunder."[15] However, those living on the other side were no less affected, as they were blinded from seeing the other behind the veil.

Through his early work as a sociologist, Du Bois single-handedly initiated a tradition of serious empirical research on Black America, which had previously remained hidden behind the veil, unpenetrated by American sociology.[16] However, after sixteen years of teaching, during which nearly 2,000 Negroes were lynched or murdered without a single assailant being punished, Du Bois later observed, "One could not be a calm, cool, and detached scientist while Negroes were lynched, murdered, and starved."[17] Disenchanted and disillusioned with his faith in the power of science and knowledge to overcome prejudice and alleviate the race problem, he left the academy and moved into the world of social critic and activist.[18] In 1909, he helped to found the NAACP, an outgrowth of the short-lived Niagra Movement, which had been formed to denounce racism in America, and in opposition to the conciliatory and conformist philosophy and practices of Booker T. Washington and his "Tuskegee machine."[19] By then a socialist, and as the NAACP's Director of Publications and Research, Du Bois developed its signature publication, *The Crisis,* into a popular weekly and for the next two decades became the leading voice in the fight to make Negroes, "politically free from disenfranchisement, legally free from caste and socially free from insult."[20] During this period he also traveled several times to Europe, visited post-revolution Russia by which he was favorably impressed, and helped to inaugurate the Pan-African Movement.

In 1934, Du Bois had a falling out with the leadership of the NAACP and resigned. He returned to Atlanta University where he served as the head of the department of sociology, establishing the journal *Phylon,* until he was forced to retire in 1944. Upon his retirement from Atlanta, the NAACP invited him back. However, his fierce independence and refusal to serve as just a titular ornament, ongoing conflicts with its secretary Walter White, and a growing red hysteria to which Du Bois refused to succumb, led the board of trustees to dismiss him once and for all in 1947. Du Bois then moved over to the much more politically active Council on African Affairs (CAA), where he continued his crusade for world peace and his aggressive criticism of American racism at home and imperialism abroad, proclaiming, "Drunk with power we are leading the world to hell in a new colonialism with the same old human slavery which once ruined us; and to a Third World War which will ruin the world."[21]

Even though the FBI began surveillance of Black Americans as early as 1917, it was only in the latter part of his life, as he began to increasingly argue that capitalism, imperialism, and racism at home and abroad were all interconnected and inseparable from one another, that Du Bois came under investigation by the FBI.[22] This is surprising given Du Bois's earlier prominence with the NAACP and Hoover's racism and belief that advocacy of racial justice was a subversive act.[23] Once under investigation, Du Bois was doubly suspect, for being both Black and red.

In February 1942, the Atlanta field office initiated an investigation of Du Bois for possible subversive activities after an informant reported that in a speech made while in Japan he had complimented the Japanese on their progress and military prowess and reportedly indicated that "when the time came for them to take over the United States, they would find they would have help from the Negroes in the United States."[24] The Baltimore, Charlotte, New York City, and Washington, D.C. offices were brought into the investigation to help with the background check and to search for any subversive activities. During its investigation, Baltimore contacted a member of the Harvard Club of Maryland and was informed not only that Du Bois had never been a member, but that no Negro had ever been a member.[25] In order to get some idea of his "attitude and tendencies," an agent from Atlanta read Du Bois's 1940 autobiographical work, *Dusk of Dawn,* and excerpted several passages on race relations, foreign relations, and Communism. Included was Du Bois's statement, "I am not and was not a Communist. I do not believe in the dogma of inevitable revolution in order to right economic wrong. On the other hand I believed and still believe that KARL MARX was one of the greatest men of modern times and that he put his fingers squarely upon our difficulties when he said that economic foundations, the way in which men earn their living, are the determining factors in the development of civilization and the basic patterns of culture."[26] After a little more than a year, in April of 1943, Atlanta indicated that extensive investigations had failed to reveal any evidence of subversive activities on Du Bois's part and closed the case.[27]

Du Bois's file lay dormant until October 1949, when his case was reopened by the New York office, which began a Security Matter–C investigation of him and turned up allegations that he was "one of a group of individuals recently named by [DELETED] as 'Concealed Communists.'[28] In late December 1950, New York submitted a detailed twenty-three-page report of its investigation to Bureau headquarters.[29] The report noted that Du Bois was then employed as Vice Chairman of the Council for African Affairs, was a U.S. Senatorial candidate for the American Labor Party, and was reported to be a sponsor, member, and sympathetic toward numerous Communist front organizations. In addition to extensive background information, the report listed the Communist front organizations with which he had been associated. It also provided a summary of over fifty newspaper articles reporting on Du Bois's activities, including his Senatorial campaign, as well as numerous speeches, conferences, and other appearances.

Based on its findings, New York recommended that Du Bois's name be placed on the Security Index, where it would remain until his death.[30] During the remaining years of his life he was under constant and careful surveillance at home and abroad, his mail tampered with, and virtually every movement he made, speech he delivered, or article he wrote was noted and reported by the FBI or other intelligence agencies cooperating with them.[31] When Du Bois married his second wife, Shirley Graham, on February 27, 1951, and left for the Carribean on honeymoon, the FBI was informed. The following month, the Washington field office obtained a copy of his passport and sent it to the translation unit so that the visa stamps could be translated in order to determine when and where he had traveled during the two previous years.[32]

Of particular interest was Du Bois's appointment as chairman of the Peace Information Center (PIC), which served as the domestic sponsor for distribution of the Stockholm Appeal, an international petition to abolish the atom bomb. Even though in the midst of the Korean War and under attack by the Secretary of State, Justice Department, and House Un-American Activities Committee (HUAC), the PIC collected more than 2 million signatures in the United States. On February 9, 1951, the day before his eighty-third birthday, Du Bois and his associates in the PIC were indicted by federal prosecutors under the Foreign Agents Registration Act for failure to register as an agent of a foreign principle, even though the PIC had been disbanded several months earlier. The following evening, in a brief speech during his birthday party, hosted by E. Franklin Frazier at Small's Paradise in Harlem, Du Bois commented, "Thus I stand tonight facing the possibility of celebrating my future birthdays in prison, and thus relieving all 'Houses of Essex' from embarrassment. The prospect is not pleasant. Yet I continue to maintain that advocacy of peace is not treason; that I am the agent of no foreign principle and never have been; that I am the champion of no idea alien to this nation; and that I have the right within the future as in the past to fight for peace."[33]

Following Du Bois's arrest a worldwide campaign was organized in his defense, but the case never went to the jury as the presiding judge, in a surprising move not anticipated by either side, ruled that the prosecution had offered only conjecture, not evidence, and granted an acquittal before the defense had even presented its case. Touted as one of the first victories against McCarthyism, in its aftermath Du Bois observed the most frightening result of the trial:

> The absence of moral courage and intellectual integrity which our prosecution revealed still stands to frighten our own nation and the better world. It is clear still today, that freedom of speech and thinking can be attacked in the United States without the intellectual and moral leaders of this land raising a hand or saying a word in protest or defense, except in the case of the saving few. Their ranks did not include the heads of great universities,

the leaders of religion, or most of the great names in science. Than this fateful silence there is on earth no greater menace to present civilization.[34]

Throughout the case, the FBI kept careful tabs on the national campaign in Du Bois's defense and the appearances and activities of Du Bois and his wife in support of it. Documents in Du Bois's file indicate that the FBI was even secretly spying on his defense committee, keeping track of its meetings at the Hotel Breslin in New York City, reporting on its defense strategy, and surreptitiously obtaining materials that were to be used in Du Bois's defense (see Figure 2.1).[35]

Following his indictment and acquittal, Du Bois continued to be an outspoken opponent of the Korean War and what he felt were its imperialist foundations. In his estimation, the major motivating factor behind it, and other similar imperialist actions, was profit and the resulting necessity to maintain ample supplies of cheap labor and to strip colonial countries of their raw materials:

Capitalism uses these profits to bribe the workers and thinkers of the more powerful countries by high wages and privilege. In this way the imperialists seek to build a false and dishonest prosperity on the slavery and degradation, the low wage and disease and very lives of the colored peoples of Asia and Africa and the islands of the sea. And to pay the price for this they demand that we in the United States, Negro and white, give up our liberties and our sons and daughters in an endless stream to be murdered and crippled in endless wars.[36]

Toward the end of 1951, the Passport Division of the State Department advised the FBI that a refusal notice had been placed in Du Bois's file, and that the Washington field office would be informed should he make an application for a passport.[37] In addition, information from the ongoing internal security investigation was no doubt passed on to Canadian authorities, as he was detained by Canadian immigration officials and denied entrance to Canada when he attempted to attend a conference on peace, arms reduction, and trade being held in Toronto in May 1952. In response, Bruce Mickleburgh, Public Relations Director for the Canadian Peace Congress, which was sponsoring the event, stated "An Iron Curtain is being thrown around Canada."[38]

Throughout 1953 and 1954, the FBI continued to shadow Du Bois and his wife, following him on his various peace crusades and collecting and exchanging information with other government agencies and offices. On January 11, 1954, an unidentifiable source provided the FBI with a copy of a briefing paper which had been prepared for Senator William E. Jenner, Chairman of the Senate Internal Security Subcommittee (SISS), from the files of the House

Figure 2.1

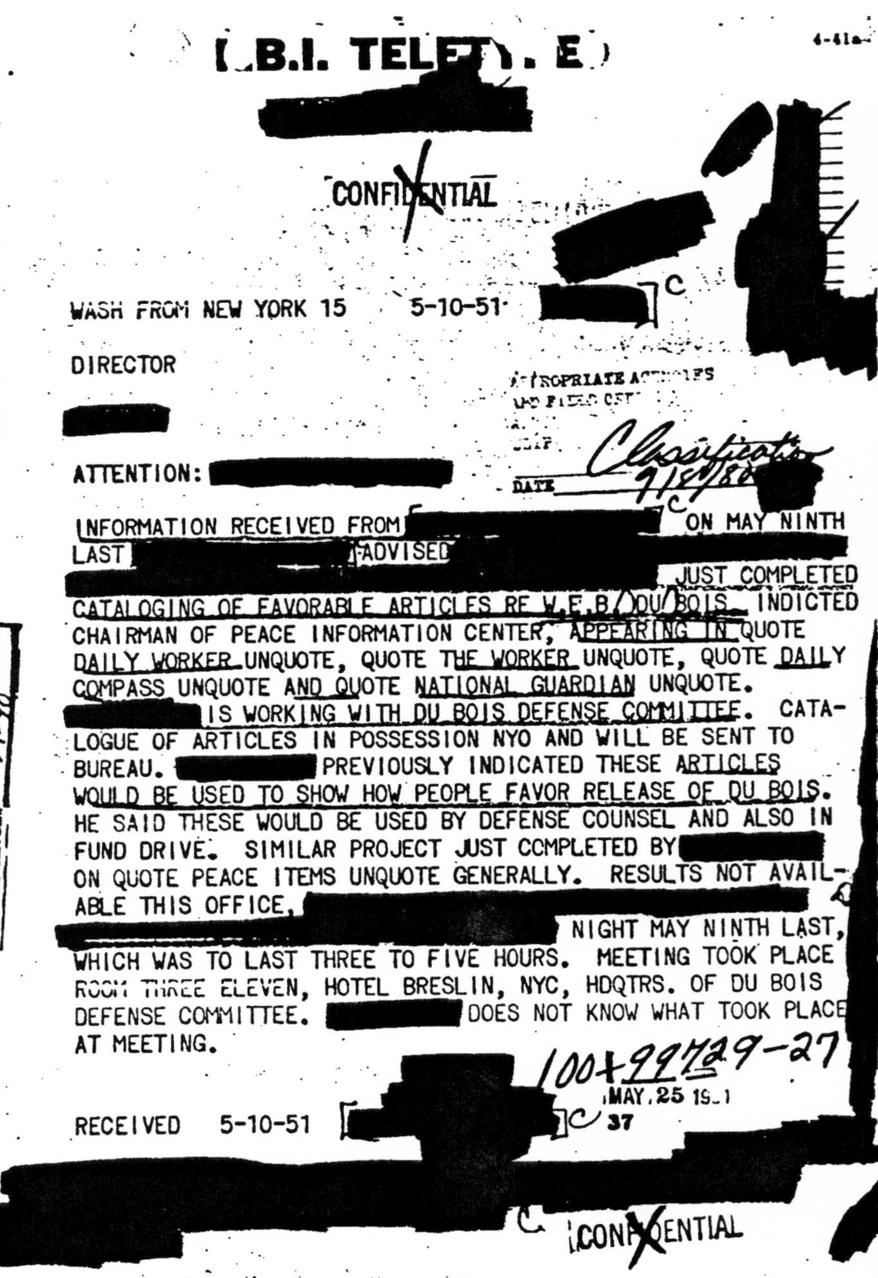

F.B.I. TELETYPE

CONFIDENTIAL

WASH FROM NEW YORK 15 5-10-51 [redacted] C

DIRECTOR

[redacted]

ATTENTION: [redacted]

INFORMATION RECEIVED FROM [redacted] C ON MAY NINTH LAST [redacted] ADVISED [redacted] JUST COMPLETED CATALOGING OF FAVORABLE ARTICLES RE W.E.B. DU BOIS, INDICTED CHAIRMAN OF PEACE INFORMATION CENTER, APPEARING IN QUOTE DAILY WORKER UNQUOTE, QUOTE THE WORKER UNQUOTE, QUOTE DAILY COMPASS UNQUOTE AND QUOTE NATIONAL GUARDIAN UNQUOTE. [redacted] IS WORKING WITH DU BOIS DEFENSE COMMITTEE. CATALOGUE OF ARTICLES IN POSSESSION NYO AND WILL BE SENT TO BUREAU. [redacted] PREVIOUSLY INDICATED THESE ARTICLES WOULD BE USED TO SHOW HOW PEOPLE FAVOR RELEASE OF DU BOIS. HE SAID THESE WOULD BE USED BY DEFENSE COUNSEL AND ALSO IN FUND DRIVE. SIMILAR PROJECT JUST COMPLETED BY [redacted] ON QUOTE PEACE ITEMS UNQUOTE GENERALLY. RESULTS NOT AVAILABLE THIS OFFICE. [redacted] NIGHT MAY NINTH LAST, WHICH WAS TO LAST THREE TO FIVE HOURS. MEETING TOOK PLACE ROOM THREE ELEVEN, HOTEL BRESLIN, NYC, HDQTRS. OF DU BOIS DEFENSE COMMITTEE. [redacted] DOES NOT KNOW WHAT TOOK PLACE AT MEETING.

100-99729-27

MAY 25 1951

37

RECEIVED 5-10-51 [redacted] C

C CONFIDENTIAL

CLASS. & EXT. BY [illegible]
REASON-FCIM II, 1-2.4.2
DATE OF REVIEW

Classification 9/18/80

Committee on Un-American Activities.[39] The paper provided a detailed picture of Du Bois's activities that was a virtual mirror reflection of that already contained in the FBI's own files.

In April 1954, J. Edgar Hoover sent a memo, classified as SECRET, to the CIA in response to its request for any information FBI files might hold as to whether Du Bois had "instigated or participated in any recent project for holding a pan-African conference."[40] The memo included copies of several CAA newsletters outlining plans being made in several Africa nations, including in South Africa by the African National Congress, to hold pan-African conferences. It indicated that Du Bois had been the founder of the first pan-African movement and was supporting these more recent efforts even though his travel restrictions would bar him from attending any of them. Hoover also indicated that the CAA may have violated the terms of the Foreign Agents Registration Act, under which Du Bois had been previously indicted, and requested any information the CIA might already have or receive in the future indicating such a violation.

In September 1955, SAC, New York forwarded a "Succinct Resume" of Du Bois's case to the Director, FBI. Following a six-page summary he recommended that Du Bois be retained on the Security Index, indicating, "Despite his advanced age it is felt that he could be, and is, used with great effectiveness by the CP. He should be retained in the SI until his effectiveness as a CP tool has terminated."[41] SAC, New York also noted that Du Bois was not currently tabbed for the Det Com Program, nor should he be.[42] By April 1956, the yearly report that New York was filing on Du Bois's investigation had grown to over fifty pages and even included a table of contents. Its summary page indicated that Du Bois, described as a concealed Communist who had joined the CP in 1944, had participated in at least twenty-nine CP front organizations, including twenty in which he served in some leadership capacity.[43]

The FBI appears to have become particularly concerned with the role it felt Du Bois was playing, or being used for, in helping to attract more Negro support for the Communist Party. In 1948, worried that the Negro vote was not "in the bag," CP officials were reportedly looking for ways to make connection with the Black community and Du Bois was identified as a sympathetic columnist. A former CP member advised that in 1949 Du Bois's works had been used in courses taught in a CP Workers School in Chicago. In 1954, top-level Party officals established the Midwest Negro Commission, with a strategy of increasing Negro voting strength by supporting the growth of Negro organizations, and Du Bois was mentioned as a prominent figure who could be used to help accomplish this program. However, while Du Bois was willing to work with whoever was supportive of his cause, including many alleged Communist front organizations, he had not yet joined the Party.

In June 1956, the FBI learned that in his testimony before the Subversive Activities Control Board, as a defense witness for the Jefferson School of Social Science, Du Bois had testified under oath that he was not then nor had ever been a member of the Communist Party. In response, a confidential memo was sent from Director, FBI to an unidentifiable official, indicating, "In the event you have not already done so, you may desire to review the above-mentioned testimony of the subject in order to consider the possibilities of prosecution of the subject of perjury." It is hard to construe this memo as anything but an act of harassment, since a brief note on an additional page attached to the memo the day after it was written indicates that the FBI had been unable to provide specific evidence to prove Du Bois's membership and therefore it was unlikely that the Department of Justice would authorize prosecution.

Shortly thereafter, Du Bois's case was once again reevaluated by New York. While it was determined that he remain on the Security Index, the case was to be closed. However, New York indicated that it would remain alert for any information showing Du Bois's continued activity in the subversive movement.[44] So, on August 8, 1958, when Du Bois and his wife were observed departing for Paris on the S.S. Liberte, the FBI kept track of his movements through information provided by reliable informants and the State Department. New York learned that the Du Bois's itinerary called for visits to Czechoslovakia, the Soviet Union, China, and Ghana. The Washington field office obtained copies of both of the Du Boises's passport files. They revealed that in 1955 the Du Boises had been denied passports because it had been alleged that they were Communists. Nonetheless, passports were issued in 1958, even though both refused to answer any questions regarding membership in any political party, including the CP, citing a recent decision set forth by the U.S. Supreme Court as grounds for their refusal.[45] On September 12, the State Department reported that Du Bois had delivered a strong anti-America speech at the Hague and the following month the Immigration and Naturalization Service (INS) placed stops on both the Du Boises upon their return.[46]

The Bureau kept close tabs on Du Bois as he continued his travels and was well received and feted throughout Eastern Europe. The legal attaché in Bonn sent a memo indicating that G-2 had reported Du Bois had been awarded the East German peace medal and received an honorary doctorate from the faculty of Humboldt University.[47] He received a similar degree from Charles University in Prague. Unable to travel to Ghana due to illness, Du Bois remained in Czechoslovakia while Shirley traveled in his stead to deliver a speech he had prepared in which he stated, "Africa awake! Put on the beautiful robes of Pan-African Socialism! You have nothing to lose but your chains! You have a continent to regain! You have freedom and human dignity to attain!"[48]

Once recovered, Du Bois also traveled throughout Russia and in early March 1959 met for two hours with Soviet Premier Khrushchev with whom he reportedly talked about peace and ways to develop closer ties and friendlier relations with the United States. Du Bois continued on to China, where his ninety-first birthday was celebrated publically with great fanfare, and was attended by Premier Chou En-lai. While in China, Du Bois spent several hours with Mao Tse Tung and dined with the Premier. The consulate in Hong Kong sent back reports chronicling Du Bois's movements in China and the deep and positive impression it had made upon him.[49] In a speech broadcast over Peiping radio Du Bois exhorted, "Come to China Africa and look around. . . . You know America and France and Britain to your sorrow. Now know the Soviet Union and its allied nations, but particularly know China. China is flesh of your flesh and blood of your blood. China is colored, and knows to what the colored skin in this modern world subjects its owner."[50]

On May 15, 1959, SAC, New York was informed by Director, FBI that Du Bois had been awarded the Lenin Peace Prize for "strengthening of peace among the people." In announcing the award, Dmitry Skobeltsyn, head of the selection committee, concluded, "Du Bois, a courageous fighter for peace and friendship among the peoples, although he is 91 years old, is full of energy and a desire to continue the struggle for peace and the happiness of the peoples with even greater vigor."[51] The *New York Times* attributed a statement to Du Bois in which he had said, "I have never been a member of the Communist party. . . . But I think Communism is the best system for all countries after this trip."[52] In an article published in *Pravda* following his reception of the award, and translated for FBI files, Du Bois reflected on the four visits he had made to the Soviet Union between 1926 and 1959 and the changes he had observed during that time, and stated, "I openly admit my prejudice. It is the rarest opportunity to be in a country and not to be subjected to insults because of one's racial origin and to enjoy respect of the things which one tried to accomplish. I am prejudiced in favor of the Soviet Union. My prejudice is based upon the things I saw and experienced."[53] And, while *Pravda* characterized Du Bois only as a prominent American scientist, writer, and public figure, the FBI memos reporting the award always made special note of his race and indicated that he was a "Negro" author and lecturer.

Du Bois returned home on the S.S. Liberte and arrived in New York on July 1, 1959. Upon learning that the prize, which included a $25 thousand premium, was to be awarded in the United States, the Bureau instructed New York to determine in advance when and where this would occur, along with the plans of the CP to capitalize on the presentation. On September 24, it advised that Premier Khrushchev was in Washington, D.C., and that Du Bois and his wife would be attending a reception for him that evening, and conjectured that this might be a propitious time for the award to be presented. While he was warmly greeted by Khrushchev, no presentation was made.[54] This was probably due to the fact that Skobeltsyn had been refused a visa to enter the United States, reportedly because American authorities did not approve the purpose of his trip; that is, presenting the Lenin Prize to Du Bois.[55]

During the next several months, the prize was not presented, though there were a couple of more false warnings. However, Du Bois was traveling around the country sharing the experiences from his travels in Eastern Europe, Russia, and China, and commenting on the impact they had had in changing his thinking. During a lecture delivered on April 10, 1960, in the Memorial Union at the University of Wisconsin, Madison, he indicated that he now saw socialism as the most successful form of government. He also continued to speak out against the red hysteria and those leaders, especially among the Black community, who were complicit in the "witch-hunting" campaigns directed against communism.[56] In his estimation, "If the American Negroes and all other Americans of all colors of skin could take into consideration everything that is today happening in the world, if they could study the history of Russia and China, if they could acquaint themselves with the teaching of Marx and Lenin, they would support socialism."[57]

In May 1960, the Bureau received information that Du Bois had once again applied for a passport, this time to travel to Ghana following an invitation by the new government to take part in its inauguration.[58] The Washington office was instructed to contact the Passport Office and learned that while Du Bois's last passport had been canceled because his travel to Communist China violated the geographical restrictions it had contained, a new one had been issued after he submitted a sworn affidavit on May 11 that he would not violate any similar restrictions contained within it or subsequently promulgated by the U.S. government.[59] Hoover then sent a memo to the Office of Security at the Department of State requesting that it furnish any information received concerning Du Bois's activities while in Ghana and sent a copy to the CIA.[60]

In the meantime, the Bureau had also learned that Du Bois would finally be presented his Lenin Prize on June 23, at the Russian Embassy, just prior to his departure for Ghana.[61] A flurry of memos between the Bureau and several of its field offices led up to the day of the ceremony, though nothing of real substance was reported in them. Upon formal presentation of the award, Du Bois stated, "I think that our meeting today will serve no useful purpose unless the Americans present here realize that our prime duty is to launch a real movement for peace in America. . . . I still dream of America as a free, democratic country where labor will be rewarded according to the work done, where no one will possess what he has not earned, where a man will be judged by his deeds, not the color of his skin, where every man can freely hold any view."[62]

On June 29, a Sabena Airlines official advised that Du Bois and his wife had departed for Prague on their way to Accra, Ghana.[63] The State Department reported to the Bureau that while in Ghana, Du Bois was the guest of honor at a dinner sponsored by the Ghana Academy of Learning and attended by the President of Ghana, Kwame Nkrumah. In a speech during the dinner, Du Bois was quoted as saying, "If you can get machines and techniques from the Soviet Union at two percent, and no strings attached, it would be crazy to borrow from the United States and Britain at four, five or six percent with resultant industry under their control and with them strutting as masters in your midst."[64]

The Du Boises were observed back in the United States in early October and FBI surveillance of their activities resumed.[65] But shortly thereafter they set out for Nigeria, where Du Bois had been invited to attend the inauguration of its first government since he was considered to be the "Father of Pan-Africa."[66] The Du Boises were only in Nigeria for two weeks. Upon their return an unidentifiable informant reported that they had no plans for public appearances for the rest of the year, but that Dr. Du Bois was preparing an "Encyclopedia Africana," an extensive study of Africa's peoples and their history and culture which he had originally conceived in 1909.[67]

Several months later, on June 22, 1961, using a pretext, a Special Agent learned from Du Bois's wife that he was then in Europe in a sanatarium for a general rest. While she would not reveal the location, an official from Scandinavian Airlines System (SAS) revealed that he had traveled to Bucharest, Rumania the week before, on a one-way ticket with no return reservations. Several weeks later, another pretext was used to contact Du Bois's wife and determine that Du Bois was not expected to return to the United States until the middle of August.[68] Following his return in late September, New

York was informed that the Du Boises had sold their house and were staying at the St. George Hotel. Through use of a pretext, one of its agents spoke with Du Bois over the phone and was informed that he and Shirley would be leaving for Ghana on October 5, where he would take a position in Accra in connection with preparing his encyclopedia which was being sponsored by the Ghana Academy of Learning.[69] One strong reason driving Du Bois and his wife to emigrate was the fear that their passports would once again be confiscated, leaving them trapped within the United States, unable to travel abroad.[70]

On November 20, 1961, the FBI learned from a reliable source that just prior to his departure Du Bois had sent a letter to Gus Hall, formally applying for membership in the Communist Party.[71] It obtained a copy of Du Bois's lengthy letter of application from the November 26, Sunday edition of *The Worker*. In it Du Bois indicated, "Today I have come to a firm conclusion: Capitalism cannot reform itself; it is doomed to self-destruction. No universal selfishness can bring social good to all." He continued, "Communism—the effort to give all men what they need and to ask of each the best they can contribute—this is the only way of human life. It is a difficult and hard end to reach—it has and will make mistakes, but today it marches triumphantly on in education and science, in home and food, with increased freedom of thought and deliverance from dogma. In the end Communism will triumph. I want to help to bring that day."[72]

In a public letter, published along side of Du Bois's, Hall enthusiastically accepted his application and, after highlighting Du Bois's international stature as an eminent American scholar, his unrelenting struggle for the freedom of the Negro, and his lifetime of commitment to the search for peace and justice around the world, responded, "You have chosen to join our Party precisely at the time when with brazen effrontery to the trends of the times, the most backward ultra-reactionary forces in our country's national life have temporarily dragooned the Supreme Court's majority into upholding the most flagrantly un-Constitutional thought control laws—the McCarran Act and Smith Act, designed to muzzle free speech, ban freedom of association, persecute Communists and suppress our Party."[73]

Hall concluded by welcoming Du Bois into the Party, suggesting, "In joining the Communist Party, you have made that association which was clearly indicated by the very logic of your life." In many ways Hall was right. Since the depression, the Communist Party had been widely recognized for its prominent role in the struggle for civil rights and racial equality, as well as its anticolonial and anti-imperialist stance.[74]

On March 14, 1962, the Washington field office obtained an unclassified Operations Memorandum sent to the State Department from the American embassy in Accra, which indicates that the Embassy had learned that Du Bois had been extremely ill during the previous few months. He was reportedly suffering from a urinary–prostate disease, complicated by the fact that he only had one kidney, and would require surgery. Plans were being made to fly him to Eastern Europe for the operation.[75] A report from New York, classified "Top Secret," indicates that Du Bois underwent three serious operations in Ghana, Bucharest, and London. Even though given only a slim chance of survival, he staged a remarkable recovery. He took his convalescence in Switzerland and China. Prior to returning to Ghana, on October 1, 1962, he and his wife were given the honor of being the first Americans to be invited to join Mao Tse-tung and other Chinese leaders in watching a half-million paraders celebrate the thirteenth anniversary of the Peoples' Republic.[76]

Du Bois returned to Ghana to continue directing work on the encyclopedia. In mid-March of 1963, an agent of the Washington field office sent to review the files of the Passport Office learned that Du Bois had applied for and been granted citizenship in Ghana the previous month. The American embassy in Accra had written Du Bois asking that he complete an Affidavit of Expatriated Person and return his American passport for cancellation. However, it reported that it had received no reply because of the subject's age (95) and "his public attitude of derision toward the United States."[77] In response, the Embassy forwarded a Certificate of Loss of Nationality of the United States to the State Department, and on March 14, 1963, under the provisions of Section S349(a)(1) of the Immigration and Nationality Act of 1952, Du Bois was officially expatriated. Upon learning of his expatriation, on May 3, 1963, SAC, New York recommended that Du Bois' Security Index card be canceled and that the stops outstanding against him with the INS and the Passport Office be removed.[78]

Du Bois died just about four months later, on August 27, the eve of the great civil rights march on Washington during which Martin Luther King, Jr. delivered his famous "I Have a Dream" speech. The final document in Du Bois's case file is a photocopy of an article clipped from *The Worker*, "Marchers Pause to Mourn Dr. DuBois; Father of Negro Liberation Movement," which reported that Ossie Davis eulogized Du Bois at the foot of the Washington Monument the next morning as the "father and great inspirer of the modern freedom movement."[79]

Even though Du Bois lived on the other side of the veil, or perhaps because of it, prior to his death he was one of the most watched persons in America. The FBI was joined in its efforts by HUAC, the CIA, Army Intelligence G-2, and the United States Information Agency (the latter removed his books from its libraries abroad).[80] Du Bois was particularly critical of HUAC, and its loyalty investigations, and with good reason. McCarthyism had a sharp racist edge to it, as those wishing to retard or stop the drive for racial equality and civil rights found it convenient to raise the red scare.[81] He asked, "What has this committee done against an un-American activity older than Communism and far more galling to Negroes, namely Jim Crow—the economic robbing of citizens based on color of skin? Nothing."[82]

Sharing the convictions of Southern segregationists, Hoover was eager to join in as a covert partner in this crusade. His racial antipathy and war on Black Americans, of which Du Bois was one of the first casualties, has been well-documented.[83] As a result, Du Bois actually found himself on the other side of a double-layered veil, one black and one red. No doubt it was the double-consciousness, acquired by virtue of his position on the other side of these veils, which offered him a unique perspective and enabled him to develop a much more critical stance regarding American society than his fellow sociologists.[84] However, this also resulted in his professional and political marginalization.

Ironically, the FBI and other agencies within the intelligence community paid far more attention to Du Bois than did his sociological colleagues. Though he was present at its creation and a member of the founding generation, Du Bois has only belatedly begun to be recognized as one of the pioneers of modern American sociology.[85] And even though he eventually became so frustrated with the limitations of academic sociology and the "white fraternity" which dominated it that he left the academy, Du Bois never left his sociological training and imagination far behind. His role as a social critic and activist was intimately tied to and guided by his conceptual and theoretical concerns.[86] Sixty years before C. Wright Mills, he recognized the importance of social historical context in sociological investigation, critiqued isolated grand theory and abstracted empiricism, and called for a sociology which would actively, critically, and courageously identify and engage the major problems facing American society.[87] His work with the NAACP and struggle for racial equality represented just such an effort, as was his critical analysis of capitalism and American society.

Throughout his life, Du Bois was never afraid to take unpopular positions and oppose the status quo, first in his opposition to Booker T. Washington, later against the Cold War and U.S. imperial policy abroad, and anti-Communism and red-baiting at home. He recognized the intersection of race, class, and gender long before it belatedly entered the sociological mainstream.[88] His tireless voice throughout the first half of the twentieth century set the tone for the era of protest, resistance, and Black consciousness and power which errupted in the decade after he died and has left a legacy which still resonates today.

NOTES

1. W.E.B. Du Bois, *The Autobiography of W.E.B. Du Bois* (New York: International Publishers, 1968), 106–107.
2. Ibid., 125.
3. Ibid., 136.
4. Francis L. Broderick, "W.E.B. Du Bois: History of an Intellectual," in *Black Sociologists: Historical and Contemporary Perspectives*, ed. James E. Blackwell and Morris Janowitz (Chicago: University of Chicago Press, 1974), 7. In *The Philadelphia Negro* Du Bois observed that such a demeanor was the not uncommon result of the impact of the continual barrage of discrimination and insult on the personalities of Black men and women. See Elliot Rudwick, "W.E.B. Du Bois as a Sociologist," in ibid., 32.
5. John H. Bracey, August Meier, and Elliot Rudwick, eds., *The Black Sociologists: The First Half Century* (Belmont, Calif.: Wadsworth, 1971), 2.
6. Du Bois, *Autobiography*, 150–152. The fund had been established in 1890 for the education of Negroes. Upon hearing that President Hayes had gone to the white-only Johns Hopkins University, made disparaging remarks toward Negroes, and indicated that the fund had been unable to find any Negro candidates with the aptitude for advanced study, Du Bois submitted an application and was rejected. He then wrote Hayes, "You went before a number of keenly observant men who looked upon you as an authority in the matter, and told them in substance that Negroes of the United States either couldn't or wouldn't embrace a most liberal opportunity for advancement. That statement went all over the country. When now finally you receive three or four applications for the fulfillment of that offer, the offer is suddenly withdrawn, while the impression still remains." He reapplied and was grudgingly given a grant, half of which, however, was to be treated as a loan.
7. Benjamin Nelson and Jerome Gittleman, "Max Weber, Dr. Alfred Plaetz, and W.E.B. Du Bois: Max Weber on Race and Society," *Sociological Analysis* 34 (1973): 308–312.
8. Du Bois, *Autobiography*, 157.
9. Ibid., 183.
10. Bracey, Meier, and Rudwick, *Black Sociologists*, 2.
11. E. Franklin Frazier, "Sociological Theory and Race Relations," *American Sociological Review* 12 (1947): 268.
12. Bracey, Meier, and Rudwick, *Black Sociologists*, 4; W.E.B. Du Bois, "Symposium on Race Friction," *American Journal of Sociology* 13 (1908): 836. Nor was it mentioned in Park and Burgess's famous "green bible." See

Rudwick, "Du Bois as a Sociologist," 25. One early group of sociologists who did not ignore Du Bois and his work were some of the early America female sociologists, particularly those associated with the Hull House, such as Jane Addams and Isabel Eaton, the latter who wrote the last eighty-two pages of *The Philadelphia Negro*. Du Bois shared an interest in the study of racism, feminism, socialism, and pacifism with the women of Hull House, many of whom were also cofounders of the NAACP. See Mary Jo Deegan, "W.E.B. Du Bois and the Women of Hull-House, 1895–1899," *American Sociologist* 19 (Winter 1988): 301–311.

13. Charles Lemert, "A Classic from the Other Side of the Veil: Du Bois's *Souls of Black Folk*," *Sociological Quarterly* 35 (1994): 386.

14. W.E.B. Du Bois, *The Souls of Black Folk* (New York: Vintage Books), 8. No doubt, Du Bois's formulation of the notion of double-consciousness was developed primarily out of his own experience as a Black man in a predominantly white America. However, he was probably aided in his conception by the influence of William James, Oswald Kulpe, and the early sociological literature on the self and consciousness. See Rutledge M. Dennis, "Du Bois's Concept of Double-Consciousness: Myth and Reality," in *Research in Race and Ethnic Relations*, vol. 9 (Greenwich, Conn.: JAI, 1996).

15. Du Bois, *Souls*, 8–9.

16. Rudwick, "Du Bois as a Sociologist," 46.

17. W.E.B. Du Bois, *Dusk of Dawn: An Essay Toward an Autobiography of a Race Concept* (New York: Schocken Books, 1968), 67.

18. Rutledge M. Dennis, "Continuities and Discontinuities in the Social and Political Thought of W.E.B. Du Bois," in *Research in Race and Ethnic Relations*, vol. 9 (Greenwich, Conn.: JAI, 1996), 9–10.

19. Benjamin Bowser and Deborah Whittle, "Personal Reflections on W.E.B. Du Bois: The Person, Scholar and Activist by Herbert and Fay Aptheker," in *Research in Race and Ethnic Relations*, vol. 9, ed. Rutledge M. Dennis (Greenwich, Conn.: JAI, 1996), 44–45. Du Bois was one of Washington's most vocal and outspoken critics, one of the few who dared to challenge him publically, writing, "So far as Mr. Washington apologizes for injustice, North or South, does not rightly value the privilege and duty of voting, belittles the emasculating effects of caste distinctions, and opposes the higher training and ambition of our brighter minds, —so far as he, the South, or the Nation, does this, —we must unceasingly and firmly oppose them." See Du Bois, *Souls,* 48.

20. Du Bois, *Autobiography*, 256.

21. Ibid., 350.

22. Kenneth O'Reilly, *"Racial Matters": The FBI's Secret File on Black America, 1960–1972* (New York: Free Press, 1989), 12.

23. Ibid., 40.

24. Federal Bureau of Investigation, *William E. B. Du Bois*, Bureau File 100-99729-1 (Washington, D.C.: FBI Freedom of Information–Privacy Acts Section). Further investigation was unable to provide confirmation that Du Bois had actually made this statement.

25. FBI, *Du Bois,* Bufile 100-99729-6.

26. FBI, *Du Bois*, Bufile 100-99729-3. This passage was taken from Du Bois, *Dusk to Dawn*, 302.

27. FBI, *Du Bois*, Bufile 100-99729-10.

28. FBI, *Du Bois*, Bufile 100-99729-13; 15. The FBI had several levels of investigation. A Preliminary Inquiry was carried out whenever it received a request to conduct a Loyalty Investigation. If any suspicious or subversive associations were turned up, a Full-Field Investigation would be ordered. Finally, several types of Security Investigations were conducted when anyone was suspected of activity deemed as threatening to the security of the United States. The most common of these were Security-C (Communist) or Security-R (Russian).

29. FBI, *Du Bois*, Bufile 100-99729-19.

30. Hoover established the Security Index in August of 1943, after Attorney General Francis Biddle ordered him to discontinue and dismantle the Custodial Detention index he had been keeping since 1939. However, instead of following his orders, he simply renamed the index the "Security Index," and ordered all SACs to quit using the term "Custodial Detention" in their files and to replace it with "Security Matter." He also indicated that the Index, and the cards prepared for it, should remain secret so that outsiders, such as the Attorney General, would not get wind of it. Athan G. Theoharis and John Stuart Cox, *The Boss: J. Edgar Hoover and the Great American Inquisition* (New York: Bantam, 1990), 200–201.

31. FBI, *Du Bois*, Bufile 100-99729-23.

32. FBI, *Du Bois*, Bufile 100-99729-23B.

33. FBI, *Du Bois*, Bufile 100-99729-33.

34. Du Bois, *Autobiography*, 386. For a more detailed account of the trial and the events leading up to it, see Gerald Horne, *Black and Red: W.E.B. Du Bois and the Afro-American Response to the Cold War, 1944–1963* (Albany: State University of New York Press, 1986), 126–183; see also Du Bois, *Autobiography*, 363–395.

35. FBI, *Du Bois*, Bufile 100-99729-27.

36. Ibid.

37. FBI, *Du Bois*, Bufile 100-99729-39.

38. FBI, *Du Bois*, Bufile 100-99729-46A.

39. FBI, *Du Bois*, Bufile 100-99729-53. The Senate Internal Security Subcommittee, often referred to as the McCarran Committee or the Jenner Committee after its respective chairmen, was the Senate's version of the much more well-know House Un-American Activities Committee. Like HUAC, it carried out investigations of alleged Communist and/or subversive activities, and held a series of public hearings, often in major cities around the nation. Even though President Truman had signed an Executive Order in March of 1948 forbidding the FBI from honoring congressional subpoenas for loyalty files, Hoover eventually relaxed his enforcement of this ban, and the FBI and HUAC regularly, albeit secretly, cooperated with one another. See Theoharis and Cox, *The Boss*, 272–275.

40. FBI, *Du Bois*, Bufile 100-99729-57. The CIA outdid both the FBI and the House Un-American Activities Committee in their interest in the mi-

nutiae of Du Bois's life. They virtually shadowed him on his trips abroad and illegally engaged in domestic surveillance of his activities at home. See Horne, *Black and Red,* 218–221.

41. FBI, *Du Bois*, Bufile 100-99729-61.

42. The Det Com Program was a plan to detain thousands of political dissidents, tagged by the FBI, if the President were ever to declare an internal security emergency. In addition to the FBI's regular agents, trusted members of local police forces and the Society of Former Special Agents of the FBI were deputized to assist in the eventuality of such an occurrence.

43. FBI, *Du Bois*, Bufile 100-99729-65.

44. FBI, *Du Bois*, Bufile 100-99729-74.

45. The decision they cited was from the case of Kent vs. Dulles, in which the Court, by a narrow five to four vote, ruled that the State Department did not have authority to deny passports to citizens because of their beliefs or associations, thereby bringing it within the ambit of due process of law and significantly reigning in its previously arbitrary and absolute authority. See Albert Fried, *McCarthyism: The Great American Red Scare* (New York: Oxford University Press, 1997), 209–210.

46. FBI, *Du Bois*, Bufile 100-99729-84.

47. FBI, *Du Bois*, Bufile 100-99729-88.

48. FBI, *Du Bois*, Bufile 100-99729-102.

49. FBI, *Du Bois*, Bufile 100-99729-92.

50. FBI, *Du Bois*, Bufile 100-99729-102.

51. FBI, *Du Bois*, Bufile 100-99729-93.

52. FBI, *Du Bois*, Bufile 100-99729-102.

53. FBI, *Du Bois*, Bufile 100-99729-99.

54. FBI, *Du Bois*, Bufile 100-99729-110; 113.

55. FBI, *Du Bois*, Bufile 100-99729-128.

56. Ibid.

57. Ibid.

58. FBI, *Du Bois*, Bufile 100-99729-136.

59. FBI, *Du Bois*, Bufile 100-99729-159.

60. FBI, *Du Bois*, Bufile 100-99729-139A.

61. Ibid.

62. FBI, *Du Bois*, Bufile 100-99729-151.

63. FBI, *Du Bois*, Bufile 100-99729-150.

64. FBI, *Du Bois*, Bufile 100-99729-157.

65. FBI, *Du Bois*, Bufile 100-99729-167.

66. FBI, *Du Bois*, Bufile 100-99729-171

67. FBI, *Du Bois*, Bufile 100-99729-172.

68. FBI, *Du Bois*, Bufile 100-99729-179; 183.

69. FBI, *Du Bois*, Bufile 100-99729-185.

70. Horne, *Black and Red*, 344.

71. FBI, *Du Bois*, Bufile 100-99729-191.

72. FBI, *Du Bois*, Bufile 100-99729-196.

73. FBI, *Du Bois*, Bufile 100-99729-197. The Smith Act, formally known as the Alien Registration Act, was passed on June 28, 1940. It gave the federal government sweeping powers to go after groups it determined to be

subversive. The McCarran Immigration and Nationality Act of 1950 was intended to tighten provisions excluding subversive aliens from the country, to grant the president power to suspend immigration of any alien or group of aliens deemed to be detrimental to U.S. interests, to make members of affiliates of the Communist Party or other totalitarian parties ineligible for naturalization, and to establish a presumption that any alien who was a member of a subversive organization within ten years previous to petitioning for naturalization was not covered by the principles of the Constitution.

74. Horne, *Black and Red*, 17.
75. FBI, *Du Bois*, Bufile 100-99729-204.
76. FBI, *Du Bois*, Bufile 100-99729-219.
77. FBI, *Du Bois*, Bufile 100-99729-222.
78. FBI, *Du Bois*, Bufile 100-99729-223.
79. FBI, *Du Bois*, Bufile 100-99729-225A.
80. Horne, *Black and Red*, 218–221.
81. Ibid., 2, 227.
82. Ibid., 203.
83. See, for example, O'Reilly, *"Racial Matters."*
84. Broderick, "History of an Intellectual," 7.
85. Paul Jefferson, "Present at the Creation: Rethinking Du Bois's 'Practice Theory,'" in *Research in Race and Ethnic Relations*, vol. 9, ed. Rutledge M. Dennis (Greenwich, Conn.: JAI, 1996), 127.
86. Dennis, "Continuities and Discontinuities," 4.
87. Dan S. Green and Edwin D. Driver, "W.E.B. Du Bois: A Case in the Sociology of Sociological Negation," *Phylon* 37 (1976): 314–317. For an extended discussion of Du Bois's conception of sociology as a science of human action in which theory and practice should be integrated, see Jefferson, "Present at the Creation." No doubt, this conception was deeply influenced by his early association with the women of Hull House and their active community-oriented vision of sociology. See Deegan, "W.E.B. Du Bois and the Women of Hull-House."
88. Betsy Lucal, "Race, Class, and Gender in the Work of W.E.B. Du Bois: An Exploratory Study," in *Research in Race and Ethnic Relations*, vol. 9, ed. Rutledge M. Dennis (Greenwich, Conn.: JAI, 1996), 208.

— 3 —

Ernest W. Burgess: Security Matter–C

Through his thirty years of collaboration with Robert E. Park, Ernest W. Burgess was a major architect of the development of the Chicago School of Sociology, as well as a contributing author to its official story. Fueled by Park's disdain for social reform and "women do-gooders" and Burgess's own desire to create an empirical social science, Chicago both dominated and defined early American sociology.[1] They left behind the social philosophizing and theoretical generalization of previous generations, broke rank with sociology's reformist roots and traditions, and lead the way in the establishment and institutionalization of sociology as a "scientific" discipline primarily concerned with the empirical investigation of society.[2]

Burgess was born in Canada in 1886, but immigrated with his parents to the United States shortly thereafter, where he received a conservative upbringing in the Midwest. He was recognized as an exceptionally bright student from early on, earning the nickname, "the little professor" in the first grade, a moniker he accepted with pride.[3] While he initially had planned to do graduate study in English following his graduation from Kingfisher College in Oklahoma, while on the train to the University of Michigan he stopped over in Chicago, was snagged by Albion Small, and never made it to Ann Arbor.[4] One of the first sociologists to be fully trained in the United States, Burgess received his Ph.D. in 1913, writing for his dissertation a critique of social Darwinism. Then, in 1916, following appointments at the University of Toledo, Kansas, and Ohio State

University, he returned to Chicago where he stayed until his retirement in 1952. Reflecting on Burgess's long career at Chicago, W. F. Ogburn, departmental chair from 1936 to 1951, commented, "Burgess is a quite unique person. He teaches a course on recreation and he never plays, he teaches a course on the family and he isn't married, and he teaches a course in criminology and he never committed a sin."[5]

At Chicago, Burgess immediately came under the influence of Park, the much older former muckraking journalist and secretary to Booker T. Washington, with whom he shared an office.[6] Upon his arrival, Burgess sought Park's assistance in preparing for an introductory course he had been assigned to teach and together they assembled a set of outlines and readings which formed the basis of their influential text, *Introduction to the Science of Sociology*. Widely referred to as the "green bible," it was intended not only as an introduction for students but also as a systematic treatise on the science of sociology, providing an outline of its intellectual domain and legitimizing it as a cumulative and organized discipline.[7]

While Park is often portrayed as the visionary leader and trailblazer in contrast to Burgess as the "patient and meticulous junior colleague who filled in all of the pertinent details," in fact, Burgess was instrumental in articulating the focus on the city with which the Chicago School is so closely associated and upon which the department's reputation was built.[8] As early as 1922, he noted, "In my judgement the research work in sociology should be oriented with reference to the utilization of the city of Chicago as a sociological laboratory."[9] Burgess and Park outlined the foundations of the human ecology, including Burgess's own contribution, the concentric zone theory of urban expansion, which would define early Chicago sociology.[10] However, in their zeal to scientize sociology and distance it from its reformist roots, neither Park nor Burgess made appropriate acknowledgment of the methodological debt they owed to the work already carried out in the city by several female sociologists, the most well-known being Jane Addams, and published thirty years earlier in *Hull House Maps and Papers*.[11] As a result, until recently, succeeding generations of sociologists have ignored the contributions of their founding mothers and mistakenly given credit for the development of many of the methodological techniques so closely associated with the Chicago sociology (i.e., social mapping, life histories, participant observation) only to the men of the Chicago School, and not its women.[12]

In addition to his collaboration with Park in the development of the Chicago School, Burgess also made pioneering contributions in several other areas including juvenile delinquency and criminology, family, and, toward the end of his life, gerontology. His article on "The Family as a Unity of Interacting Personalities" contributed to the conception of the family as a social institution whose "reality exists in the interaction of its members and not in the formalities of the law," and resulted in the recognition of family as a major subarea for the discipline.[13] In 1945, his book, *The Family: From Institution to Companionship*, became the leading text in the field. Through this work, Burgess helped to construct a sociological conception of the family free of the psychological and psychiatric dependence typical of his day.[14]

During much of his career, Burgess also found himself in the midst of the debate over quantitative versus qualitative methodology, a debate which intensified with the arrival of Ogburn in 1927 and the retirement of Park in 1933.[15] Burgess tended to sympathize more with the qualitative side and worried that "the prestige of statistics as *the one* scientific method has naturally led in sociology and I suspect in psychology and the other social sciences to a naïve and uncritical application of quantitative measurement to mental and social phenomena."[16] However, rather than taking either side, Burgess served as a calming and judicious presence, arguing that "the methods of statistics and the case study are not in conflict with each other; they are in fact mutually complementary."[17] As a full professor he sat in on Ogburn's statistics course and employed statistics in his own research. Working with the Chicago Census Committee in 1924, he helped to develop the modern census track.[18] He was the first sociologist to apply factor analysis to sociological data, and the first professor of sociology at Chicago to make use of the computer.[19]

In addition to his work at Chicago, Burgess was also active in several professional associations. He served as Secretary to the American Sociological Society during the period of its Chicago dominance from 1920 to 1930, and was elected President in 1934. From 1936 to 1940 he served as editor of the *American Journal of Sociology*. He also helped to establish the National Council on Family Relations, the Gerontological Society, and helped found the Society for the Study of Social Problems.

Though he contributed to the empiricist rhetoric which was increasingly coming to define the identity of the professional sociologist, Burgess struggled with the relationship between reform and empirical sociology, as indicated by the title of his intended autobiography, *I Renounce Reform and the Reformer: The Story of a Conflict of Social Roles*. Characterized as a "social reformer who had little faith in social work," he had also lived at Hull House for a while and held a deep personal admiration for Jane Addams, even though he never recognized her as a professional sociologist and colleague.[20]

A "little man, with a soft shy smile," he often took the side of the underdog, joining their organizations and lending his name to their causes.[21] And though generally conservative and reserved in his demeanor, his seemingly insatiable intellectual curiosity led him to be unusually open to and interested in new ideas and developments. In response to the Bolshevik revolution, he learned to read and speak Russian. He was particularly interested in the impact of communism on the family and visited the Soviet Union several times. This interest in Russian society, and his association with several related organizations considered to be subversive, eventually led him to be charged with disloyalty by a Congressional committee.[22] It also led the FBI to place him on their Security Index as a communist.

Burgess did not come under the formal scrutiny of the FBI until 1943. By then he was in his late fifties and already well established as a prominent sociologist with a nationally recognized reputation as being one of the architects of the Chicago School. However, during the 1940s and 1950s he was the subject of several FBI investigations, including an Employee Investigation, a Loyalty Investigation, and two Internal Security Investigations, which scrutinized his activities as far back as the early 1930s.

While his name had turned up in some other cases, the first formal investigation concerning him was based on a request sent to the Bureau by the Office for Emergency Management for an Employee Investigation following his application to serve as a public panel member with the War Labor Board in Chicago.[23] On September 6, 1943, the Bureau sent a memo charging SAC, Chicago with conducting the investigation and instructing the Cincinnati, Kansas City, Oklahoma City, and Washington, D.C. field offices to provide assistance. The Bureau was particularly concerned that "an individual who may be identical with the applicant is mentioned on page 10 of the Monthly Summary of General Intelligence at Chicago dated February 15, 1943, re Communist Activities."[24] Burgess's name had also been mentioned in reports on internal security and espionage with regard to Russia.

The Oklahoma City field office reported that Kingfisher College, which Burgess had attended from 1904 to 1908, was no longer in existence, and its records had been transferred to Oklahoma University.[25] Records obtained from the Registrar there indicated that Burgess had been an excellent student and that his grades had averaged 92 percent during the four years he was at Kingfisher. Oklahoma also learned that from 1908 to 1909 he and his sister had been employed as instructors by the Northwestern Academy in Carrier, Oklahoma. Burgess had taught math and English and was said to be "an outstanding young instructor in the academy, of good moral habits and was a brilliant student."[26]

Kansas City was able to report only that Burgess had been employed as an assistant professor of sociology from September of 1913 to August of 1916 at a salary of $1,200 per year, as they were unable to locate anyone to be interviewed who knew him at the time.[27] Meanwhile, Cincinnati investigated Burgess's time at Ohio State, where he had been employed as an assistant professor of economics and sociology at a salary of $2,000 during the academic year of 1915–1916.[28] Cincinnati reported that he was considered "loyal, capable and highly intelligent by fellow employees," and that neighborhood, credit, and criminal checks were all negative.

A Special Agent from the Washington, D.C. office was sent to the State Department to check passport records and was advised that between 1930 and 1935 Burgess had made three trips to Europe.[29] During this time he had been in Russia from June 10 to October 1, 1930, and visited again in 1935. Washington also noted that Burgess had been listed in Elizabeth Dilling's *The Red Network*, under the subheading "Who is Who in Radicalism." Finally, an examination of the Dies Committee records indicated that Burgess and his sister Roberta were listed as members of the Chicago Repertory Group of the New Theater Group, said to be a Communist front organization, and that he was listed as a signer of an open letter to the Mayor of Stalingrad which had been issued in June 1943 by the National Council of American Soviet Friendship (NCASF).[30]

On October 5, 1943, as the field office formally charged with conducting the investigation, Chicago provided the most comprehensive report, including information that "Confidential Informants report applicant active in Russian War Relief and reported a Communist Party member" (see Figure 3.1).[31] A check with the Bureau of Immigration and Naturalization revealed that Burgess had first arrived in the United States on April 5, 1888, but had not obtained his citizenship until June 26, 1924. Chicago agents interviewed Burgess's references, Robert Burns and John Larkin, both with the War Labor Board, who testified to his integrity, national reputation as a sociologist, and qualifications to serve as a public panel member with the Board.

Several neighbors from Burgess' apartment building were interviewed, including an intimate friend, Mrs. Irving W. Durfee, who reported that Burgess "gives approximately one-half of his income away, giving it to charitable institutions and to various boys' organizations . . . being interested in the prevention of juvenile delinquency."[32] Durfee also indicated that she believed Burgess had made at least three trips to Russia but thought he was mainly interested in its family set-up and not its political situation. She stated that he was not a Communist, but as a sociologist would naturally be interested in the Communists purely from an academic point of view.

Figure 3.1

FEDERAL BUREAU OF INVESTIGATION

Form No. 1
THIS CASE ORIGINATED AT BUREAU

FILE NO. 77-2805

REPORT MADE AT	DATE WHEN MADE	PERIOD FOR WHICH MADE	REPORT MADE BY
CHICAGO, ILLINOIS	10/5/43	9-13,16,18,20,21-43	[redacted] CSJ:kh (b7C)
TITLE: ERNEST WATSON BURGESS			CHARACTER OF CASE: EMPLOYEE INVESTIGATION OFFICE FOR EMERGENCY MANAGEMENT PANEL MEMBER PUBLIC OEM

SYNOPSIS OF FACTS:

Applicant born 5-16-86, Tilbury, Ontario, Canada. Naturalized Circuit Court of Cook County, Chicago, Illinois, June 26, 1924. Obtained Ph.D. University of Chicago 6-10-13. Employed by University of Chicago in Sociology Department from July, 1916 to present time. University official and colleagues recommend very highly as qualified, loyal and above reproach as to morals and reputation. Neighbors speak very highly of applicant and also recommend. Listed in "Who's Who in America". Credit and criminal negative. Confidential Informants report applicant active in Russian War Relief and reported a Communist Party member.

ALL INFORMATION CONTAINED HEREIN IS UNCLASSIFIED DATE 3-8-94 BY 9803 [redacted] (b7C)

- RUC -

REFERENCE: Bureau file No. 77-28993
Letter from Bureau to Chicago dated September 6, 1943.

DETAILS: AT CHICAGO, ILLINOIS

A check at the Bureau of Immigration and Naturalization in the New Post Office Building, Chicago, Illinois, revealed that the applicant was born in Canada on May 16, 1886 and that he first arrived in the United States on April 5, 1888. He first declared his intention of applying for citizenship on March 12, 1920 and filed his petition on March 26, 1924, obtaining his citizenship by naturalization through the Circuit Court of Cook County on June 26, 1924.

EDUCATION

APPROVED AND FORWARDED: [signature] SPECIAL AGENT IN CHARGE

ENCLOSURE — DO NOT WRITE IN THESE SPACES

77-28993-19

31 NOV 29 1943

COPIES OF THIS REPORT

5 - Bureau

2 - Chicago

Miss Irene Carter and Miss Bertha Favard, two "maiden ladies" also living in the building who had known Burgess for thirty years, characterized him as a very generous man who was cultivated "to the fingertips," and stated that it would be impossible "to find a pinhole in his armor."[33] However, they revealed that Burgess and his sister owned a summer place at the dunes along Lake Michigan which was an exact copy of a Russian *isba* (i.e., the home of a Russian peasant). They also reported that his sister owned a collection of rare Russian books and that both spoke some Russian.

Agents were also sent to the University of Chicago to check with the registrar as well as to interview several of his colleagues, including sociologists William Ogburn and Herbert Blumer and anthropologist Robert Redfield. Through the registrar's office Burgess's student and employment records were reviewed, though the title of his Ph.D. thesis was mistakenly reported as "Socialism Its Functions in Social Evolution."[34] Ogburn, who was then serving as chairperson of the department, characterized Burgess as a hard worker who in his opinion was "a reserved fellow who is not a good mixer and who keeps to himself."[35] Blumer noted Burgess's prominence in the field and considered him to be of unquestionable loyalty. Both men were aware of his trips to Russia, but, like Durfee, they indicated that his interest was purely professional and academic. Redfield, who was Park's son-in-law and therefore very familiar with Burgess, concurred with Ogburn and Blumer, noting that for recreation he believed that Burgess "applied the social sciences which he studied . . . in his relief and welfare projects."[36] All three recommended him highly.

Information obtained from Captain Walter H. Will of the Michigan City police department presented a much different picture. On November 14, 1932, Will had reported that, "he had been advised by a confidential informant that E. W. BURGESS had a large library in his home at Beverly Shores, Indiana, consisting of nothing but communistic articles and books; further that all magazines and newspapers taken by BURGESS were Communistic."[37] The identity of the informant was not revealed and Will did not know whether Burgess attended Communist meetings. However, Chicago noted that on July 29, 1942, a confidential informant, possibly the files of the American Legion National Headquarters at Indianapolis, had advised that Burgess was a member of the Communist Party and a member of the Chicago Forum on Russian Affairs.[38] Confidential informants also reported that Burgess was listed as one of the many pro-Soviet tutors at the University of Chicago and as a sponsor of the Chicago Committee of Russian Relief, as well as the Teachers Committee of the Veterans of the Abraham Lincoln Brigade, which was reported to be a Communist front.[39] A cover letter attached to the report noted that Blumer and Ogburn were also members of the Teachers Committee and that Ogburn's name had appeared in an FBI report entitled "Communist Activity in the United States from the American Legion Files."

Based on the information contained in Chicago's Employee Investigation report, particularly that he was a member of the Communist Party, the Bureau then initiated an internal security investigation of Burgess, under the caption "Security Matter–C," and FBI surveillance of his background and activities continued. On March 7, 1944, Chicago submitted a report on this investigation which contained all the information from the Employee Investigation as well as some new additions.[40] Confidential informants stated that Burgess was a member of the Chicago Forum on Russian Affairs and provided a copy of a letterhead from the Joint Anti-Fascist Refugee Committee which listed Burgess as a sponsor of the organization, said to be a Communist front. It was also reported that on June 18, 1943, Burgess had spoken at a meeting of the Chicago Council on American–Soviet Relations. The report concluded with a physical description, likely taken from Burgess's Selective Service record, noting that he had an appendectomy scar and, under "Peculiarities," that he spoke Russian.

Based on the findings of the Security Investigation, Burgess was placed on the FBI's Security Index. On April 19, 1944, Hoover sent a confidential memo notifying SAC, Chicago to prepare a 5 inch by 8 inch white card captioned "Communist" for filing in the field office's Confidential Security Index Card File, and instructing him that "the caption of the card prepared and filed in your Office must be kept current at all times and the Bureau immediately advised of any changes made therein in that connection."[41]

Burgess remained on the Security Index for the next two years, after which, on August 5, 1946, the Bureau instructed Chicago to reopen the case to determine the nature of Burgess's current activities, noting, "In the event you find that the subject is now inactive, the advisability of continuing the Security Index card should be reconsidered by your office."[42] Almost a year later, Chicago reported that no evidence of current Communist activity had been uncovered and recommended that Burgess's Security Index card be canceled. On July 21, 1947, Burgess was taken off the Index and his card relocated to his investigative case file.[43]

FBI interest in Burgess remained dormant for the next two and one-half years until February 1950, when, in accordance with the provisions of Executive Order 9835, the Bureau received a request for a Loyalty Investigation following Burgess's application to serve as a Special Consultant with the National Institute of Health (NIH).[44]

No doubt aware of the prevailing Cold War climate, in his letter of application Burgess had called attention to his affiliation with the National Council of American Soviet Friendship and its affiliate the Chicago Council of American Soviet Friendship (CCASF). He outlined his limited participation in both and indicated, "For a full statement on these activities and my attitude to communism see my testimony before the Broyles Seditious Activities Commission."[45]

In response to the request, on February 21, 1950, the Bureau instructed SAC, Chicago to conduct a full field investigation of Burgess's loyalty beginning with a review of activities reported earlier in his Security Matter–C case file.[46] Three months later, Chicago submitted its report based on information collected from over twenty confidential informants and accompanied by twelve attachments of various exhibits of evidence, including copies of letters, letterhead, and pamphlets from several organizations. The report confirmed Burgess's membership in the NCASF and its Chicago affiliate and noted he had been a member of its Initiating Committee in 1943 and served on its Speakers Bureau until 1945.[47] In addition, Burgess was said to have been a sponsor, member of the advisory board, or lecturer for several reported Communist front organizations.

Chicago also obtained a document entitled "New Russia," which announced two slide presentations and lectures to be delivered by Burgess and his sister on November 15, 1933, under the auspices of the Park–Burgess Lectures series and the Chicago Urban League. Based on their travels and research in Russia, Burgess spoke on "New Men, New Crimes: Crime in the Soviet Union," and his sister on "Moscow 1933: Everyday Life in Moscow."[48] Burgess and his sister had just returned from Russia, where they had conducted several weeks of participant observation, sharing a small apartment with a Russian family in one of the new residential areas for workers and participating in their daily routines and family life. The summer before they had also spent time in several Soviet villages.

Chicago agents were sent back to the University of Chicago. Ogburn was recontacted and repeated his admiration for Burgess and absolute confidence in his loyalty. He noted Burgess's academic interest in Russia and indicated the likelihood that Burgess "undoubtedly has come in contact with other groups in the United States who are also interested in Russia and communism." But he also advised that "for the last 6 or 7 years, due to the difficulty of obtaining factual material on Russia, Professor BURGESS has largely lost interest in research concerning Russia and communism."[49] Charles E. Merriam, Professor Emeritus of Political Science, acquainted with Burgess since 1916, described him as "a very conservative individual," and said that he could not conceive of him being disloyal to the United States.[50]

Several other faculty, staff, and students were interviewed, all attesting to his loyalty; none could provide any derogatory information or evidence of Communist activity or affiliation. Residents in his apartment building reported the same, though agents were unable to recontact Miss Irene Carter and Miss Bertha Favard, as the latter was deceased and the former in a home for the feebleminded.

For its part, the Indianapolis field office was charged with recontacting Captain Will of the Michigan City police to see if it could obtain more information on Burgess's library and activities.[51] Will could no longer recall the identity of the informant who had originally furnished the information. However, one of the field office's confidential informants, who had been a former public official in Beverly Shores, advised that in 1947 Burgess had been asked to write an article on the town to be included in a program for the Fireman's Dance. He claimed that the article was very pro-Russian and that Burgess had compared Beverly Shores with a famous Russian seacoast resort and recommended that to improve itself, Beverly Shores should become more like its Russian counterpart.

Indianapolis also interviewed Louise Van Hess Young, a summer resident of the Dunes whose deceased husband had been a math professor at Chicago and had known Burgess for thirty-five years. Burgess and his sister were frequent visitors at her summer home and eventually she moved in with them in their home in Chicago. She had no doubts about his loyalty, but during the interview she expressed considerable doubts about the Loyalty Program and described the FBI as an organization of "snoopers." Her comments were duly recorded on the administrative page attached to the Indianapolis report, no doubt destined for a file of her own.

In support of the investigation, the Springfield field office obtained certified copies of the transcribed proceedings of the Illinois Seditious Activities Investigation Commission's hearings on the investigation of the University of Chicago and Roosevelt College held during April and May 1949.[52] Otherwise known as the Broyles Commission, this was the testimony to which Burgess had referred in his letter to the NIH. Burgess, who had publicly opposed the Commission, was subpoenaed to testify before it concerning the affidavit he had submitted in response to star witness and conservative Hearst reporter Howard Rushmore's accusations of his affiliation with several Communist front organizations.[53] The exchanges between Burgess and J. B. Matthews, brought in from Washington, D.C. to serve as Chief Investigator and Interrogator, were often contentious:

Dr. Matthews: "Are you aware of the fact that the Chicago Council for American–Soviet Friendship, as a branch of the National Council for

American–Soviet Friendship, is on the Attorney General's list of subversive of communist organizations?"

Mr. Burgess: "I am."

Dr. Matthews: "It isn't necessary to show you the document or would you like to see it?"

Mr. Burgess: "I see my name is here with many prominent persons throughout the country. Three United States Senators—who apparently do not agree with the Attorney General that this organization is subversive."

Dr. Matthews: "Are you implying that you are going to establish innocence by association?"

Mr. Burgess: "But it seems to me if you imply guilt by association you should also—be able to prove innocence by association."

Dr. Matthews: "You then accept guilt by association?"

Mr. Burgess: "I am not saying that. I am—I don't subscribe to either one, but if one is brought forward, then the other should also be brought forward."[54]

Burgess further argued that the Attorney General had made a mistake in listing the Council as subversive, and read statements of support which had been sent to it in 1944 by President Roosevelt, and 1945 by General Eisenhower.[55] Burgess also read a statement which he had prepared outlining his views on Communism:

I have never been and am not now a communist. I have never been and am not now in sympathy with communism. In all the 33 years I have taught at the University of Chicago, I have never heard of a single member of the faculty who was accused or even suspected of being a communist. Communism as exemplified at present in the Soviet Union, combines three principles. I am opposed to all three. First, communism educates State socialism and ultimately communism. Although socialism has been tried for over thirty years in the Soviet Union, its results are very inferior, both in productivity and in, especially in, the quality of goods to those of our American Economic System. Second, communism in the Soviet Union has maintained a political dictatorship, with a one party government, and the final power in the hands of the Politburo. Third, the communist party has abolished freedom of speech and freedom of teaching in every country where it has taken over power. American citizens should prize their heritage of freedom of speech and of teaching, and should be fearful of attempts to restrict and limit it.[56]

Hoover pal and protege Guy Hottel, SAC for the Washington, D.C. field office, forwarded Washington's report in early July 1950. In addition to rechecking Burgess's passport records with the State Department, Washington also checked the files of the House Committee on Un-American Activities. HUAC files revealed that in April

1949, just prior to his testifying before the Broyles Commission, Burgess had joined fifty leading professors and instructors in signing a letter, a copy of which was published in the *Daily Worker*, opposing the Broyles Bill, which was characterized as intending to outlaw the Communist Party, imprison Communists and members of Communist fronts, and impose thought control throughout the educational system. In 1943, he had signed a letter, issued by the NCASF, protesting anti-Soviet slander and calling for complete national unity to win the war. Burgess's name also appeared in exhibits taken from 1941 and 1942 issues of *Social Work Today* and *Soviet Russia Today*, both cited as Communist fronts by HUAC, and he was listed as a contributor to the Commonwealth College in 1933, cited as a "Communist Enterprise" by the Attorney General under Executive Order 9835.

On July 19, 1950, with the Loyalty Investigation completed, Hoover sent copies of the reports from the four field offices to James E. Hatcher, Chief of the Investigations Division of the Civil Service Commission with a request to "Please advise this Bureau of the ultimate disposition which is made of this case."[57] Copies were also sent to the Justice Department, in accordance with the attorney general's request, in 1948, that he be informed of all cases where there is evidence of membership in the Communist Party by a government employee.[58] Then, the following month, Chicago was instructed to reopen its internal security investigation of Burgess:

> As the loyalty investigation of Burgess has been completed you should now consider him as a Security Matter subject and authority is granted to contact your confidential informants and reliable sources of information, including those affiliated with educational institutions. You may also contact the registrars' offices of such institutions as set forth in SAC Letter 128, Series 1948. Prior Bureau authority must be obtained before interviewing any students, employees or persons otherwise affiliated with educational institutions who are not covered by the above categories.[59]

Chicago did not complete its investigation until late February 1951, but in the meantime, on October 25, 1950, Joseph McElvain, Chairman of the Federal Security Agency's Board of Inquiry of Employee Loyalty, sent an inquiry to the Bureau, requesting, "Since it is apparently impossible for you to advise us of the identities of these informants, we request that you supply us with sufficient background information concerning them, which may reflect upon their veracity, so that this Board will have some actual information which will assist us in evaluating the informants' credibility."[60]

Background information was assembled for several of the informants, the most important being Louis F. Budenz. Former editor of the *Daily Worker* turned police informer, Budenz had advised the New York field office in May 1950 that "Professor Ernest W. Burgess was one of the four hundred persons he considered concealed Communists."[61] Hoover instructed New York to contact Budenz, who was then interviewed on December 2, 1951. Budenz stated he had met Burgess in Chicago at a closed meeting of the Communist Party sometime in 1938 or 1939. He recalled that Morris Childs, leader of the CP in Chicago at that time, had introduced Burgess to him as a Communist.[62] Budenz also suggested that the Bureau contact Frank Meyer, who had been doing graduate work at Chicago and knew Burgess from 1934 to 1938. Meyer claimed to have been a leader of the University student and faculty sections of the CP and was not aware of any Communist activity on Burgess's part. He indicated that he believed Burgess to have been "clean" during the period he knew him.

On December 16, Hoover forwarded the background information on informants to the Civil Service Commission, with copies to McElvain and Assistant Attorney General James M. McInerney.[63] The names of all confidential informants, including Budenz of course, were not revealed. A couple of weeks later, McElvain wrote Hoover requesting additional details concerning information provided by "Confidential Informant New York [DELETED]," unknown to him to be Budenz. In particular, the Board was interested in information which might "reflect upon the ability of the informant to identify a person from a photograph after the lapse of a period of twelve years when it appears that the relationship was of short duration and when the importance of the meeting is not set forth."[64] Hoover sent an urgent request to New York asking for further details on the credibility and reliability of the information.[65] Though not immediately available, when recontacted, Budenz indicated that he had seen Burgess a number of times, heard his name often mentioned by CP officials, and felt that he knew him well enough to recognize him after a few years. For the information and guidance of the Loyalty Board, New York also noted that Budenz was a self-admitted former member of the Communist Party who had furnished the FBI reliable information in the past. On January 27, 1951, this information was duly passed on so the Board could complete its deliberations.[66] However, it would be another year before the FBI would be informed that Burgess had been reviewed favorably by the Board of Inquiry and determined to be "Eligible on loyalty."[67]

In the meantime, on February 28, 1951, Chicago submitted its report on its reopened security investigation of Burgess.[68] In the detailed eighteen-page document, Chicago brought Burgess's security file up to date, incorporating the most recent information concerning his reported Communist front affiliations which had been listed in the Loyalty Investigation, the Broyles Commission testimony of Rushmore, and the accusations of Party membership obtained from Budenz. The only previously uncovered piece of information was a note that in March 23, 1945, Burgess had participated in a roundtable concerning the outlawing of discrimination sponsored by the Chicago Council Against Racial and Religious Discrimination.

Once again Burgess was placed on the Security Index as a Communist and remained there even after the Civil Service Commission had reported him eligible on loyalty on February 13, 1952.[69] Burgess had retired in 1951, but FBI interest in his activities continued and on June 8, 1953, Chicago reported to the Bureau that he had been subpoenaed to appear before the closed hearings on "Communist Infiltration into Education" being conducted in Chicago by the Jenner Committee. However, when called, Burgess stated that he wanted a public hearing so that the public would know why he was subpoenaed and "in order to do what I can to counteract the rising tide of public hysteria."[70] He then got up, left the closed hearing room, and distributed a mimeographed statement to the reporters waiting outside condemning the Committee's action and giving evidence of his own loyalty. The Bureau obtained a transcript of Burgess's statement to the Committee but warned, "Because it was heard only in executive session and was furnished confidentially to the Bureau, the contents of this Volume should not be set forth in any communication which may be disseminated outside of the Bureau."[71]

Burgess's file was once again updated in April 1955. Because "no information has been developed tending to show BURGESS as being in a leadership capacity in any front group," on June 28, 1955, he was removed from the Security Index.[72] However, in March 1956, the Miami field office was given permission to interview him at his Palm Beach home in connection with a Loyalty Investigation of Herbert Blumer, but only after Chicago furnished detailed information on Burgess's background and Communist Party and front activities.[73]

In addition to Blumer's loyalty, Burgess was also questioned about his own activities and once again denied ever being a member of the Communist Party, knowing any of its members, or attending any of its meetings.[74] He stated that he had given his name freely for use by several welfare organizations. However, he denied knowing that any of the organizations with which he had been associated were Communist fronts, for example the Chicago Council of American Soviet Friendship, until 1949, when he had been called before the Broyles Commission. He discussed his three trips to Russia, indicating that during his 1933 trip he had conducted a study of crime and juvenile delinquency in Russia in which he had gained access to the records of a criminal psychopathic institution in Moscow. He had contacted psychiatrists because "they actually believed that criminal behavior was based upon human behavior patterns, although they openly followed the Communist Party line that economic and social trends were the actual causes of crime and juvenile delinquency." He also stated that "he felt that the psychiatrists would give him a truer picture in this regard and did not contact Russian sociologists because they followed the Communist Party line strictly, . . . and therefore would not give him any information of value to his study."[75] Finally, he also noted that in association with his employment as a consultant for the Federal Security Agency in 1951, he had been afforded a hearing in connection with his activities and had been absolved of any disloyalty.

The Washington field office checked to see whether Burgess was still serving as a consultant with the government, and, when they discovered he was not, informed the Bureau that they would take no further action. By then Burgess was seventy years old and his health was starting to deteriorate. Nonetheless, he continued writing on gerontological issues until his death at age eighty in 1966.

There is a certain irony that Burgess, one of the architects of the Chicago School of Sociology, with its human ecology model that has been regularly taken to task for supporting the status quo, legitimizing capitalism, and mystifying some of the central features of American society, would become a target of FBI surveillance and suspicions and even be officially listed on its Security Index as a Communist.[76] Further contributing to the irony, Burgess and J. Edgar Hoover shared much in common. Both spent their entire lives as bachelors, one living with his mother, the other his sister. Both men were consummate bureaucrats who devoted their entire lives to building and maintaining a single institution.

As a role model in the development of the sociologist as "benevolent technocratic analyst," Burgess did not see the relationship between sociology and capitalism as problematic and was more inclined to cooperate with its social and political institutions than critique them.[77] Hoover, on the other hand, was much more aware of the critical potential of sociology and tended to have a rather suspicious regard for sociologists. And while Burgess's Russian interests and organizational affiliations were no doubt purely academic or the innocent result of his support for the underdog, to Hoover and the FBI they appeared to be the activities of a Communist.

Burgess never broached the issue of McCarthyism, the Loyalty Program, or the FBI in any of his sociological writings, nor discussed their impact on the discipline or his own work. And with the exception of a chapter on the Russian family included in *The Family*, he never published any major works based on the research he did during his travels to the Soviet Union. However, through his testimony before the Broyles Commission and his courageous refusal to testify in closed session before the Jenner Committee he made it quite clear that he saw these activities as a fundamental threat to the democratic values of the nation and the intellectual freedom of the academy.

NOTES

1. Martin Bulmer, *The Chicago School of Sociology: Institutionalization, Diversity, and the Rise of Sociological Research* (Chicago: University of Chicago Press, 1984), 68.

2. As Louis Coser has noted in "American Trends," in *A History of Sociological Analysis*, ed. Thomas Bottomore and Robert Nisbet (New York: Basic, 1978), 311–312, the history of early American sociology is the history of the Chicago School. Several excellent accounts of this history exist including Bulmer, *The Chicago School*; Ruth Shonle Cavan, "The Chicago School of Sociology, 1918–1933," *Urban Life* 14 (1983): 407–420; Mary Jo Deegan, *Jane Addams and the Men of the Chicago School, 1892–1918* (New Brunswick, N. J.: Transaction, 1988); Robert E. L. Faris, *Chicago Sociology, 1920–1932* (Chicago: University of Chicago Press, 1967); and Dennis Smith, *The Chicago School: A Liberal Critique of Capitalism* (New York: St. Martin's, 1988). Lester Kurtz, *Evaluating Chicago Sociology: A Guide to Literature* (Chicago: University of Chicago Press, 1984), provides a comprehensive overview of Chicago sociology as well as an extensive annotated bibliography of works evaluating it.

3. Donald J. Bogue, introduction to *The Basic Writings of Ernest W. Burgess*, ed. Donald J. Bogue (Chicago: Community and Family Study Center, 1974), xii.

4. Ibid., xiii.

5. As quoted in Bulmer, *The Chicago School*, 187.

6. Park taught his first course at Chicago in 1914, "The Negro in America." However, even though he provided some of the most influential and definitive intellectual leadership of the Chicago School, he did not receive a full-time appointment in the department of sociology until relatively late in his career. For a detailed account of Park's life and contributions to Chicago sociology, see Winfred Raushenbush, *Robert E. Park: Biography of a Sociologist* (Durham, N. C.: Duke University Press, 1979). No similarly comprehensive biographical work has been completed on Burgess. In response to an FOIA request on Park, the FBI indicated that it could locate no information pertaining to him in its files.

7. Ibid., 81–82. No doubt the book received its nickname for the color of its cover as well as its heft and breadth. A sophisticated and demanding text by today's standards, it was organized around fourteen sociological themes and included 196 readings drawn from the likes of Spencer, Simmel, and Durkheim. It was one of the first sociology texts to include psychoana-

lytic concepts. Each chapter is followed by a set of discussion topics and essay questions. The book immediately became the most widely used text of its day and was last republished in 1970.

8. Herbert Blumer, "Ernest W. Burgess," *American Sociologist* 2 (1967): 148; Bogue, "Introduction," xiv; Bulmer, *The Chicago School*, 128.

9. As quoted in Martin Bulmer, "The Early Institutional Establishment of Social Science Research: The Local Community Research Committee at the University of Chicago, 1923–1930," *Minerva* 18 (1980): 65.

10. Burgess's theory of concentric zones is developed in his contribution to the book, *The Growth of the City: An Introduction to a Research Project*, in which he originally presented at the eighteenth annual meeting of the American Sociological Society in 1923.

11. In response to a FOIA request on Jane Addams, the Bureau did not release any files on Addams herself, but did release approximately 185 pages from a case file on the Women's International League for Peace and Freedom (WILPF). The case file, which had been routed to Hoover (then serving as Special Assistant to the Attorney General) and stamped "General Intelligence," consists primarily of documents and reports from the Bureau's surveillance of the Fourth International Congress of WILPF held in Washington, D.C., April 30 to May 4, 1924. As President of WILPF and Chairperson for the Congress, Addams's name is mentioned several times in what appear to be verbatim transcripts of the meetings. Included also is a copy of her Presidential Address, in which she indicates that perhaps it was a bit too soon to bring the WILPF Congress to the United States, noting,

> I am sorry to speak a word of apology. Ever since you landed some of you must have felt certain currents of intolerance never before encountered at our previous congresses. May I assure you that Americans are not by nature and training less tolerant than the people in those other countries, who treated us with such fine and unwavering courtesy. But a survival of war psychology is an unaccountable thing; it constitutes a new indictment, if one were needed, of the devastating effects of war upon the human character. . . . Perhaps we ought to have accepted the invitation of our British Section to meet in London, where free speech and free assemblage are once more firmly reestablished.

Copies of the report were also forwarded to the Office of Naval Intelligence. See Federal Bureau of Investigation, *Women's International League for Peace and Freedom*, Bureau File 61-1538-46, 50 (Washington, D.C.: FBI Freedon of Information–Privacy Acts Section).

12. Deegan, *Jane Addams*, 66; Kurtz, *Evaluating Chicago Sociology*, 22–23. As Deegan indicates in her book, this was part of a much broader and ongoing process whereby a gendered division of labor was institutionalized within the discipline of sociology, with the men recognized as social scientists while the women were marginalized as social workers. Generally, the process was fueled by fears of feminization in academia as more women were entering higher education. At Chicago, it was further exacerbated by a fight over the issue of sex-segregated education. See also Barbara Laslett, "Biography as Historical Sociology: The Case of William Fielding Ogburn," *Theory and Society* 2 (1991): 522.

13. Ernest W. Burgess, "The Family as a Unity of Interacting Personalities," in *The Basic Writings of Ernest W. Burgess*, ed. Donald J. Bogue (Chicago: Community and Family Study Center, 1974a), 145.

14. James W. Trent, "A Decade of Declining Evolvement: American Sociology in the Field of Child Development, the 1920s," *Sociological Studies of Child Development* 2 (1987): 24.

15. Because the popular legacy of the Chicago School has primarily celebrated the development of its qualitative methodology, the considerable quantitative tradition at Chicago, as reflected in the inscription from Lord Kelvin on its Social Science Research Building erected in 1929, "When you cannot measure your knowledge is meager and unsatisfactory as a primarily qualitative one," has often gone unrecognized. In fact, what distinguishes the Chicago School is not its qualitative methodology but rather its commitment to developing and employing a diverse set of methods, qualitative and quantitative, for the empirical analysis of social reality. For a detailed discussion of the quantitative tradition at Chicago, see Martin Bulmer, "Quantification and Chicago Social Science in the 1920s: A Neglected Tradition," *Journal of the History of the Behavioral Sciences* 17 (1981): 312–331.

16. Ernest W. Burgess, "Statistics and Case Studies as Methods of Sociological Research," in *The Basic Writings of Ernest Burgess*, ed. Donald J. Bogue (Chicago: Community and Family Study Center, 1974c), 368.

17. Ibid., 373.

18. Bulmer, *The Chicago School*, 156–159.

19. Bogue, "Introduction," xix.

20. Deegan, *Jane Addams*, 144–152.

21. Edward Shils, "Some Academics, Mainly in Chicago," *American Scholar* 50 (1981): 184.

22. Bogue, "Introduction," xii.

23. Federal Bureau of Investigation, *Ernest Watson Burgess*, Bureau File 77-28993-1 (Washington, D.C.: FBI Freedom of Information–Privacy Acts Section).

24. Ibid.

25. FBI, *Burgess*, Bufile 77-28993-3.

26. Ibid.

27. FBI, *Burgess*, Bufile 77-28993-2.

28. FBI, *Burgess*, Bufile 77-28993-4.

29. FBI, *Burgess*, Bufile 77-28993-5.

30. Martin Dies, Democrat from Texas, was the first chair of the House Un-American Activities Committee. Like its Senate counterpart, the committee was often referred to by the name of its chair. Dies presided over hearings on alleged Communist power and influence as early as 1938 to 1940.

31. FBI, *Burgess*, Bufile 77-28993-9.

32. Ibid.

33. Ibid.

34. Ibid. The actual title as published in 1916 was *The Function of Socialization in Social Evolution*. It is easy to see how in its ardor to seek out subversiveness the FBI might have made such an obviously Freudian slip.

However, as indicated earlier, since inaccuracies are not uncommon among FBI files, and most sources and their reliability are not identifiable, this instance serves as an additional reminder that information taken from them must be regarded with great caution.

35. Ibid.

36. Ibid.

37. Ibid.

38. The report makes reference to several Confidential Informants, all of whose identities as well as code names are blacked out. However, on the final page of the report, which would be removed if it was to be disseminated outside the FBI in order to protect the identity of its informants or hide any illegal procedures though which the information was obtained, the only source listed is the American Legion Headquarters. Even here the name of the actual contact making its files available is blacked out.

In 1940, Hoover established the American Legion Contact Program using Legion members to enable the FBI to operate a network of domestic informers dispersed in every small town and big city across the nation. Particularly directed to monitor and report any sources of radical dissent, by 1943 over 60 thousand Legionnaires had been recruited. The program continued to operate "as a latter day Inquisition" until 1966. See Athan G. Theoharis and John Stuart Cox, *The Boss: J. Edgar Hoover and the Great American Inquisition* (New York: Bantam, 1990), 224–229.

39. Since this information appears to have come from several different confidential sources, but only one, the American Legion, is listed under "Sources of Information," there is a good chance that some of it was actually obtained by Bureau agents themselves using illegal procedures such as break-ins.

40. Federal Bureau of Investigation, *Ernest Watson Burgess*, Bureau File 100-287323-1 (Washington, D.C.: FBI Freedom of Information–Privacy Acts Section).

41. FBI, *Burgess*, Bufile 100-287323-2.

42. FBI, *Burgess*, Bufile 100-287323-4.

43. No information recording the results of Chicago's reopened year-long investigation of Burgess appears in the files released. Apparently, no formal case report was forwarded to the Bureau and therefore would not have been included in the information released. The FOIA requests were only submitted to Bureau headquarters and would only cover information actually residing there. Details of this period of the investigation are probably available though the Chicago office from its own file on Burgess (Chicago 100-13891).

44. Federal Bureau of Investigation, Ernest Watson Burgess, Bureau File 121-22014-1 (Washington, D.C.: FBI Freedom of Information–Privacy Acts Section). Executive Order 9835 was issued by President Truman on March 22, 1947. It initiated a loyalty-security program for federal employees, giving Hoover and the FBI presidential sanction and wide-ranging licence to carry out its security investigations, and charged the Attorney General with establishing a list of foreign or domestic groups, associations, organizations, and so on, designated as totalitarian, Fascist, Communist, or subver-

sive. In effect, it established anti-Communism as the functional orthodoxy of the nation, and laid the foundations for McCarthyism. Albert Fried, *McCarthyism: The Great American Red Scare* (New York: Oxford University University, 1997), 24, 28–30.

45. Ibid.

46. FBI, *Burgess*, Bufile 121-22014-3.

47. FBI, *Burgess*, Bufile 121-22014-4X.

48. Ibid.

49. Ibid.

50. Ibid.

51. FBI, *Burgess*, Bufile 121-22014-5.

52. FBI, *Burgess*, Bufile 121-22014-9.

53. Howard Rushmore was one among a number of reporters organized by J. B. Matthews, who had served as Staff Director of HUAC, to support McCarthy. The group provided McCarthy with information, some of which came from special access afforded them by Hoover to FBI files, and also helped to write his speeches. See Theoharis and Cox, *The Boss*, 311.

54. Seditious Activities Investigation Commission, *Special Report: Investigation of the University of Chicago and Roosevelt College* (Springfield, Ill.: State of Illinois, 1949), 218–219.

55. Ibid., 219–220. Roosevelt had stated, "I am gratified to you and to all others who are celebrating American–Soviet Friendship day for the words of support and confidence I have received. There is no better tribute we can hold out to our allies than to continue working in ever growing accord to establish a peace that will endure." Eisenhower said, "American–Soviet Friendship is one of the corner stones on which the edifice of peace should be built. To achieve this friendship, nothing is more important than mutual understanding on the part of each of the traditions, and customs of the other. As an American soldier and lover of peace, I wish your Council the utmost success in the worthy work it has undertaken."

56. Ibid., 227–228.

57. FBI, *Burgess*, Bufile 121-22014-13.

58. Ibid.

59. FBI, *Burgess*, Bufile 121-287323-9. Actually, Chicago had requested and been given permission to reopen its Security Matter-C investigation of Burgess in February, but then quickly closed it once the Loyalty Investigation was begun. See FBI, *Burgess*, Bufile 121-287323-7; 8.

60. FBI, *Burgess*, Bufile 121-22014-14.

61. FBI, *Burgess*, Bufile 121-22014-15. Budenz was one of the FBI's paid informers and was know by his controllers in the agency to be inclined to make sensational charges which could not be fully substantiated by the facts. However, this information was withheld in order not to compromise his credibility with the public as a star anti-Communist witness. Ellen Schrecker, *Many Are the Crimes: McCarthyism in America* (New York: Little, Brown, 1998), 230–231.

62. FBI, *Burgess*, Bufile 121-22014-22.

63. FBI, *Burgess*, Bufile 121-22014-27;28.

64. FBI, *Burgess*, Bufile 121-22014-28.

65. FBI, *Burgess*, Bufile 121-22014-29.
66. FBI, *Burgess*, Bufile 121-22014-32;34.
67. FBI, *Burgess*, Bufile 121-22014-35.
68. FBI, *Burgess*, Bufile 100-287323-11.
69. FBI, *Burgess*, Bufile 100-287323-10;14.
70. FBI, *Burgess*, Bufile 100-287323-15;16.
71. FBI, *Burgess*, Bufile 100-287323-17. Hoover developed a set of elaborate procedures to protect the nature and scope of Bureau activities from outside scrutiny. He was particularly anxious that Congress not find out the extent to which he had infiltrated it and was surveilling its members and activities. He was also interested in protecting those members with whom he had established a "personal and confidential" relationship. Theoharis and Cox, *The Boss*, 201–203. Copies of the testimony were not released with Burgess's file.
72. FBI, *Burgess*, Bufile 100-287323-19;20.
73. FBI, *Burgess*, Bufile 100-287323. Also Federal Bureau of Investigation, *Herbert George Blumer*, Bureau File 138-3450-5.
74. FBI, *Burgess*, Bufile 100-287323-22.
75. Ibid.
76. See Kurtz, *Evaluating Chicago Sociology*, 26–29. Also Alvin W. Gouldner, *The Coming Crisis of Western Sociology* (New York: Basic, 1970); James D. Miley, "Critical Dimensions in Human Ecology: Ideology in American Sociology," *Urban Life* 9 (1980): 163–185; and Julia Schwendinger and Herman Schwendinger, "Sociologists of the Chair and the Natural Law Tradition," *Insurgent Sociologist* 3, no. 2 (1973): 3–18.
77. Kurtz, *Evaluating Chicago Sociology*, 78–79; Smith, *The Chicago School*.

— 4 —

William Fielding Ogburn: Scientist, Statistician, Schizophrene

Upon his retirement in 1951, *Time* magazine characterized William Fielding Ogburn as "the top social statistician in the U.S."[1] A pioneer in the application of multivariate analysis, later refined by Samuel Stouffer and Paul Lazarsfeld, Ogburn once wrote in his diary, "My worship of statistics had a somewhat religious nature. If I wanted to worship, to be loyal, to be devoted, then statistics was the answer for me, my God."[2] A member of the "second generation" of American sociologists, throughout his career he was a vigorous and outspoken advocate of the use of quantitative methods and statistics as a means of creating a more empirical and "objective" discipline.[3] Ogburn joined Park and Burgess in their crusade to purge the intellectuality, emotion, and bias he felt to be associated with the social philosophizing and reform interests of the preceding generation of male American sociologists, as well as their female colleagues and contemporaries at Chicago. As one of the founding fathers of scientism in American sociology,[4] he argued in his address to the American Sociological Society upon being elected president in 1929, "Sociology as a science is not interested in making the world a better place in which to live, in encouraging beliefs, in spreading information, in dispersing news, in setting forth impressions of life, in leading multitudes, or in guiding the ship of state. Science is interested directly in one thing only, to wit, discovering new knowledge."[5]

Ogburn was born in 1886, in Butler, Georgia, into a well-to-do merchant planter's family. However, his father died only six years later and he spent the rest of his childhood being raised by his mother in relatively impoverished circumstances. In 1902, at age sixteen, he entered Mercer College, graduating in 1905. Following Mercer, he took a teaching position at the Morton School for Boys and then as assistant principal at the Darlington School, staying in Georgia until he moved north to begin his graduate studies at Columbia University in 1908.[6]

As a graduate student at Columbia, Ogburn came under the tutelage of Frank Giddings, head of the department of sociology and one of the first sociologists interested in quantitative methods as a means of developing a more scientific sociology.[7] Eventually becoming his star student, it was through Giddings and one of the founders of econometrics, Henry L. Moore, that Ogburn was introduced to the significance of science and statistics and the importance of objectivity over emotion. Nonetheless, upon finishing his Ph.D. in 1912, when he left to take a position at Reed College in Portland, Oregon, he still carried with him a desire to "make the world a better place to live."[8] While at Reed, Ogburn spent large amounts of time with students and characterized his teaching as "a mild indoctrination of a liberal or radical social philosophy."[9] He sported an interest in socialism and participated in a variety of social reform efforts, working with the unemployed, posing as an unemployed man and visiting lumber camps, helping to found the Oregon Civic League, and lecturing to the Industrial Workers of the World (IWW). One of his most prized possessions in life was a three-volume edition of the works of Karl Marx, inscribed to him by the Portland chapter of the IWW.[10]

However, this commitment was not to last, as he became increasingly caught up in professional ambitions and concerned with being pigeonholed forever at Reed. In 1917, Ogburn accepted an appointment at the University of Washington. After one year, and with the outbreak of World War I, he then moved to Washington, D.C., and went to work as head of the cost-of-living section of the National War Labor Board, and a short time later as a Special Agent for the Bureau of Labor Statistics. During his year and one half in Washington, D.C., Ogburn led the way in the development of methods for analyzing family budgets and constructing price indexes. He published seventeen articles and was subsequently offered a position at Columbia in 1919.

With his return to Columbia, Ogburn resolved to abandon his earlier reform interests and to dedicate himself solely to the pursuit of science: "My problem as I saw it at Columbia was to indoctrinate only scientific method. . . . My social action I confined largely to organizational work in the advancement of science in the social discipline."[11] One of the first American sociologists to have developed an interest in Freud, and having himself undergone psychoanalysis, he increasingly began to discount social reform efforts as a "rationalization" of hopes for greater equality as well as a source of emotional bias and distortion which undermined the standards of scientific research.[12] He turned instead to what would become the fundamental task informing his life's work, understanding the processes underlying social change and social invention. In 1922, he published his most famous work, *Social Change: With Respect to Culture and Original Nature*, in which he introduced the concept and coined the phrase "cultural lag."[13] Eventually he would profess, "I shall be bold. I claim that the problem of social evolution is solved and that I have played a considerable part in solving it."[14]

Ogburn stayed at Columbia until 1927, when, having achieved national prominence as a quantitative sociologist, he was hired away by Chicago. His recruitment was a conscious and unanimous move by the Chicago faculty, including Burgess and Park, calculated to strengthen the quantitative dimension of its program and to help maintain its national reputation as the leading sociology program in the country.[15] Nonetheless, he encountered a much more hostile attitude to statistics than he had anticipated, or experienced at Columbia. No doubt this hostility was fueled in part by his energetic participation in the department's ongoing debate over quantitative versus qualitative methods, and a tireless advocacy of measurement which was gaining him the reputation of a methodological zealot.[16]

Ogburn was appointed chairperson of sociology at Chicago in 1940, and remained so until 1947 when Burgess took the helm. At Chicago he was known for browbeating his colleagues for their lack of scientific rigor, as well as the rather jealous guarding of his time from students. Prominently displayed in his office for any who might venture in to consult with him was a sign which stated, "He who takes my time steals the one thing he can never return."[17] Still, he exerted a considerable influence on his students and colleagues, and through them the increasingly quantitative and scientistic direction in which the discipline of sociology was developing. After Talcott Parsons convinced Samuel Stouffer, Ogburn's most accomplished student, to leave Chicago to run the Social Relations Laboratory at Harvard, Stouffer wrote back, "One consolation to you personally should be the knowledge that something of the scientific spirit of which you are America's greatest exemplar in our field will be brought into a new environment and diffused even more widely."[18]

Ogburn was also a leader in the construction of a new dimension in the role for the academic sociologist, that of professional consultant and government servant. In 1929, he was appointed as Director of Research for President Herbert Hoover's Research Committee on

Social Trends, a landmark in social investigation and for many years a standard reference for social scientists and government agencies.[19] He also held positions as research consultant to the National Resources Committee, advisor to the Resettlement Administration, Director of the Consumer's Advisory Board of the National Recovery Administration, and chairperson of the U.S. Census Advisory Committee.[20] However, noting the potential dilemma arising from the contradictory demands for value-free objectivity on the part of the scientist versus the inherently value-laden judgement and policy recommendations expected of the consultant, he was always careful to claim a conscious and self-imposed separation between the two. He drew on his familiarity with Freud in his attempt to resolve this dilemma and protect the integrity of his role as scientist from being undermined by that of the policy advocate: "The key to the solution I worked out for myself. . . . I turned with admiration to the schizophrene!"[21] The resultant and discomfiting schizophrenia has remained grafted onto the identity of American sociology ever since.

Ogburn came under the formal scrutiny of the FBI in the spring of 1950, while he was conducting a survey, under the auspices of the University of Chicago, of the dispersal of industry in and around American cities in order to find out whether industries were located close to city centers or out in suburban areas. The survey consisted of eight items and asked how many miles a plant was located from the center of the nearest city, how long the plant had been in operation at its current address, and the plant size.[22] However, upon receiving the survey, an unidentifiable official of E. I. Dupont deNemours & Company furnished a copy to a Special Agent of the Chicago field office and advised that "his company was not answering the questionnaire since it was considered that the information being sought could be of interest to enemies of the United States" (see Figure 4.1).[23]

Chicago forwarded copies of the survey to the Bureau, which tried to determine whether the study was being carried out for a government agency.[24] The office of the secretary of defense was contacted and reported no knowledge of such a study. It suggested that the National Security Resource Board (NSRB) be contacted. The security officer of the NSRB reported that the agency had no formal contract with the University of Chicago but did note that Ogburn was known to officials of the NSRB and had occasionally furnished it with copies of various studies carried out by the university.

On May 26, 1950, Director, FBI sent SAC, Chicago, a memo with reference to the industrial questionnaire circulated by Ogburn.[25] The memo indicated that in January 1948, he had been one of twenty-one sponsors of the "Committee of One Thousand" which had been

Figure 4.1

C
O
P
Y

Name of company_______________

Address of plant_______________

Year plant began operations at this address_______________

Are the number of employees under 500______, between 500 and 2,500______, over 2,500______?

If located in or near a metropolis, give name of city and distance in miles from the center of the metropolis:

Name of city_______________Distance_______________

If not in a metropolis or near one, then state the number of miles to the town or city center that is nearest:

Name of town_______________Distance_______________

set up to abolish the House Un-American Activities Committee. Chicago was instructed to provide the Bureau with a summary of all information on Ogburn appearing in its files.

Two months later, on July 24, Chicago submitted a memorandum to the Director, under the subject heading, "INTERNAL SECURITY–MISCELLANEOUS."[26] The memo indicates that even though there had been no formal investigation directed at Ogburn before, the Bureau's surveillance activities cast such a wide net that he had been caught within it a number of times. The memo lists several references to Ogburn, taken from the indices of the Chicago office and dating back to October 1941, when an anonymous source made available a cardex file maintained in the Offices of the United Spanish Aid Committee, which shared offices with the Veterans of the Abraham Lincoln Brigade. According to the informant, the cardex file offered a structural picture of the individuals affiliated with the United Spanish Aid movement and the capacities in which they served. Ogburn was listed as a member of the Teachers Committee of the Spanish Refugee Relief Committee, which at one time had sponsored a relief ship to the Loyalists in Spain.

The memo indicates that an unidentifiable source had reported Ogburn to have been a sponsor of the National War Time Conference of the Professions, the Sciences, the Arts, and the White Collar Field held in 1943 at the Biltmore Hotel in New York. The source described the conference as a Communist-inspired gathering. Chicago's files further indicate that on May 25, 1944, Ogburn had sent a letter to the Bureau which discussed the effect of aviation on the organization of the FBI's work and how it might be used to expedite some aspects of the Bureau's work.[27]

Also in 1944, T-2, a "very confidential" source, provided materials which indicated that Ogburn had written a letter to Oskar Lange, a former professor at Chicago who had given up his American citizenship to become the Polish ambassador to the United States. These materials appear to have been obtained from inside the Polish embassy.[28] In the letter, Ogburn thanked Lange for his presentation to the Institute of Social Research, saying, "Our people are most appreciative of what you said, and I was particularly impressed with the plans and emphasis you gave various courses."[29] On July 25, 1945, a pretext phone call made by a Chicago agent to the offices of the Midwest Division of the American Committee for Yugoslav Relief, designated a Communist organization by the attorney general, revealed that Ogburn was a sponsor of the group.

Chicago had also collected several clippings from local newspapers concerning Ogburn's views on the atomic bomb. During a University of Chicago Roundtable Discussion broadcast on Sunday,

August 8, 1945, just two days after the dropping of the bomb on Hiroshima, Ogburn "termed the bomb the most important invention of all times and predicted sweeping economic and social changes in the atomic age comparable to those created by the industrial revolution." He also warned that the "United States will be the world's most hated power if it tries to sit on the secret of the atomic bomb."[30] On October 22, 1945, Ogburn addressed a meeting of the Independent Citizens Committee of Arts, Sciences, and Professions and urged the scientific investigation of the likely effects of an atomic bomb on the structure of American society. He recommended the decentralizing of American cities as a possible defense against atomic war and pointed out that because Russia's cities were much smaller and scattered over a much larger area they would probably suffer less in this regard.

In 1946, Chicago had obtained a copy of a booklet put out by the Woodrow Wilson Foundation, "The Politics of Atomic Energy," written by Harry Gideonse, Raymond Fosdick, and Ogburn. Ogburn wrote the third section of the booklet, "If International Action Fails," in which he concluded that the atomic bomb should be banished by a world government. He also published a detailed discussion of his views on sociology and the atomic bomb in the January 1946 issue of the *American Journal of Sociology*, though it was never picked up by the FBI.[31] In it, he claimed that Hiroshima had ushered in a new age, the atomic age, which would impact many of our social institutions. And while it was the function of the natural scientists to make the bomb, it was that of the social sciences to determine its likely social consequences. Intimating the need for a sociological Manhattan Project, he argued, "No doubt, if sociologists had the two-billion-dollar fund, which the physicists and engineers had to finance constructing the bomb, then in several years' time they could advise adequately on the social adjustments to this new source of power."[32]

In May 1946, the New York field office had obtained a copy of the Branch membership of the American Association of Scientific Workers (AASW) from a "highly confidential source." In it, Ogburn was listed as a member of the Chicago branch. He was subsequently interviewed by a Special Agent from the Chicago field office. During the interview he advised that he had served as president of the Chicago chapter of the AASW for a one-year period in 1938 or 1939, and had remained an active member until 1945, when he resigned. He stated he had resigned from the organization "because there were some members in the organization who were 'radical' in that they proposed the use of force to make people accept social changes."[33] He also indicated that the failure of the organization to accomplish its purpose of causing scientists to become more aware of the social aspects of their activities had also contributed to his resignation. Chicago's memorandum concludes with a note that, according to Elizabeth Dilling's *The Red Network*, Ogburn was an advisor to the Pioneer Youth of America, which was characterized as a Communist-influenced group for young people, and a defender of various educators dismissed from their posts for "disaffectionists [sic] activities" toward the United States.

The memorandum was placed in the Bureau's files and became a permanent part of Ogburn's record. On January 26, 1951, in response to a request for information from the State Department, the Bureau forwarded a verbatim copy of the Chicago memo.[34] Similar documents were prepared for the United States Information Agency (USIA) on July 9, 1954, and the State Department once again on March 8, 1956. All were accompanied by the warning, "The foregoing information is furnished to you as a result of your request for an FBI file check and is not to be construed as a clearance or a nonclearance of the individual involved. This information is furnished for your use and should not be disseminated outside of your agency."[35]

FBI attention returned to Ogburn again, on October 9, 1958, when one of the FBI's liaisons sent information from the Passport Office notifying the Washington field office that Ogburn had been issued a passport in June for an August trip to the United Kingdom, Belgium, West Germany, France, and Morocco. It was specially noted, "In the passport application filed June 12, 1958, Mr. Ogburn denied present and past membership in the Communist Party." Scribbled by hand at the bottom of the report is the instruction, "Find out why this was referred to us."[36] One negative and six prints of Ogburn's passport photo were also forwarded.

In late November, a Special Agent from the Washington field office was sent over to the Passport Office where an unidentifiable official from the legal section of the Passport Office "made available" Ogburn's passport file.[37] The agent learned that in 1951, the office had received information of a "derogatory security nature" regarding Ogburn. No doubt this was why the FBI had been flagged to receive information concerning his passport application some seven years later. Based on this information, SAC, Washington, sent a memo, under the heading "Security Matter–C," to his counterpart in Chicago requesting, "Inasmuch as subject's passport file contains a notation that the FBI has information of a derogatory security nature, Chicago is requested to furnish WFO with all pertinent information to subject. P."[38]

Chicago forwarded a classified confidential eleven-page report on January 30, 1959, once again summarizing the information in its files.[39] A synopsis indicates, "Source in 1944 described WILLIAM

FIELDING OGBURN as broad-minded, but did not believe he was a Communist." The report is primarily a repeat of the information listed in the original Chicago memo, with an appendix listing some additional information on the nature of several of the organizations determined to be Communist affiliated with which Ogburn was associated or which he had sponsored.[40] The only other information not previously mentioned in earlier reports was that the FBI had in its possession a document dated February 27, 1935, with a notation that Ogburn had been the faculty director of a Student Anti-War Conference.

Upon receiving Chicago's report, Washington carried out a supplementary investigation of its own.[41] Using a "suitable pretext," one of its agents surreptitiously learned that Ogburn and his wife maintained an apartment in Washington, D.C., but that they were residing in Tallahassee, Florida, while he was teaching at Florida State University. He had been serving as a visiting professor and would not return until the middle of June. Washington also contacted several informants in its area familiar with the activities of CP members and organizations and was informed that Ogburn was not known to any of them. On February 19, 1959, Washington submitted its final report on Ogburn to the Bureau, concluding, "Subject does not meet the criteria for inclusion in the Communist Index. It being noted that subject has not had any reported activity in any subversive organization since the 1940's."[42] The Bureau forwarded the information to the State Department. One month later, on April 29, 1959, Ogburn died in a Tallahassee hospital following an emergency operation.

Though Ogburn never commented specifically on Hoover and the FBI, in a 1948 essay on freedom and organization he recognized that American society had become organized to a degree unprecedented in history, and posed the question of how its tradition of liberty could be reconciled to the ideology of organization. Indicating that there were times when this ideal was in jeopardy of being reduced to little more than a rhetorical ritual, he noted, "Thus, when our orators are speaking eloquently about liberty in connection with Lincoln and the Constitution, radicals are dismissed from their jobs, not because of anything that they have done but because of what others say they think. Some of our talk about freedom is merely a devotional to ancient gods."[43]

Taking advantage of his theory of the schizophrene and abandoning the role of scientist and the mantra of value-free objectivity he believed fundamental to it, he argued that the social philosophy undergirding our highly organized society should rest on a substructure of individual rights and liberties and pointed out the peril of unbridled organizational authority, (e.g., such as that wielded by Hoover and the FBI): "For there is serious danger of abuse of organizational authority, as the history of intolerance shows, unless it is safeguarded by a system of justice which protects the rights and liberties of individuals."[44]

NOTES

1. See Barbara Laslett, "Unfeeling Knowledge: Emotion and Objectivity in the History of Sociology," *Sociological Focus* 5 (1990): 417.

2. Quoted in ibid., 422.

3. Barbara Laslett, "Biography as Historical Sociology: The Case of William Fielding Ogburn," *Theory and Society* 2 (1991): 511–512.

4. Ibid., 533.

5. William Fielding Ogburn, "The Folkways of a Scientific Sociology," in *Studies in Quantitative and Cultural Sociology* (Chicago: University of Chicago Press, 1930), 2. See also William Fielding Ogburn, "Three Obstacles to the Development of a Scientific Sociology," *Social Forces* 8 (1930): 347–350.

6. Like Burgess, no comprehensive biographical treatment of Ogburn has been completed, even though, as Laslett notes, his papers are relatively well-preserved and organized in the archives at Chicago. All that exist are relatively brief overviews such as those provided by Laslett in her articles, and the occasional references in accounts of the Chicago school or introductions to compilations of Ogburn's work.

7. Martin Bulmer, *The Chicago School of Sociology: Institutionalization, Diversity, and the Rise of Sociological Research* (Chicago: University of Chicago Press, 1984), 9. Early on, beginning with the work of Richmond Mayo-Smith in the 1880s, Columbia was known as the home of statistical methods in sociology. Originally an editorial journalist, Giddings began teaching sociology at Columbia in 1893 and continued the tradition into the early 1900s. However, he was never able to build as influential a department of sociology at Columbia as existed at Chicago. In large part this was due to his dogmatic viewpoint and domineering personality, which bred considerable resentment among the rest of the faculty. See also Seymour Martin Lipset, "The Department of Sociology," in *A History of the Faculty of Political Science, Columbia University,* ed. Robert G. Hoxie (New York: Columbia University Press, 1955); and Floyd Nelson House, *The Development of Sociology* (New York: McGraw-Hill, 1936).

8. Laslett, "Biography as Historical Sociology," 518.

9. Quoted in ibid.

10. Otis Dudley Duncan, introduction to *On Culture and Social Change* by William F. Ogburn (Chicago: University of Chicago Press, 1964), ix.

11. Quoted in Laslett, "Unfeeling Knowledge," 422.

12. Ogburn felt that psychoanalysis might be used as a tool to help uncover and guard against the unconscious biases that threatened objectivity in science. See William F. Ogburn, "Bias, Psychoanalysis and the Subjective in Relation to the Social Sciences," *Publication of the American Sociological Society* 17 (1922), 62–74. His continuing interest in and study of

analysis led him to become an original member of the Board of Trustees of the Institute for Psychoanalysis in Chicago, and serve as its president between 1942 and 1947.

13. Even though it has been the subject of great controversy, Ogburn's concept of "cultural lag" has since become a part of the pantheon of common concepts in sociology (mentioned in virtually every introductory text), and has also penetrated popular vocabulary. For a detailed discussion of the development of the concept and his theory of social change, see Toby E. Huff, "Theoretical Innovation in Science: The Case of William F. Ogburn," *American Journal of Sociology* 79 (September 1973), 261–277. For a listing of additional sources, see Lester Kurtz, *Evaluating Chicago Sociology: A Guide to Literature* (Chicago: University of Chicago Press, 1984), 92, 110, 160.

14. As quoted in Duncan, Introduction, xiv.

15. Bulmer, *The Chicago School*, 171.

16. Ogburn observed in his journal, "On coming to the U. of C. I found a much more hostile attitude towards statistics than I ever had at Columbia. Yet I fought the battle, taught all the statistics in the Sociology Department, and participated generally in the statistical work of University Committees." As quoted in Laslett, "Biography as Historical Sociology," 516. See also Duncan, Introduction, xx.

17. Laslett, "Biography as Historical Sociology," 523.

18. Ibid., 520.

19. Roscoe C. Hinkle and Gisela J. Hinkle, *The Development of Modern Sociology: Its Nature and Growth in the United States* (New York: Random House, 1954), 46. Commissioned in 1929 by Herbert Hoover, the massive study, involving hundreds of social scientists and examining virtually every area of American life, was primarily concerned with social change and represented American social sciences coming of age in the realm of policy and government.

20. Dennis Smith, *The Chicago School: A Liberal Critique of Capitalism* (New York: St. Martin's, 1988), 167–168.

21. As quoted in Laslett, "Unfeeling Knowledge," 423. For Ogburn, schizophrenia was not an illness, but a strategy which enabled him to compartmentalize the normative expectations associated with each role and thereby offset the contradictions resulting from the potential role conflict between sociologist as scientist and sociologist as policy advocate and/or social activist. Laslett, however, questions his claim to have successfully and so thoroughly separated the two. See Laslett, "Biography as Historical Sociology," 516.

22. Federal Bureau of Investigation, *William F. Ogburn*, Bufile 100-148350-2 (Washington, D.C.: FBI Freedom of Information–Privacy Acts Section).

23. FBI, *Ogburn*, Bufile 100-148350-1.

24. FBI, *Ogburn*, Bufile 100-148350-3.

25. Ibid.

26. FBI, *Ogburn*, Bufile 100-148350-4. See also FBI, *William F. Ogburn*, Bufile 100-29013-1 (Washington, D.C.: FBI Freedom of Information–Privacy

Acts Section). This file consists of a report prepared in 1954 by the correlation clerk and summarizes the information on Ogburn appearing in FBI files. Though there is little in addition to the Chicago memorandum, it does provide a more detailed account of each of the references and therefore offers greater insight into FBI investigative and surveillance practices. In addition to those activities reported in the Chicago memo, the 1954 report also notes that, in 1946, a search of a residence conducted by the Los Angeles office had turned up a document entitled, "A Brief History of the CCASF (Chicago Council of American Soviet Friendship)," and a list of names of "Leading Chicagoans" on which Ogburn appeared. And, in 1950, Ogburn was among those listed on the Advisory Board of the American Civil Liberties Union.

27. No doubt this memo was based on his interest in technology and social change and research he was conducting at the time on the social impact of aviation. See William F. Ogburn, "Aviation and Society," *Air Affairs* 1 (1946), 10–20; and William F. Ogburn, Jean L. Adams, and S. C. Gilfillan, *The Social Effects of Aviation* (Boston: Houghton Mifflin, 1946).

28. Confidential informants are not identified by name in any FBI report that might be circulated outside the Bureau. Instead, they are referred to by code, such as T-1, T-2, and so on. However, in documents released in response to FOIA requests, there is often included an administrative page which, for internal identification purposes only, originally listed the code number and then the name of each confidential informant. These names of course are almost always blacked out.

29. FBI, *Ogburn*, Bufile 100-148350-4.

30. FBI, *Ogburn*, Bufile 100-29013-1; FBI, *Ogburn*, Bufile 100-148350-4. The clippings were taken from the August 13, 1945, editions of the *Chicago Daily News* and *Chicago Daily Tribune*.

31. While the FBI set up extensive clipping operations to identify and collect information appearing on suspect individuals and/or activities from newspapers across the country, academic publications received much less attention unless specifically brought to its notice by a confidential informant or other external source.

32. William F. Ogburn, "Sociology and the Atom," *American Journal of Sociology* 51 (1946), 268. Ogburn was one of just a few social scientists addressing the social consequences of the bomb and proposing that social scientists pick up where the natural scientists had left off and help harness the social forces of atomic awareness to create a new society. He served as a member of the Committee on Social Aspects of Atomic Energy, set up by the Social Science Research Committee in 1946 and funded by the Carnegie and Rockefeller Foundations. The Committee sponsored two studies published in 1947: "American Opinion on World Affairs in the Atomic Age," and "The Problem of Reducing Vulnerability to Atomic Bombs." See Paul Boyer, "Social Scientists and the Bomb," *Bulletin of the Atomic Scientists* 41 (1985), 31–37.

33. FBI, *Ogburn*, Bufile 100-148350-4.

34. Federal Bureau of Investigation, Bufile 62-60537-23800 (Washington, D.C.: FBI Freedom of Information–Privacy Acts Section). It is not clear

from the documents to what file this number refers. It appears to be a rather large file, perhaps containing a record of other similar requests for information from the State Department and other government agencies.

35. FBI, Bufile 62-60527-46473. This proviso, or one similar, was routinely attached to any information sent outside the Bureau.

36. FBI, *William F. Ogburn*, Bufile 100-35330-1 (Washington D.C.: FBI Freedom of Information–Privacy Acts Section).

37. FBI, *Ogburn*, Bufile 100-35330-2.

38. Ibid.

39. FBI, *William F. Ogburn*, Bufile 100-430091-1 (Washington, D.C.: FBI Freedon of Information–Privacy Acts Selection). The report was classified confidential because information furnished within it "could reasonably result in identification of informants of continuing value and compromise future effectiveness." Almost forty years later, many of the sources of information and the identity of all of the informants have been blacked out, as is typical in virtually all documents released by the FBI, regardless of their age or contemporary importance.

40. Included are the American Association of Scientific Workers, the Cultural and Scientific Conference for World Peace, the Independent Citizens Committee of the Arts, Sciences and Professions, and the United Spanish Aid Committee. See FBI, *Ogburn*. Bufile 100-430091-1.

41. FBI, *Ogburn*, Bufile 100-430091-2.

42. Ibid.

43. William Fielding Ogburn, "Thoughts on Freedom and Organization," *Ethics* 58 (1948): 260.

44. Ibid.

— 5 —

Robert and Helen Lynd: From Middletown to Moronia

Robert Straughton and Helen Merrell Lynd's classic study of small-town white America, *Middletown*, was one of the first sociological works to be widely promoted and distributed among the general public.[1] Much to the chagrin of John D. Rockefeller's Institute of Social and Religious Research, which had originally commissioned the work but refused to publish it upon completion because of its "savage attack on religion," it came out with front page reviews in the *New York Times* and *Herald Tribune*, and decked the window display at Brentanos. In his review, entitled "A City in Moronia," H. L. Mencken characterized it as "one of the richest and most valuable documents ever concocted by American sociologists," but also noted, "What it reveals is a man of almost unbelievable stupidities. Well-fed, well-dressed, complacent and cocksure, he yet remains almost destitute of ideas. The things he admires are mainly mean things, and the things he thinks he knows are nearly all untrue."[2]

Not surprisingly, many local residents were somewhat chaffed by the "cold," "cynical," and "hickish" portrayal of Muncie, the Indiana, community which the study was about. Nonetheless, it was given a place of honor, along with the copies of the Bible and the Methodist Creed, in the cornerstone of a Methodist Church constructed shortly following its publication and remained there even though a local editor called for a public campaign to "get that damned book out."[3]

While Robert Lynd argued that their critical portrayal of Muncie reflected nothing more than the efforts of the disinterested investigators fulfilling the duties of objective social scientific observation, its tone would suggest that it was also influenced by the somewhat elite, if not effete, perspective of two native Midwesterners who had been transported to the more cosmopolitan and urbane East and would choose to live most of their lives on New York City's Central Park West.[4]

Considered one of the most radical sociologists of his time, Robert Lynd was born in New Albany, Indiana, about 150 miles south of Muncie on the Ohio River, and given a strict Christian moral upbringing. He attended Princeton University and, though never happy there, received his bachelors in English in 1914. After becoming disenchanted with a budding career as a publisher for Scribner's and Sons following World War I, he decided to go into the ministry and entered the Union Theological Seminary in 1920. During the summer of 1921 he volunteered as a student preacher for an oil camp at Elk Basin, Wyoming. Jumping into camp life much as an anthropologist might, he published an account of his experiences as well as an exposé of the wretched conditions in the western oil camps, which called for a series of improvements. The latter caused a furor among Standard Oil officials, who offered to build a marble Carnegie library in Elk Basin if Lynd would withdraw it. When Lynd refused, John D. Rockefeller, Jr. published a personal response in which he tried to claim that the conditions at Elk Basin were not typical, but agreed with Lynd that "the twelve-hour day and the seven-day week should no longer be tolerated."[5]

Helen Merrell was born in LaGrange, Illinois, to Congregationalist parents who along with their strict Christian beliefs were committed to embracing all of humanity, regardless of race, sect, or nationality. Self-described as an impetuously lying and guilt-ridden child, a rebel from the start who flunked the fifth grade, Merrell went on to excel at Wellesley College where she was deeply influenced by Hegelian philosopher Mary S. Case and graduated Phi Beta Kappa in 1919. She and Robert met in passing while hiking on New Hampshire's Mt. Washington, and while neither mentioned their names, Helen struck up a conversation about Veblen's *Theory of the Leisure Class.* The next day Robert climbed back to the mountain top to get her address from the logbook there. They were married in 1921 and moved to New York where Helen obtained her M.A. from Columbia University.[6]

The confrontation over the Elk Basin articles notwithstanding, the Rockefeller Foundation's Institute of Social and Religious Research asked Robert to direct a small city project to study religious life in America.[7] In 1924, the Lynds moved to Muncie, and after overcoming early objections expanded the study beyond the rather narrow religious boundaries initially outlined by the Institute to encompass an examination of the impact the terrific social changes of burgeoning capitalism and its attendant industrialization were having on all aspects of the daily life of the community. Muncie was chosen for its "middle-of-the-road" quality and homogenous population, including an unusually small foreign-born and Negro population for an industrial city.[8] What made *Middletown* such a pioneering and influential work in community studies was the breadth of its analysis and the use of an anthropological methodology that till then had been reserved for the study of so-called "primitive" cultures. In 1935, the Lynds returned to Muncie for a follow-up on their original study, this time to investigate the impact of the depression and the community's response to it.[9] Together, the two studies represent a chronicle of the life and times of an American community unprecedented in American sociology.

Following *Middletown*, the Lynds found themselves in the unusual position of having completed one of the seminal studies of their discipline at the beginning of their careers, even before either had received their Ph.D. Robert received his Ph.D. from Columbia in 1931, the same year he was given a position there. His dissertation consisted of six chapters of *Middletown*, but only after he and Helen went through the "fake process" of putting a blue pencil through every line she had written.[10]

After the Middletown studies, Robert Lynd only produced one other major work, *Knowledge for What? The Place of Social Science in American Culture*, a critical appraisal of the contemporary state of the social sciences in which Lynd called for social scientists to become critics of the status quo, not its high priests.[11] He argued that it is the role of social science to be troublesome, and noted that "no culture can be realistically and effectively analyzed by those who elect to leave its central idols untouched."[12] Like Du Bois, Lynd foreshadowed the critique Mills would offer a generation later of the rise of abstracted empiricism and grand theory, although Lynd's analysis reflected an elitist, centralizing, and controlling tendency with which in all probability Mills would not have been comfortable.

Lynd himself was deeply concerned with America's growing "pecuniary culture" and, as a pioneer in both consumer research and advocacy, helped to establish the Consumers National Federation.[13] However, as a radical without a party or a movement, he was politically homeless.[14] Following World War II, his increasingly academic embitterment and intellectual pessimism with the scientistic direction sociology was taking brought on a depression which kept him from completing the major treatise on power in America which he had hoped to write. Eventually, he did publish an outline of his observations in the course of a critical review of Mills's *The Power Elite*.[15]

Though Helen Lynd was much less recognized than her husband for her contributions to *Middletown* and her work beyond it, one might argue that it was she who went on to be the more productive of the two. After *Middletown*, she was offered a position at the newly established Sarah Lawrence College and had a formative influence on its innovative development and open curriculum. However, Columbia did not afford Helen the same opportunity as Robert to use her part of *Middletown* as her dissertation. As a result, she only received her Ph.D., in history, relatively late in her career for her thesis on *England in the Eighteen-eighties: Toward a Social Basis for Freedom*, a sweeping social historical case study of personality and social structure and the interaction of ideas, material changes, and social movements. With an intellectual breadth that extended considerably beyond the limits of sociology and cut across philosophy and psychology, she also produced a still insufficiently appreciated work, *On Shame and the Search for Identity*, an unusually modern treatment of the relationship between personality and society in which she critiques Freud and Parsons for neglecting the role of social values in shaping the self.[16]

Robert Lynd came under formal scrutiny by the FBI as the result his application to become a consultant for the Office of Emergency Management. On February 21, 1942, following a Special Inquiry from the office, Hoover sent a letter instructing the New York office to lead an investigation of him.[17] The Washington and Newark field offices were instructed to assist and a memo setting out information already contained in Bureau files was included, indicating, "The derogatory information contained therein, should be included in the applicant report submitted by the New York Office."

Newark was charged with investigating Lynd's activities during his undergraduate years at Princeton.[18] Scholastic records obtained there showed that prior to entering the university he had been a below-average student, but once in college went on to graduate with honors in English. One of his former English professors, Charles W. Kennedy, indicated that Lynd "appeared to be a very intelligent young man and was above the average student in his class," and observed that he was very sincere in his work and had made the most of his college opportunities. A check with the alumni secretary's office turned up records which showed that when once asked by the student paper to comment on his experiences at Princeton, Lynd had replied that he was surprised Princeton did not admit Negroes and suggested that its students were "snobbish to a certain degree in comparison with other schools."[19]

Washington was requested to examine the Dies Committee records for any references to Lynd.[20] Over thirty listings were discovered, chronicling activities from 1937 to 1940, including membership in such organizations as the American Committee for Democratic Freedom and the American Council on Public Affairs. He had also signed numerous petitions and sponsored activities of organizations such as the American Civil Liberties Union, the American Committee to Protect the Foreign Born, and the Consumers Union. The information was forwarded to New York for inclusion in its final report.

On June 26, 1942, New York submitted its report, a virtual biography in itself, providing a detailed account of Lynd's education, employment and salary history, character, and suspect or derogatory activities. An interview with an unidentifiable person in the registrar's office at the Union Theological Seminary determined that while there Lynd was an excellent student, always considered to be "worthwhile, open-minded, keenly intelligent, fearless but tactful, and forceful without being opinionated."[21] The FBI also learned that between 1920 and 1921 Lynd had attended courses at the New School for Social Research, studying current economic theory and the objective study of social relations. He also spent several semesters at Columbia, both before and after *Middletown*, taking sociology courses for his doctorate degree.

A friend and colleague who had first met Lynd at Union Theological and known him for over twenty years indicated that Lynd was an "individual of very tender conscience," whose disillusionment with the terrible consequences of World War I had caused him to enter the ministry.[22] However, Lynd left the ministry with the thought that he could better serve his fellow men in a teaching position. Another long-time friend indicated that Lynd was very liberal in his views but was not a "radical or red," and declared, "He is a strong defender of freedom of speech and will not tolerate any restraint of this democratic freedom. This love for freedom and his defense of other individuals, . . . often has given LYND the above mentioned reputation of being Communistically inclined, and as a result of this he has signed petitions protesting against all curtailments of life and liberty."[23]

The FBI also contacted an associate with whom Lynd had worked at the Social Science Research Council, first as secretary and then executive director, where he was employed from 1927 until he left to take his position at Columbia. In the associate's estimation, Lynd was the "best man on the earth" who wanted the whole world to be reformed. He suggested that as a result "LYND is impractical in his views because he sees things in too big a light." He went on to say that Lynd was "always striving for the eradication of poverty and disease from the United States, although in his estimation he desires them to be abolished along democratic lines."[24] He also noted that Helen Lynd was just like her husband, but more tough-headed in her ideas.

Several of Lynd's early employers—Publishers Weekly, Scribner's, B. W. Huebsch Publishing Company, and the Commonwealth Fund—were also contacted. And though it was noted that while at Scribner's he was often impatient with its "passe" methods and that many of the older businessmen at Scribner's considered him to be a "leftist" because of his rather radical views on things, all his former employers gave him high praise and recommended him for any position in the government for which he might apply.

At Columbia, a member of the department of sociology who claimed that Lynd was invited to become a member of the faculty on his recommendation characterized Lynd as a very forceful and extraordinary person with a forthright manner who never soft-pedaled anything and always told people exactly what he thought. He further characterized Lynd as "a veritable whale of work" who felt it almost immoral to take a day off and who was less interested in theory than practice. And while Lynd possessed a sympathy for downtrodden people, he knew of no un-American connections which Lynd might have with fascistic or communistic groups.

New York also obtained information from several confidential informants, two of which were also from Columbia University. Confidential informant T-1 indicated that he doubted Lynd's judgement, since "in his desire for social reform LYND seems to strive for impossible ideals and situations." T-2 noted that Lynd saw many good things in Soviet Russia and that Lynd had signed an enormous amount of petitions of so-called "front" organizations and other groups defending various freedoms, but was no longer signing them as promiscuously as he once had. T-2 also noted that on occasion Lynd's "desire for perfectness might lead him at times to annoy a fellow colleague."[25]

Confidential source T-3, the morgue of the *New York Times*, indicated that in October 1937 Lynd had signed an open letter from the American Friends to Aid Spanish Democracy charging that a pastoral letter from the Catholic hierarchy had shown "open hostilities toward the principle of popular government, freedom of worship, and the cooperation of Church and State, and attempted to justify a military rebellion against a legally elected government."[26] From T-3 it was also learned that in December 1939 Lynd had denounced a report published by an investigator for the Dies Committee in which some consumer groups were described as "Communist transmission belts." That same month he had also signed a letter to the Faculty

Committee on Student Affairs at City College of New York requesting that Earl Browder, then Secretary of the Communist Party, be permitted to speak at the College Civil Liberties Forum. The faculty committee denied the request.

Confidential source T-4 was the memorandum which had been sent with the original charge outlining the information contained in Bureau files. As requested in the original memo, under T-4 New York listed the derogatory activities identified from Bureau files. In February 1937, Lynd had signed an open letter recruiting members for the American Committee for the Defense of Leon Trotsky. In March 1938, he was the signer of a letter to Borough President Stanley M. Isaac, complimenting him for standing by his appointment of S. W. Gerson, formerly a *Daily Worker* reporter, to his staff and endorsing his action for refusing to dismiss Gerson from public service simply because of his membership in a political party. In 1940, Lynd was reported to be one of sixty-two signers of a pamphlet, "In Defense of the Bill of Rights," protesting the efforts being made by the U.S. government to silence and suppress the Communist Party. Lynd was also listed as a sponsor for a meeting of the American Committee for Friendship with the Soviet Union, as a member of the Board of the American Committee for Democracy and Intellectual Freedom, and as a sponsor of the National Committee for Academic Freedom. Derogatory information from T-4 concluded with the note that a reliable confidential source who was well acquainted with Lynd, "considers him as being 'Leftist' in his views, and would definitely label him as a fellow traveler."[27]

From confidential source T-5, the files of the New York Field Division, it was learned that Lynd was listed as a member of the board of directors of the Institute of Propaganda Analysis, the money for which was provided by Good Will Industries. T-5 characterized some of the officials of the Institute as having "Leftist tendencies." Robert and Helen Lynd were also both listed as having signed a petition to President Roosevelt under the letterhead of the American Committee for the Protection of the Foreign Born, protesting the Hobbs Concentration Camp Bill and the denying of jobs to Americans of foreign birth. Robert was also listed as a member of the American–Russian Institute for Cultural Relations with the Soviet Union, which, originally organized in 1926, was reported to have worked closely with the Soviet Union Society for Cultural Relations with Foreign Countries, located in Moscow. His name had also been found in the New York office of the National Federation of Constitutional Liberties.

Confidential informants T-6 and T-7 are listed as residing in the same building as the Lynds at 75 Central Park West. T-6 suggested that among the other residents of the building the Lynd family had the reputation of being "reds and Communists." However, she had never heard either make any un-American statements but did report that during a strike by the building's elevator operators both had refused to use the elevator while it was being operated by the management, insisting instead on walking up to their apartment. T-7, who had known Lynd for about a year, stated that in reaction to his own critical observations about the Soviet Union, Lynd had responded "what an excellent country it was and how the workers and the people who lived there were very happy under the Soviets."[28]

New York concluded its report by noting that the Lynds had no record of criminal activity and that their credit record was listed as "fair." Two undeveloped leads noting the Lynds' Muncie activities and Robert's summer experience at Elk Basin were referred to the Indianapolis and Denver field offices for further investigation. Indianapolis reported that the Lynds had stayed at the Roberts Hotel for part of the time they were in Muncie, and had rented space form the Western Reserve Life Insurance Company for their offices. Several persons contacted, including a member of the local Chamber of Commerce, had nothing but the highest regard for "Bob" Lynd and not the slightest doubt concerning his loyalty.[29] Denver was unable to locate any information on Lynd's Elk Basin activities.[30]

Based on the information collected, New York concluded that Lynd was "reputed to be impractical, wishful thinker type, and alleged radical."[31] Unfortunately, at this point the FBI file on Robert Lynd ends. Additional information was released by the Department of Army's Intelligence Division, General Staff United States of America (GSUSA), and the Office of Naval Intelligence. This information had been in FBI files, but since it came from another agency it was sent to them for FOIA processing. In 1950, GSUSA had been investigating the American Civil Liberties Union, of which Lynd was a committee member, and Naval Intelligence had been investigating the American Investors Union, of which he was a sponsor. While GSUSA indicated that the ACLU's "roster of officers, directors and committee members listed on letterheads consists of many who have been in revolt against the established order in varying degrees, either chronically or sporadically," neither agency presented any new information concerning Lynd himself. There is likely more information in FBI files to be released on Lynd, for example, concerning the eventual recommendation made to the Federal Emergency Management Agency in response to its Special Inquiry. And it is hard to believe that the FBI collected no further information on Lynd given the nature of his continuing activities up to and beyond the height of the Cold War and the red scare of the McCarthy period, neither of which had yet come into full force.

With ironic similarity to the academic community which gave her lesser recognition than her husband, the FBI also directed less effort to investigating Helen Lynd's activities, even though they would seem to have been of a potentially more serious nature. Helen Lynd came under scrutiny in 1948, when the Bureau received allegations concerning Communist infiltration and instruction at Sarah Lawrence College.[32] The Bureau obtained a copy of the college's directory and reviewed its files for any derogatory information concerning members of the faculty. Helen Lynd was listed as having signed a statement in February 1941 urging the defeat of a bill to bar the Communist Party on the ballot in New York. That same year she was also listed as a member of the board of the American Committee to Save Refugees and a sponsor of the Fifth National Conference of the American Committee for the Protection of the Foreign Born. In 1942, she was listed as a member of the executive board of the Joint Anti-Fascist Refugee Committee, and in 1944, as a sponsor of the Independent Citizens Committee of the Arts, Sciences and Professions, which was reputed to be a "well-known Communist front group."[33]

Based on this information, on September 1, 1948, Director, FBI initiated a Security Matter–C investigation and instructed New York to conduct "a most discreet" inquiry of Lynd to determine her background and activities. Authority was granted to use reliable and established sources as well as contact an unidentifiable male informant from Sarah Lawrence who had previously contacted the FBI and indicated his willingness to cooperate with them where his assistance could be of value. It was also noted, "If you feel additional contacts are necessary to fully determine whether subject is dangerous or potentially dangerous to the security of this country, you should first obtain Bureau authority for such contact."[34]

New York submitted its report six months later, in late March 1949.[35] A brief biographical sketch drawn from the volume *American Women for 1937–38* was included, followed by a similar sketch of Robert Lynd taken from *Twentieth Century Authors*. In addition to the activities already identified, New York noted that in December 1940 Lynd had testified at an open hearing held by the Committee for Defense of Public Education, condemning the Rapp–Coudert investigation into communism in the New York City public schools. In February 1942, she had joined a group of 152 staff members of area colleges in petitioning the U.S. Senate to defeat the Lend–Lease Bill. Lynd was also listed, with her husband, among the sponsors of an ad placed in the *New York Times* on March 3, 1945, by the Veterans of the Abraham Lincoln Brigade, entitled "For America's Sake Break with Franco Spain." In 1946, she and Robert were listed as sponsors of the Committee on Education of the Council for American–Soviet Friendship.

Gaining access through an employee, New York checked the records of the Manhattan Board of Elections and learned that Lynd had registered as a Socialist Party voter in 1933. In 1936, she and her husband had both registered as voters of the two major parties, and from 1944 through 1948 were both registered as members of the American Labor Party. An agent was also sent to the New York Public Library to check the reference catalog for a listing of the books Helen Lynd had written. Several were examined, including *England in the Eighteen-eighties*, in which it was noted that several statements by Karl Marx and Frederick Engels were quoted "but the author does not appear to have stressed the quoted opinions of MARX and ENGELS out of proportion to their proper place in English political life."[36] Of the *Middletown* studies it was noted that the problems of concentration of wealth and labor–management relations were emphasized in both volumes.

Along with its report, New York sent a request to contact additional sources in New York and Los Angeles to fully determine whether or not Lynd represented a security risk. Permission was granted on April 18, though both offices were cautioned to be "very circumspect in the handling of these interviews."[37] Unfortunately, at this point in the file five pages have been withheld in their entirety, including the main body of the Los Angeles report, so it is impossible to determine the content of these interviews.

While both Lynds were ardent champions of the freedom of expression and critical of any attempts to suppress it, Helen was by far the more outspoken and public of the two in her advocacy. Thus, during the summer of 1949, while she was still under investigation by the FBI, she published a strongly worded denunciation of the dismissal of several professors by the University of Washington, against the recommendations of the Faculty Committee on Tenure, on the basis of their political affiliation with the Communist Party.[38] Lynd suggested that the target of attack was not just Communists but anyone who might be liberal in thought or engage in progressive social action. She observed, "With the worst that anyone can say about the Communist Party, I cannot discover any reading of this evidence about what has happened at the University of Washington that supports the belief that there can be more dictatorial power over teachers in the United States by the Communist Party than by Boards of Regents."[39] Her conclusion was that when Communists were made the focus of attack, "the main damage is done, not to Communists, but to all independent thought and action."[40]

In 1951, she spoke out once again, this time addressing the growing climate of repression, warning "the attempt to confine American democracy to a single stereotype is disloyal to the whole animus of the American tradition, and that freedom in a democracy is not a dispensable luxury to be enjoyed at such times as the society is secure and untroubled, but rather, is itself the basis of security and survival."[41] She also criticized the loyalty program and McCarthy's anti-Communist campaign, arguing, "In the process of this suppression, we are in danger of ourselves being the agents of destruction of freedom by adopting those methods of making thought serve political ends which we deplore in Communist countries."[42]

Given her outspoken positions, Lynd was not surprised when, toward the end of 1951, the local chapter of the American Legion attacked the college and sent a delegation to meet with Harold Taylor, president of the college, and Harrison Tweed, chairman of the board of trustees, calling for her dismissal. Rather than conceding to their demands, the board ignored the charges and instead issued a statement on academic freedom.[43] However, this was not the end of her troubles, as two years later, in March 1953, she was summoned to testify, along with twelve other faculty from the college, before the Jenner Committee, the Senate Internal Security Subcommittee charged with investigating subversive influences in the educational process. Frightened and insecure at the prospect of testifying at a formal hearing, and much to her regret afterward, she chose not to challenge the committee by taking the fifth and answered Senator Jenner's question whether or not she had ever been a member of the Communist Party.[44]

Lynd's testimony before the Jenner Committee once again piqued the FBI's interest in her and the Director sent a memo to New York indicating that Lynd had testified that she had never been a member of the Communist Party or attended any of its meetings, but did admit past connections with the League of American Writers, the League of Women Voters, and the Cultural and Social Conference for World Peace.[45] Noting that Lynd was not included on the Security Index, New York was instructed that information concerning her testimony should not be set out in any investigative report, and was informed that a review of the testimony suggested no further investigative action. In September of 1955, Lynd's file was once again reviewed in relationship to her connection with the Fund for the Republic's Committee on Fear in Education.[46] The only new information was garnered from the anti-Communist newsletter *Counterattack*, which indicated Lynd was among six college professors who had been barred from testifying in support of eight teachers suspended by the New York City Board of Education when they refused to state whether or not they were members of the Communist Party.[47]

Helen Lynd's opposition to government loyalty programs and McCarthyism was neither purely political nor self-serving, but rooted in her life-long inquiry into the nature of creativity and discovery and the social processes and individual circumstances which foster them. Toward the end of her life she observed, "I am inclined to think that any important creative insight to which voice is given encounters enough encrusted custom and authority that it may often necessitate rebellion, if it is to be more than an idea in somebody's head or a portrait in somebody's studio."[48] Robert Lynd shared similar views, though in his case growing out of his interest in the sociology of knowledge and the place and possibility of social science in society. He concluded, "Social science cannot perform its function if the culture constrains it at certain points in ways foreign to the spirit of science; and at all points where such constraints limit the free use of intelligence to pose problems, to analyze all relevant aspects of them, or to draw conclusions, it is necessary for social science to work directly to remove the causes of these obstacles."[49] Unfortunately, many social scientists would choose to cooperate with the FBI and various other investigators and investigating committees, or just quiescently stand by, rather than resist the climate of fear and intellectual repression and engage in the kind of courageous and spirited defense of free and critical inquiry of which the Lynds, and especially Helen, were such ardent defenders.

NOTES

1. Irving Louis Horowitz, "Lynd, Robert S. and Helen Merrell," in *International Encyclopedia of the Social Sciences: Biographical Supplement*, vol. 18, ed. David L. Sills (New York: Free Press, 1979), 471.
2. H. L. Mencken, "A City in Moronia," *American Mercury* 16 (1929): 379.
3. In his introduction to their follow-up study a decade later, Robert Lynd claims that the book was generally well received in Muncie. However, this claim seems to be contradicted by other reports, though by the time the Lynds returned to Muncie the controversy had died down. See Robert S. Lynd and Helen Merrell Lynd, *Middletown in Transition: A Study in Cultural Conflicts* (New York: Harcourt, Brace, 1937), xii–xiii; Alden Whitman, "Robert S. Lynd, Co-Author of Middletown Dies," *New York Times*, 3 November 1970, p. 38.
4. Robert S. Lynd and Helen Merrel Lynd, *Middletown: A Study in Contemporary American Culture* (New York: Harcourt, Brace, 1931), xiii–xviii.
5. Lynd's first article, "Crude-Oil Religion," appeared in *Harper's* in its September 1922 issue and is a lively anecdotal and largely ethnographic account of his summer ministry at Elk Basin. The second, "Done in Oil," *The Survey: Graphic Number* 49 no. 3 (1922), was much more critical and well-documented, drawing not only upon Lynd's own observations but also Bulletin 297 of the United States Bureau of Labor Statistics on Wages and Hours of Labor in the Petroleum Industry, which had been published in 1920 by the Government Printing Office. Rockefeller's response, "A Prom-

ise of Better Days," accompanied Lynd's article. For a more detailed account of these experiences and their influence on later work, especially *Middletown*, see Straughton Lynd, "Robert S. Lynd: The Elk Basin Experience," *Journal of the History of Sociology* 2 (1979–1980): 14–22.

6. Veblen probably would have been somewhat amused to hear the story that for a while after the Lynds met and married every Wellesley girl carried with her a copy of his book while on trips. For a more detailed account of Merrell Lynd's life see Mary Jo Deegan, "Helen Merrell Lynd (1896–1982)," in *Women in Sociology: A Biography Sourcebook* (Westport, Conn.: Greenwood, 1991) and her own autobiographical account, Helen Merrell Lynd, *Possibilities*, rev. ed. (Youngstown, Ohio: Inkwell Press, 1983). No doubt he would have been less amused to learn about FBI interest in his work. Only two pages were released in response to an FOIA request on Veblen. They indicate that Veblen's writings were investigated by the Department of Justice during World War I, while he was working for the Food Administration, on complaints that he was pro-German. At issue was the character of his book, *The Nature of Peace*. During the war Veblen was also consulted concerning his view of the possibility of a crop shortage in the Northwest resulting from a shortage of labor and indicated that, "prosecutions of members of the I.W.W. should be dropped except in a few individual cases where the proof of unlawful action was very strong." Finally, it was noted that in 1919 the Chief of the Secret Service forwarded to the Department of Justice a communication he had received indicating, "Veblen is alleged to be the man chosen to perform in America the work done by Lenine [*sic*] and Trotsky in Russia." No further information or details were made available. Federal Bureau of Investigation, *Thorstein Veblen*, Bureau File 62-30348 (Washington D.C.: FBI Freedom of Information–Privacy Acts Section).

7. It remains a mystery why, following this confrontation, the Rockefeller Foundation's Institute of Social and Religious Research would then ask Lynd to direct their study. Lynd's son, a labor lawyer, suggests it represented an attempt to "remove an outspoken shop-floor militant by making the man a foreman." Whatever the reason, it backfired when the Institute refused to publish the results but then smugly gave Lynd permission to look for another publisher telling him that they were sure he would not be able to find one. See Straughton Lynd, "Father and Son: Intellectual Work Outside the University," *Social Policy* 23, no. 3(1993): 8.

8. Lynd and Lynd, *Middletown*, 8–9. To further insure this homogeneity was not compromised, no black families were included among the 164 working- and business-class families interviewed, and the responses of black students among the 1,500 high school students survey were excluded from tabulation. See ibid., 507–509.

9. Lynd and Lynd, *Middletown in Transition*. What they found was a much less optimistic community just beginning to recover from the social and economic devastation of the Depression, with a much more concrete and decided stratification between the working and business classes, though this latter observation may have been as much a reflection of their own developing sociological sensitivities and growing interest in class as any

real transformation in the relations that had always existed.

10. Lynd, *Possibilities*, 38.

11. Robert Engler, "Knowledge for What? Indeed," *Journal of the History of Sociology* 2 (1979–1980): 126.

12. Robert S. Lynd, *Knowledge for What? The Place of Social Science in American Culture* (Princeton: Princeton University Press, 1939), 226.

13. Lynd had also been responsible for the consumption study included in *Recent Social Trends*, the report of the President's Research Committee on Social Trends. His was one of the few chapters with a critical perspective, which, only after extensive argument, escaped Director of Research William F. Ogburn's pure empiricism. For a more detailed account of this neglected area of Lynd's scholarship, see Mark C. Smith, "Robert Lynd and Consumerism in the 1930's," *Journal of the History of Sociology* 2 (1979–1980): 99–120.

14. S. M. Miller, "Struggle for Relevance: The Lynd Legacy," *Journal of the History of Sociology* 2 (1979–1980): 62.

15. Robert S. Lynd, "Power in the United States," *The Nation* 182 (1956): 408–411.

16. Deegan, "Helen Merrell Lynd," 274.

17. Federal Bureau of Investigation, *Robert S. Lynd*, Bureau File 77-15837-1 (Washington, D.C.: FBI Freedom of Information–Privacy Acts Section).

18. FBI, *Robert Lynd*, Bufile 77-15837-2.

19. Lynd described his Princeton experience as "an intellectual vacuum for me." According to his wife, he did not make a fraternity and felt rejected and left out. This resulted in a sense of marginalization which influenced him for the rest of his life. See Gillian Lindt, "Introduction—Robert S. Lynd: American Scholar-Activist," *Journal of the History of Sociology* 2 (1979–1980): 2; Lynd, *Possibilities*, 33.

20. FBI, *Robert Lynd*, Bufile 77-15837-3. Martin Dies was an early member of the House Un-American Activities Committee, which held several public hearings in major cities across the country, including New York, for the purpose of determining the extent of Communist presence and "subversive" influence among American professors and school teachers.

21. Ibid.

22. FBI, *Robert Lynd*, Bufile 77-15837-6.

23. Ibid.

24. Ibid.

25. Ibid.

26. Ibid.

27. Ibid.

28. Ibid.

29. FBI, *Robert Lynd*, Bufile 77-15837-7.

30. FBI, *Robert Lynd*, Bufile 77-15837-8.

31. FBI, *Robert Lynd*, Bufile 77-15837-6.

32. Federal Bureau of Investigation, *Helen Merrell Lynd*, Bureau File 100-357382-1 (Washington, D.C.: FBI Freedom of Information–Privacy Acts Section).

33. Ibid.

34. FBI, *Helen Lynd*, Bufile 100-357382-2.
35. Ibid.
36. Ibid.
37. Ibid.
38. Helen Merrell Lynd, "Truth at the University of Washington," *The American Scholar* 18 (1949): 346–353. The article was one of four in a forum, "Communism and Academic Freedom," concerned with academic freedom and political affiliation with special reference to the University of Washington case.
39. Ibid., 352.
40. Ibid., 353.
41. Helen Merrell Lynd, "What is Democratic Loyalty?," reprinted in *Toward Discovery* (New York: Hobbs, Dorman, 1965), 144.
42. Helen Merrell Lynd, "Realism and the Intellectual in a Time of Crisis," *The American Scholar* 21 (1951–1952): 28.
43. Lynd, *Possibilities*, 48; Ellen Schrecker, *No Ivory Tower: McCarthyism and the Universities* (New York: Oxford University Press, 1986), 213.
44. Lynd, *Possibilities*, 49.
45. FBI, *Helen Lynd*, Bufile 100-357382-NR.
46. Ibid.
47. *Counterattack: Facts to Fight Communism* was established by three former FBI agents and published weekly by the American Business Consultants, Inc. Supported financially by right-wing groups, it was dedicated to publishing current "facts" exposing communist activity in the United States and those persons it claimed to be involved in this activity. Its sources of information included communist publications, the FBI, HUAC and other government files, and letterheads of organizations designated as subversive.
48. Lynd, *Possibilities*, 59. For an outline of her observations and assumptions concerning creativity and discovery, see Chapters 1 and 2 of *Possibilities*.
49. Lynd, *Knowledge for What?* 249.

— 6 —

E. Franklin Frazier: Enfant Terrible

E. Franklin Frazier, the grandson of a self-emancipated slave, his mother an ex-slave, spent his entire lifetime struggling to emancipate himself and sociology from the obstacles, indignities, and injustices of the system of apartheid which continued to enslave American society and all its institutions during his lifetime. An outspoken critic of the racist doctrines which, cloaked in pseudoscientific guise, permeated early American sociology, after a long and prolific career he became the first African American to be elected president of the American Sociological Association. Frazier liked to describe himself as an *enfant terrible* committed to "destroy the illusions which keep colored people in bondage."[1] Even after his death, Frazier has remained a center of controversy, labeled by some as a sociological "Uncle Tom" for his supposed posthumous underwriting of the Moynihan report, and celebrated by others as one of America's most prominent "Black sociologists," even though he would have vigorously opposed this moniker, having argued that "such recognition is as much the product of the racist mentality as the Negro restrooms in the Montgomery airport are."[2]

In 1894, the year Frazier was born in Baltimore, Maryland, 135 Blacks were lynched in the South. He developed an early awareness of these injustices through his father, a self-educated bank messenger and "race man" who kept a scrapbook of newspaper clippings of the achievements and abuses of Negroes. A brilliant student from the beginning, as he walked past Johns Hopkins University on his way to grammar school the younger Frazier would spit on its buildings, knowing that because of his color he would not be admitted to study within the segregated confines inside its gates. He was the top student in his grammar school class and in 1912 was awarded his high school's only scholarship to Howard University.[3]

At Howard, Frazier found himself under the shadow of a white board of trustees and a president who expected a docile conformity from its students. Courses on Afro-American history were prohibited. Nonetheless, he continued to be an excellent student, nicknamed "Plato" by his peers, and, as he recounted in his later years, "When my curiosity to learn everything was at fever heat, my course of study embraced a wide range of courses, including mathematics and physical science, literature, Latin, Greek, French, German as well as the social sciences with the exception of sociology because I heard it was not presented in a serious fashion."[4] During his four years at Howard, Frazier became politically active and participated in the Political Science Club and the Intercollegiate Socialist Society. He graduated cum laude in 1916.

After Howard, Frazier spent a year teaching math at the well-known Tuskegee Institute, but could not abide by the ethic of industrial education and political accommodation of its founder, Booker T. Washington, who once stated, "If education does not make the Negro humble, simple, and of service to the community, then it will not be encouraged."[5] No doubt his frustrations were only exacerbated when he was forbidden by the director of the academic department to walk across the campus with books under his arm because "white people passed through the campus and would get the impression that Tuskegee Institute was training the Negro's intellect rather than his heart."[6]

Frazier spent the next two years teaching at Southern high schools, then did a brief stint doing "colored work" at the segregated Camp Humphreys in Virginia after unsuccessfully trying to avoid being drafted to serve in a war which he felt "was essentially a conflict between imperialistic powers and in view of the treatment of the Negro in the United States, the avowed aim, to make the world safe for democracy, represented hypocrisy on the part of America."[7] He refused to join other prominent African Americans, such as W.E.B. Du Bois, in supporting the war and in 1918 wrote and published at his own expense a small antiwar pamphlet entitled *God and War.*[8]

In 1919, Frazier entered Clark University to do graduate work in sociology, studying under two of the leading advocates of scientific racism, Frank Hankins and G. Stanley Hall. Nonetheless, and perhaps in reaction to Hankins and Hall, he continued his political interests and wrote his thesis on "New Currents of Thought among the

Colored People of America," with particular sympathy for a newly emerging Afro-American radicalism and a voice that foreshadowed the tone of Black nationalism which would be heard several decades later.

After a year as a research fellow with the New York School of Social Work studying the city's Negro longshoreman, he spent a year at the University of Copenhagen as a Fellow of the American Scandinavian Foundation.[9] Frazier was the Foundation's first Negro fellow, but was only chosen after an all-night debate by the election committee, and his name and photograph were excluded from its announcement of awardees for 1921–1922.[10]

Upon his return from Denmark, Frazier married Maria Ellen Brown, the daughter of a distinguished Baptist leader, and took a position as an instructor of sociology at Morehouse College. He was also appointed Director of the fledgling Atlanta School of Social Work, and during the next five years built the school from the ground up, serving as administrator, recruiter, and fundraiser, as well as raising admissions standards, teaching courses, and systematizing the curriculum. However, his uncompromising refusal to conform to the demeaning expectations of Southern "race etiquette" and his outspoken opposition to segregation and support of the civil rights movement led the very board of trustees he had helped to establish to ask for his resignation. Frazier refused and in March 1927, the board fired him.[11] A few months later, when preparing to move to Chicago at the invitation of Robert Park, an article that Frazier had written several years earlier suggesting that Southern white racist behavior exhibited the same characteristic as insanity was finally published. He received several death threats and was forced to flee Atlanta, with a .45 caliber pistol in his belt.[12]

At Chicago, Frazier, already a seasoned scholar, encountered a much different atmosphere than he had at Howard, Clark, and in Atlanta. Park ignored letters from Atlanta suggesting he was a "bad nigger" and invited him to Chicago to carry out a study on the Negro family. For his dissertation, Frazier used Burgess's concentric theory model to study the gradient patterns of social life among the Negro community in Chicago.[13] In 1929, Frazier took a position at Fisk University in the department of social science, under the leadership of Charles Johnson. As a Research Professor of Sociology at Fisk, he continued the research he had begun on the Negro family in Chicago and eventually, in 1932, published his findings in the classic *Negro Family in the United States*. Characterized by Burgess as the most important contribution to the literature on the family since *The Polish Peasant*, the book also represented a "severe indictment of the American civilization for what it had done to Negroes in this country."[14]

In 1934, Frazier was invited back to Howard, as chair of the sociology department, where he joined the most distinguished group of black scholars ever assembled on one campus.[15] Even though he had a strong dislike for administrative and managerial duties, Frazier reorganized the sociology department and reconstructed its curriculum. A forceful and often abrasive man, he also made a deep impression on his students. As one student observed, "We do not revere Professor Frazier because he was a doddering, outspoken, kindly gentleman who led up to learning with a gentle hand. Professor Frazier was an irascible man, and a brilliant and demanding teacher. He growled and roared. . . . But the heart of the attraction was his respect and profound understanding of what a teacher was and could be. It simply came down to this: he valued the student."[16]

Like Du Bois, it was Frazier's conviction that the scientific investigation of African-American life and the critique of the social economic organization of American life were the proper domain of the social sciences. He also felt such investigations could offer an institutional identity for Negro universities. And while he failed in his dream to establish such a center of research at Howard, he was able to pursue such an agenda through his own scholarship. In 1949, he published *The Negro in the United States*, his monumental and comprehensive treatment of black–white relations, for which he received the John Anisfield Award given in recognition of the most significant book on the subject of race relations published each year. The book was reviewed as "more up-to-date and factual than *American Dilemma*, far wider in scope than *Black Metropolis*."[17]

In 1951, Frazier took a leave from Howard to travel to Paris where he spent the next two years serving as the director of the Division of Applied Social Science for the United Nations Educational, Scientific, and Cultural Organization (UNESCO), overseeing research on interactions between people of different racial and cultural backgrounds.[18] While there, he also spent considerable time in the Paris cafes, writing what would become his most controversial work, *Black Bourgeoisie*, in which he repeated hopes from earlier work that the Black middle class, through its economic gains, would raise up the entire community. But he also expressed his fear that economic interests would divide the Afro-American community along class lines. He criticized the preoccupation with conspicuous consumption and the fixation on an imitation of white values shared by much of the Black middle class, but also noted that its failure to provide leadership for the Black masses was largely due to its precarious class position as a result of its social isolation caused by racism and white oppression. The book stirred up considerable controversy, especially within the Black community, some members of which felt Frazier was turning on his own.[19]

Throughout his life, Frazier not only disregarded the "race etiquette" of the South, and sometimes his own community; he also ignored the growing "red etiquette" which spread across the country at large. His stock response to accusations of Communist sympathies was, "I am a Marxist only in so far as every scientist is a Darwinian. I make use of economic interpretations without joining any party."[20] Not surprisingly, his unwillingness to succumb to the red hysteria and disassociate himself from suspected Communist-influenced associates and organizations brought him to the attention of J. Edgar Hoover and the FBI. In addition, as an outspoken African American like Du Bois, he, too, was caught in the early crossfire of Hoover's war on Black America.[21] As a result, beginning in the early 1940s and continuing to the end of his life, he was subject to three major security investigations by the FBI.

On August 25, 1941, Hoover sent a memo to Assistant Attorney General Matthew McGuire indicating that the name of E. Franklin Frazier appeared on the active indices of several possibly subversive organizations and asking whether any investigation should be conducted by the Bureau.[22] Like all faculty at Howard, Frazier was considered to be under the authority of the Department of Interior and therefore subject to the Public Employees Loyalty Program established by the Congress. Given the go-ahead, Hoover instructed SAC, Washington to conduct an Internal Security investigation of Frazier.[23]

Washington submitted its report in February 1942, documenting both Frazier's Communist front affiliations as well as his activities in support of racial equality for Black Americans.[24] A confidential source reported that on May 1, 1937, Frazier had attended a rally organized by the Communist Party of the District of Columbia and spoken on the history of Labor Day and the conditions under which Negroes currently lived and worked. Confidential informants reported that Frazier's name was on a phone list maintained by the American Peace Mobilization and that he had sponsored a conference on civil rights held in April 1940 under the auspices of the Washington Committee for Democratic Action. On November 11, 1941, the *Daily Worker* had carried an article indicating that thirty-five Negro leaders, including Frazier, had written a letter to the President urging the release of Earl Browder, onetime general secretary of the Communist Party.[25] Frazier was also reported to be interested in the National Negro Congress and on the editorial board of *Science and Society*, reputed to be under the control of the Communist Party. An agent sent to consult the files of the Dies Special Committee on Un-American Activities determined that he had also been a member of the Marian Anderson Citizens Committee and a contributor to *New Masses*.

Several of Frazier's associates at Howard were also interviewed. The consensus was that Frazier was a "strong racialist" but was not a member of the Communist Party. And while one informant stated that he believed Frazier to be a "crazy racialist" who would follow any movement or organization with a strong racial interest, all his other associates indicated that his interest in Communism was only scholarly. On February 16, 1942, Frazier himself was interrogated and denied membership in the Committee for Democratic Action, Peace Mobilization, Negro Congress, or Communist Party. At the conclusion of the interrogation he observed, "I am a social scientist, and I don't belong to any isms. I study human behavior, and that is my chief interest in society. That is all I have to say."[26]

In its report to the Bureau, Washington's SAC, S. K. McKee, attached a memo with additional information obtained from a highly confidential source which said that Frazier's name appeared on the indices of the Capitol City Forum and noted his association with the National Socialist Workers, Keep Out of War Committee, and League of Industrial Democracy.[27] It was also noted that he was on the active indices of the United American Spanish Relief Committee and had contributed two dollars in February of 1939. Hoover forwarded the information on Frazier to the Federal Security Agency, which reported back that "inasmuch as we find nothing in these reports showing that the above employee [*sic*] has engaged in any activities which might properly be characterized subversive or disloyal to our Government, they have been exonerated and we are filing the reports without further action."[28] Hoover then closed the investigation, indicating that no administrative action was to be taken against Frazier.

However, several months later Frazier once again came to the attention of the FBI, this time under suspicion of espionage following his request for twelve blueprint copies of a map of various government buildings in Washington, D.C. The employee who made the copies became suspicious when he could not locate Frazier's name in the local telephone book and reported his worries to the Washington field office. Once Washington identified Frazier it reviewed his files, noting his previous possibly subversive associations, but concluded, "In view of the fact that subject's identity has been determined and there is no indication of any un-American activity and subject's background is well known in this field division, this case is being closed upon the authority of the Special Agent in Charge."[29] Hoover forwarded the information to the Federal Security Agency and no further action was taken.[30]

Yet another addition to Frazier's file was made when J. W. Vincent, SAC, New York, forwarded copies of thirty-two talks, including one by Frazier, given at the Congress of American–Soviet Friendship held in New York City on November 6 and 7, 1944. Frazier delivered his talk as part of the Nationalities Panel, stating, "American Negroes are so thoroughly assimilated to American ways of thinking and feeling that they have shared most of the American prejudices toward Russia. Of course, the more sophisticated among them have seen through the propaganda and if they have not accepted the economic philosophy of Soviet Russia, they have regarded it with considerable sympathy."[31] He went on to observe, "Despite propaganda about the dire economic and moral consequences of a communistic society, the Negroes knew that a society that treated all races as equals possessed some virtue."[32] Though Frazier harbored no illusions, he did hold hopes for a common humanity:

> The racial ideologies of Nazi Germany have been rejected by the civilized world not only because of their absurdity but because of the barbarism which they have inspired and I am afraid because they have been used against the white races. But the truth of the matter is that all racial ideologies act as barriers to a universal moral order. A universal moral order can be achieved only when the conceptions which members of various nations and races have of other nationalities and races include a conception of themselves. It is thus that a common humanity is created.[33]

Frazier's file lay dormant for the next ten years until February 12, 1953, when SAC, Washington was once again asked to review its files on him following a request by Hoover for a name check on the employees of Howard University.[34] At approximately the same time the Federal Security Agency also requested a name check on Frazier in relation to his position with UNESCO, and the two requests were carried out in conjunction with one another. Two weeks later, Washington sent the Director a detailed confidential memo listing its findings.[35] A report filed in 1950 indicated that Frazier had been listed as a guest lecturer at the George Washington Carver School in New York City, declared by the attorney general as falling under the purview of Executive Order 9835. In 1951, Frazier had been listed as a member of the Planning Committee of the National Committee to Repeal the McCarran Act and had also signed an open letter urging President Truman to send a message to Congress asking for the immediate and outright appeal of the Act.

Also in 1951, Frazier had joined 200 notables from 33 states in calling for the withdrawal of the persecution of W.E.B. Du Bois for failure to register under the Foreign Agents Registration Act. The plea was ignored and when the trial was about to open, Frazier once again joined in an effort to support Du Bois, claiming that he had never been a "Foreign Agent" and indicating that his prosecution was designed to "intimidate into silence other leaders of our people who speak out boldly for full democratic rights for Negro Citizens."[36] Frazier's name had also been placed on a list entitled "Suspected Communist Party (D.C.)," which had been submitted to the Washington Bureau in September 1950.

In early March 1953, this information was forwarded to the Federal Security Agency and Assistant Attorney General Warren Olney III, and on March 26, SAC, Washington was instructed to open its second investigation of Frazier, this time a Full-Field Investigation.[37] On April 7, Washington responded that Frazier was on leave of absence from Howard while serving in Paris as the Chief of the Division of Applied Science for UNESCO.[38] The Bureau then converted the case to a Loyalty Investigation under the auspices of Executive Order 10422 (United Nations Loyalty Order), and in late June charged Washington with leading the new and much broader inquiry.[39] Fifteen offices across the country, from Atlanta and Boston to St. Louis and San Francisco were brought into the investigation, and since Frazier had listed extensive travel in Central America, South America, and Europe on his loyalty form, Hoover also contacted the State Department's Office of Security and requested an investigation of Frazier's foreign activities.[40]

Through the investigations of its various field offices, the Bureau retraced Frazier's life. Baltimore checked out his childhood years.[41] An agent sent to Frederick Douglass High School, known as Baltimore High School when Frazier had attended it forty years earlier, was advised that there was no record of any disciplinary action taken against him. A former teacher recalled that Frazier had been an above-average student who was an independent thinker. When asked to clarify what he meant by "independent thinker," the teacher indicated that he meant that Frazier "did not accept too readily what was told him but rather inquired for himself and made up his own mind."[42] Baltimore also reported that in 1938 Frazier had attended the Eastern Regional Conference of the National Negro Congress, which, according to the Senate Special Committee on Un-American Activities, constituted the Communist front movement in the United States among Negroes.

The Mobile, Alabama, field office contacted the Tuskegee Institute and reported that Frazier had a good reputation there and no criminal record.[43] The Cleveland office was unable to locate any records of his employment with the West Steel Casting Company during the summer of 1917, but did report that in 1948 his name had appeared on an ad placed in the *Cleveland Press* by the Civil Rights Congress, cited by the attorney general under the purview of Executive Order 9835, demanding the defeat of the Mundt Bill.[44] Richmond was unable to locate any records of Frazier's employment with St. Paul's Normal and Industrial School in Lawrenceville, Virginia, from 1917 to 1918, but did locate a school official who remembered Frazier as being "of brilliant mind."[45]

Boston confirmed Frazier's M.A. work at Clark University in Worcester, but did not find any record of his reported employment with a local steel mill.[46] Boston also noted that Frazier had contributed a couple of articles to *Science and Society*, including a review of the Lynds' *Middletown in Transition*, published in the summer of 1937. In its 1948 report, the California Committee on Un-American Activities had joined the Special Committee on Un-American Activities in citing *Science and Society* as a Communist publication claiming it to be "Communist initiated and controlled, or so strongly influenced as to be in the Stalin Solar System."[47]

Atlanta investigated Frazier's period with Morehouse and the Atlanta School of Social Work.[48] His former associates generally characterized him as a loyal American citizen of excellent character, reputation and associates, a strong believer in the fundamental principles of democracy, and an outstanding sociologist. Three associates familiar with the circumstances under which Frazier had left in 1927 claimed that he had resigned the Directorship after Dr. John Hope, then President of the Atlanta School of Social Work, had "objected to the fact that Dr. FRAZIER had shown a lack of sufficient administrative ability and was apparently being distracted from his duties as Director by outside interests such as speeches and writings."[49] However, only one of the three declined to recommend him for a position of trust and confidence, stating that Frazier was too argumentative and antagonistic and that "possessed with this personality and disposition, he might easily be misunderstood and even suspected of possessing un-American sympathies due to his ill-advised remarks concerning political theories."[50] The informant was unable, when asked, to provide more definite facts as to the basis of this judgement. Atlanta informants familiar with the activities of the Communist Party in Georgia advised they were not acquainted with Frazier.

Chicago agents confirmed Frazier's education and employment as a research assistant at the University of Chicago from 1927 to 1929, but found no one still there who had been personally acquainted with him.[51] A confidential informant did make available an October 1943 newsletter of the Chicago Council of the Arts, Sciences, and Professions, which indicated that Frazier was an officer (Vice-President) of the National Council of Arts, Sciences and Professions, cited as a Communist front by the Congressional Committee on Un-American Activities in 1950. It was also noted, in the *Daily Worker*, that in February 1945 he had returned to Chicago as the principal speaker at Du Sable High School's celebration of Negro History Week.

Memphis was unable to locate any records of Frazier at Fisk University, as its personnel records for the period in question were rather sketchy.[52] However, a university official remembered him and considered him to be "one of the outstanding sociologists in the U.S. or in the world," and entirely loyal to the United States.[53] A female member of the department of sociology and close associate of Frazier's noted that "probably many people would be irritated by FRAZIER inasmuch as he is completely frank and outspoken in his attitude and completely honest in all opinions which he offers."[54] However, she believed he was anti-Communist and would only defend the rights of the Communist Party in order to preserve the American democratic ideals of free speech. A lifelong friend of Frazier's concurred in this assessment, adding that Frazier's in-laws, with whom he identified, were known to be very conservative and anti-Communist.

New Orleans reported on Frazier's membership on the Board of the Southern Conference Educational Fund, which he had listed on his loyalty form.[55] Informants familiar with the Fund advised that it was originally an adjunct of the Southern Conference for Human Welfare before the latter's demise in 1948. Political differences and negative publicity from the House Committee on Un-American Activities had resulted in its dissolution, but the Fund had continued on as a separate and independent organization, devoted primarily to race relations and campaigning against discrimination and segregation in education.

Since Frazier had taught at the University of Southern California during the summer of 1948, Los Angeles was also brought into the investigation.[56] Its agents determined that he had taught an intercultural workshop for the education department. The 1948 Report of the California Committee on Un-American Activities was also checked and showed Frazier to have been affiliated with, or given support to, the American Youth Congress, cited under Executive Order 10450.[57] However, local informants familiar with CP activities in the area had no information concerning him. Even the San Juan office was brought in as Frazier had spent a few weeks, while on sabbatical in 1949, at the University of Puerto Rico, Rio Piedras, collecting material on race relations in the Caribbean. A brief acquaintance there reported that Frazier was "a liberal thinker as regards race relations, but not the type of person who would embrace Communism."[58]

As the Bureau deadline for completing the investigation drew near, Hoover sent Airtels to New York and Washington urging them to submit their reports immediately or report the reason for delay. He also reminded the State Department's Office of Security of the investigation and requested its report "at your earliest convenience."[59]

New York submitted its report indicating that, in addition to attending Columbia University's New York School of Social Work, Frazier had been employed there from 1943 to 1951 as a visiting lecturer during the winter and summer quarters. He had also served as a visiting professor of sociology at New York University during the summers of 1944 through 1951. While all of his associates contacted considered him to be loyal, New York's informants advised that Frazier had been a member of various Communist front groups, including the Committee for a Democratic Far Eastern Policy, the National Council of American–Soviet Friendship, and the Council on African Affairs, all designated under Executive Order 10450.

New York also reported that an article in the *Daily Worker* indicated that in 1945 Frazier had signed a statement commending the War Department's stand on the question of rendering Communists and Communist sympathizers eligible for Army commissions. Another article said that in 1947 he had joined 100 prominent citizens in a letter which opposed all legislation that would curtail the civil rights of Communists and called upon Congress to defeat punitive measures being directed against the Communist Party. New York also obtained a copy of a petition, signed by Frazier, which had been presented on May 17, 1950, to the General Assembly of the United Nations and the Commission on Human Rights. The petition suggested that the House Committee on Un-American Activities, aided and abetted by the Executive Branch and the courts, had engaged in an attempt to repress the rights of individuals to freedom of speech and association.[60]

Finally, old records maintained by the New York City Police Department showed that Frazier had been arrested on May 6, 1921, in front of the Capitol Theater, at 51st and Broadway, and charged with disorderly conduct for picketing the showing of the anti-Negro film, *Birth of a Nation*. He received a suspended sentence which was later overturned by the Appellate Court of the State of New York. Bureau files also noted that almost twenty years later, in 1939, Herbert Blumer, whom Frazier had cited as a reference in his loyalty form, had joined Ernest Burgess and H. F. Gosnell in testifying in support of a request by the NAACP that a Chicago showing of the movie be discontinued.[61]

Washington did not submit its report until September 2, 1953.[62] Once again, Frazier's associates and coworkers described him as an outstanding spokesman with an excellent professional reputation and of unquestioned character who was undoubtedly loyal. However, the Director of Administration of the Library of Congress during the time Frazier was a research fellow in 1943 and 1944, indicated that he was "not one of the most charming representatives of his race or of humanity in general," explaining that Frazier was "antipathetic and extremely blunt."[63] On the other hand, a former colleague from Fisk characterized him as one of the most brilliant scholars in America, outspoken and courageous. Neighbors offered similar characterizations. A check of metropolitan police records indicated that between 1937 and 1951 Frazier had been cited for ten minor traffic violations, forfeiting bonds from three to ten dollars.

Files from another government agency, perhaps G-2, indicated Frazier had introduced well-known singer Paul Robeson at a Negro Freedom Rally held in Turner's Arena on October 13, 1949. Robeson later described Frazier as "a fearless and independent thinker." Robeson was said to be a long-time member of the Communist Party and reported to be engaged in secret international work in connection with his concert tours. Information gleaned from the *Daily Worker* indicated that in late 1950 Frazier was active in supporting U.S. recognition of China and its admittance to the United Nations, and that in March 1951 he had joined ninety faculty from the University of Chicago in urging President Truman to recognize the People's Republic.

An updated review of the files of the House Committee on Un-American Activities reflected that Frazier was among the signers of the Stockholm World Appeal to outlaw atomic weapons. HUAC files also indicated that he was a sponsor of a National Conference for a "Cease Fire" in Korea. On September 14, Washington submitted an addendum to its initial report, forwarding the results of a final interview with an acquaintance of Frazier's who reported that he was a "whole-hearted patriotic American," who did not "belong to the left-wing crowd."[64]

Hoover bundled copies of all the fifteen reports the Bureau had received from its field offices together and forwarded them to the assistant attorney general and the Investigations Division of the U.S. Civil Service Commission as required under 10450.[65] In the meantime, the Bureau was informed by UNESCO headquarters that Frazier had returned to the United States in early September and was no longer employed by the organization.[66] As a result, on September 30, 1953, Hoover closed the investigation and notified the State Department's Office of Security that its foreign investigation, yet to be completed, could be discontinued.[67] He then asked SAC, Washington, to ascertain from confidential sources whether Frazier was still employed at Howard, who duly did so by making a pretext telephone call to Frazier's secretary.[68]

While the Bureau had discontinued its investigation of Frazier, he was not to be left alone. In February 1954, the Jenner Committee requested a name check on Frazier. A seven-page memo outlining all the instances of reported Communist front affiliation or subversive activity collected in his files since 1941 was prepared and forwarded to the Committee.[69]

Frazier's file lay dormant for the next several years until May 1961, after Alfred Metraux, chief of UNESCO's Division of Social Sciences, had approached Frazier to direct a study in the United States and South Africa on industrialization and race relations. The Civil Service Commission contacted the FBI and requested that its earlier investigation be completed and results be made available to the International Organizations Employees Loyalty Board. For the third time, Frazier was to be the subject of a major security investigation as his case was reopened and Hoover asked the State Department's Office of Security to complete its previously discontinued investigation.[70]

Once again the field offices were put on Frazier's trail and reports began to flow in from across the country documenting his activities since the last investigation. Honolulu reported that Frazier had been in Hawaii for a few weeks in the summer of 1954 to attend a sociological conference on race relations financed by the Ford Foundation.[71] New Orleans reported that in April 1954, Frazier had signed an open letter to Senator Jenner protesting the unfairness of his Committee's hearings and condemning his attack on the Southern Conference Educational Fund as "an attack upon the Negro Community of this Nation."[72]

In 1958, Frazier had signed another open letter, this time to the U.S. House of Representatives, protesting HUAC plans to hold hearings in Atlanta. The letter reflected his concern that the red hysteria was being used as a smoke-screen to hide efforts to maintain the racist segregation in the South and intimidate those individuals and organizations from challenging it by painting red all those would stand up for equality and justice for blacks:

> We are acutely aware of the fact that there is at the present time a shocking amount of un-American activity in our Southern states. To cite only a few examples, there are the bombings of the homes, schools, and houses of worship of not only Negroes but also of our Jewish citizens; the terror against Negroes in Dawson, Ga.; the continued refusal of boards of registrars in many Southern communities to allow Negroes to register and vote; and the activities of White Citizens Councils encouraging open defiance of the United States Supreme Court.[73]

However, Frazier and his colleagues did not believe these were the un-American activities that the Committee planned to investigate, saying that they were "alarmed at the prospect of this committee coming South to follow the lead of Senator Eastland, as well as several state investigating committees, in trying to attach the 'subversive' label to any liberal white Southerner who dares to raise his voice in support of our democratic ideals."[74]

New York reported that in 1954 Frazier had been listed as a sponsor of a "Statement for the Defense of Democracy," mailed out by the National Council of the Arts, Sciences and Professions, which had been cited as a Communist front by both HUAC and the Internal Security Subcommittee of the Senate Judiciary Committee.[75] The statement was a scathing denunciation of the congressional witch-hunt and McCarthyist fearmongering which was marching across the land:

> The spirit of intolerance is abroad in our land.
>
> Congressional committees, in the guise of "investigations," have conducted a systematic persecution of people for their political beliefs and associations. The time-honored principle that a person is innocent until proven guilty has been discarded in favor of a procedure which imputes guilt and imposes punishment without trial.
>
> Minority opinion is being suppressed by such devices as blacklisting, dismissal from employment, even jailing for "conspiracy to teach and advocate" a minority viewpoint on social affairs.
>
> Books are banned because of the political views of their authors. Works of art are threatened with destruction. Artists and scientists with minority views are prevented from traveling abroad by an arbitrary withholding of passports. Ministers are pilloried and smeared for joining in social welfare movements. A congressional committee has set itself up as judge of what should be the content of a textbook on medical practice.
>
> By no stretch of the imagination can actions such as these be justified as a defense of democracy. On the contrary, they constitute an assault on our basis freedoms. Unless checked in time they will extend the "black silence of fear" to all areas of American life and destroy the democracy we are striving to preserve and develop.[76]

To make possible a return to the basic principles of democracy, the statement called for the abolition of the attorney general's list of "subversive organizations," the repeal of the Smith, McCarran, and Taft-Hartley Acts, the abandonment by Congress of the "inquisitorial probing into the beliefs, opinions and political affiliations of individuals," the reinstatement of teachers dismissed on loyalty grounds, the cessation of blacklisting, the discontinuance of book banning, the abandonment of passport and visa restrictions on the basis of political beliefs and associations, and amnesty for those in jail on charges of conspiracy to teach and advocate their political views.

Washington reported that during the course of another investigation, in August 1954, Frazier had advised Special Agents that he had become a member of the Council of African Affairs in the early 1940s. During that time he had supported Paul Robeson for head of the council as he felt Robeson's opponent was an opportunist and of low moral integrity. Frazier advised the agents that he had a file at his office containing materials on the Council and furnished them a number of items from it. When asked whether he would appear before a hearing of the Subversive Activities Control Board, he indicated reluctance because of his positions at Howard and UNESCO, and the unfavorable publicity that might surround such an appearance.[77]

In November 1961, after receiving a letter that his clearance had been delayed due to possible "derogatory information" that had been passed on to the loyalty board, an exasperated Frazier wrote Metraux, "Why is it necessary to fingerprint an American scholar each time that he undertakes some scholarly task for an international organization."[78] In response to the possibly derogatory information, the International Organizations Employees Loyalty Board sent Frazier an eleven-page interrogatory requesting additional detailed and specific information on his beliefs and affiliations. By then, fed up and struggling with cancer, he refused to answer. In March 1962, Metraux, unable to wait any longer, assigned the project to the Institute of Race Relations in London. Deeply embittered but with his fighting spirit still intact, Frazier wrote Metraux a letter denouncing the FBI's harassment: "As soon as I am well enough, I intend to write a letter to the Secretary of State and I shall even go further and inform the learned societies in the United States about this action on the part of the FBI. How can American scholars and intellectuals participate in an international organization if they have got to be subjected to a lot of foolishness initiated by policemen?"[79]

Frazier never fully recovered and died before he could fulfill his intentions. The last item which appears in Frazier's file is a photocopy of an obituary from *The Worker*, announcing his passing on May 30, 1962, and declaring, "The sum total of Dr. Frazier's professional life represented significant blows against racism, colonialism and human indignities of all kinds; he lived and wrote and taught resistance to these abominations. He did all these things effectively, he lived well and left a seemly heritage."[80] Upon his death, Howard University's student newspaper, *The Hilltop*, eulogized that Frazier had been "a person *and* a personality," who "had anger for the sufferings, sympathy for the frustrations, and ironic stinging ridicule for the affectations and weaknesses of his people."[81]

Three years after his death, Frazier was once more embroiled in controversy with the release of the infamous Moynihan report. While the report documented the consequences of racism on Black family life, in a classic case of blaming the victim it identified the "tangle of pathology" of the black family as the cause of the "deterioration of the fabric of Negro society."[82] Sloppy scholarship on Moynihan's part, and selective quotations drawn out of context from Frazier's work, led him to be misleadingly characterized as the "father" of the report and the pathology model of the Black family. This resulted in accusations of racist scholarship which have left an undeserved cloud over his reputation as a scholar, social critic, and activist.[83]

Though criticized for underrating the impact of African social heritage on the development of the Black family and community, Frazier advanced the level of sociological research on race relations, turning it from its racist and biological focus to one which considers the interaction between social organization and culture as the basis of understanding the development of Black America.[84] Throughout his life, though continually hounded by self-appointed guardians of ideological purity and conformity from both sides of the color line, Frazier always saw himself as a champion of humanity whatever its color—red, white, or black: "I am not interested in the color of the future Americans, although I have some sentiment in regard to the continuation of civilization to which men of any color can be heirs."[85]

NOTES

1. As quoted in Anthony Platt, *E. Franklin Frazier Reconsidered* (New Brunswick, N.J.: Rutgers, 1991), 179. *E. Franklin Frazier Reconsidered* offers the most authoritative and extensive account of Frazier to date and presents a detailed discussion of his life and work, contributions and controversies.

2. John Hope Franklin, "The Dilemma of the American Negro Scholar," in *Soon One Morning: New Writings by American Negroes, 1940–1962*, ed. Herbert Hill (New York: Knopf, 1963), 71.

3. The award was to be given to the best graduate each year. Frazier actually finished third in his class, but two female students who had received higher grades were passed over. Arthur P. Davis, "E. Franklin Frazier (1894–1962): A Profile," *The Journal of Negro Education* 31 (1962): 430.

4. As quoted in Platt, *E. Franklin Frazier Reconsidered*, 28. At the time, sociology was being taught by Kelly Miller, a politically cautious reformist who was closely associated with Booker T. Washington.

5. As quoted in ibid., 32

6. Ibid., 33.

7. Ibid., 35

8. Ibid., 38–39.

9. Frazier was deeply impressed by the comparative rigor and academic openness of the Scandinavian universities in comparison with their American counterparts, as he indicated in a brief correspondence from Copenhagen. See E. Franklin Frazier, "Scandinavian vs. American Universities," *The Nation* 114 (1922): 597. "Here the university is certainly no 'nursery' where 'babes' are fed adulterated truth. A socialist lectures at the

university. The students—no older than ours—can listen to any speaker they choose for their clubs—anarchist, atheist, Bolshevist, nihilist, communist, or cannibalist. But, perhaps, our American students are weak-minded and must be taught Santa Claus religion, Ray Stannard Baker's history, Gompers' labor policies, and Gary's economics lest thinking within the university walls will disable the ship of state."

10. Davis, "Profile," 431. See also Platt, *E. Franklin Frazier Reconsidered*, 56.

11. Platt, *E. Franklin Frazier Reconsidered*, 75. At the time, as the result of a campaign of his detractors, Frazier was also denied a position at Fisk.

12. E. Franklin Frazier, "The Pathology of Race Prejudice," *Forum* 70 (1927): 856–862. Frazier had to submit the article to several journals before it was accepted. For a more detailed account of this episode, see Platt, *E. Franklin Frazier Reconsidered*, 84.

13. See E. Franklin Frazier, *The Negro Family in Chicago* (Chicago: University of Chicago Press, 1932).

14. G. Franklin Edwards, "E. Franklin Frazier," in *Black Sociologists: Historical and Contemporary Perspectives*, ed. James E. Blackwell and Morris Janowitz (Chicago: University of Chicago Press, 1974), 95.

15. Henry P. Charles, "Abram Harris, E. Franklin Frazier, and Ralph Bunche: The Howard School of Thought on the Problem of Race," *National Political Science Review* 5 (1995): 41. This concentration was not coincidental as the racist policies of the segregated academy of the 1930s left Black faculty, no matter how talented, with nowhere else to go. Other distinguished scholars at Howard included Ernest Everett Just, Alain L. Locke, Sterling A. Brown, William H. Hastie, Charles H. Houston, Charles R. Drew, Merze Tate, Rayford Logan, Charles Thompson, Mordecai Johnson, Lorenzo Turner, Charles Wesley, Howard Thurman, Percy Julian, William Leo Hansberry, Mercer Cook, Abram Harris, and Ralph Bunche. In the 1940s, government service and white elite universities lured many away.

16. As quoted in G. Franklin Edwards, "E. Franklin Frazier: Race, Education, and Community," in *Sociological Traditions from Generation to Generation*, ed. Robert K. Merton and Matilda White Riley (Norwood, N.J.: Ablex, 1980), 124.

17. Davis, "Profile," 434. Frazier contributed a minor paper to Myrdal's classic study, but played a critical role in its final stages when asked to give a detailed criticism of the final manuscript, indicating that notwithstanding earlier misgivings he had been pleasantly surprised and agreed with Myrdal that the study contained lots of dynamite and that the "explosion should take place upon its publication." See Platt, *E. Franklin Frazier Reconsidered*, 107.

18. In 1944, Frazier had served as Chair of the UNESCO Committee for Social Scientists, which was asked to define race and the various fields of race-relations research. This second appointment gave him the opportunity to develop a global perspective on race relations and eventually resulted in the publication of *Race and Culture Contacts in the Modern World*, an interdisciplinary and multicultural investigation of interpersonal relations and contacts between groups with divergent racial and cultural backgrounds.

19. Attention to *Black Bourgeoisie* has tended to focus primarily on Frazier's critique of the Black middle class and has resulted in an oversimplified and distorted conception of his work. Throughout his life he developed a very complex analysis of the Black middle class which included but was by no means limited to its failure to provide the progressive political consciousness and leadership of the Black community which he had envisioned. See Bart Landry, "A Reinterpretation of the Writings of Frazier on the Black Middle Class," *Social Problems* 26 (1978): 211–222. Martin Kilson, "The Black Bourgeoisie Revisited," *Dissent* 30 (1983): 85–96, offers a more recent and optimistic assessment of Frazier's political consciousness and the ability of his work to have a progressive impact on American society and race relations.

20. As quoted in Davis, "Profile," 435.

21. Kenneth O'Reilly, *"Racial Matters": The FBI's Secret Files on Black Americans, 1960–1972* (New York: Free Press, 1989).

22. Federal Bureau of Investigation, *Edward Franklin Frazier*, Bureau File 101-1603-1 (Washington, D.C.: FBI Freedom of Information–Privacy Acts Section). Public Law 135 was the Hatch Act.

23. FBI, *Frazier*, Bufile 101-1603-2.

24. FBI, *Frazier*, Bufile 101-1603-3.

25. Ibid.

26. Ibid.

27. FBI, *Frazier*, Bufile 101-1603-4.

28. FBI, *Frazier*, Bufile 101-1603-5.

29. FBI, *Frazier*, Bufile 101-1603-6.

30. FBI, *Frazier*, Bufile 101-1603-7.

31. Ibid.

32. Ibid.

33. Ibid.

34. FBI, *Frazier*, Bufile 101-1603-8.

35. FBI, *Frazier*, Bufile 101-1603-9.

36. Ibid.

37. FBI, *Frazier*, Bufile 101-1603-11, 12, 13.

38. FBI, *Frazier*, Bufile 101-1603-12.

39. Truman signed Executive Order 10422 on January 9, 1953. It extended the scope of Executive Order 9835 to include the United Nations, and prescribed procedures for making available to the secretary general loyalty and security information on U.S. citizens employed by or seeking employment with the United Nations.

40. Federal Bureau of Investigation, *Edward Franklin Frazier*, Bureau File 138-825-1 (Washington, D.C.: FBI Freedom of Information–Privacy Acts Section).

41. FBI, *Frazier*, Bufile 138-825-18.

42. Ibid.

43. FBI, *Frazier*, Bufile 138-825-8.

44. FBI, *Frazier*, Bufile 138-825-11. Frazier had reported his summer employment with West Steel on his loyalty form, but the company's employee records only went back to 1930.

45. FBI, *Frazier*, Bufile 138-825-6. Since Lawrenceville had no credit agency and town records did not predate 1926, Richmond agents were unable to investigate Frazier's credit and criminal records there.
46. FBI, *Frazier*, Bufile 138-825-20.
47. Ibid.
48. FBI, *Frazier*, Bufile 138-825-13.
49. Ibid. As indicated earlier, Platt's more recent investigation has shown that this account is not fully accurate, and places a much more benign, and perhaps self-serving, face on the actions of Hope and the board of trustees than appears to be warranted by the facts.
50. Ibid.
51. FBI, *Frazier*, Bufile 138-825-19.
52. FBI, *Frazier*, Bufile 138-825-17.
53. Ibid.
54. Ibid.
55. FBI, *Frazier*, Bufile 138-825-9.
56. FBI, *Frazier*, Bufile 1380825-12.
57. FBI, *Frazier*, Bufile 138-825-10.
58. FBI, *Frazier*, Bufile 138-825-23.
59. Executive Order 10450 was signed on April 27, 1953 by President Eisenhower. It is largely a refinement of Executive Order 9835 and provides further details concerning the security requirements for government employment.
60. FBI, *Frazier*, Bufile 138-825-28.
61. FBI, *Frazier*, Bufile 138-825-4.
62. FBI, *Frazier*, Bufile 138-825-52.
63. Ibid.
64. FBI, *Frazier*, Bufile 138-825-44.
65. FBI, *Frazier*, Bufile 138-825-52.
66. FBI, *Frazier*, Bufile 138-825-45.
67. FBI, *Frazier*, Bufile 138-825-51.
68. FBI, *Frazier*, Bufile 138-825-15, 16.
69. FBI, *Frazier*, Bufile 138-825-54.
70. FBI, *Frazier*, Bufile 138-825-57, 59.
71. FBI, *Frazier*, Bufile 138-825-62.
72. FBI, *Frazier*, Bufile 138-825-64. During its 1954 hearings, the Jenner Committee had investigated the SCEF and made statements which the petitioners felt were disparaging to the Negro people, imputed disloyalty to the Fund, and smeared its leadership.
73. Ibid.
74. Ibid.
75. FBI, *Frazier*, Bufile 138-825-69.
76. Ibid.
77. FBI, Frazier, Bufile 138-825-70. While it is not indicated in the Washington report, this information was likely gathered as part of the FBI's Internal Security–Africa investigations.
78. As quoted in Platt, *E. Franklin Frazier Reconsidered*, 210.
79. Ibid., 212.

80. FBI, *Frazier*, Bufile 101-1603.

81. As quoted in Davis, "Profile," 433–434.

82. See William Ryan, *Blaming the Victim* (New York: Vintage, 1976), for an extended discussion of the ideology of blaming the victim underlying the Moynihan report and how it has permeated social scientific and social policy discourse.

83. Anthony Platt, "E. Franklin Frazier and Daniel Patrick Moynihan: Setting the Record Straight," *Contemporary Crises* 11 (1987): 265–277, provides a detailed account of Moynihan's misuse of Frazier's work. For a conflicting account which associates Frazier with Moynihan, see Arthur Mathis, "Contrasting Approaches to the Study of the Black Family," *Journal of Marriage and Family* 40 (1978): 667–676. Dorothy Smith Ruiz Cumming and Robert G. Cumming, "Cultural Ideology and the Moynihan Report," *The Western Journal of Black Studies* 17, no. 2 (1993): 65–72, provides an analysis of the ideological underpinnings of the Moynihan report.

84. Clovis E. Semmes, "The Sociological Tradition of E. Franklin Frazier: Implications for Black Studies," *The Journal of Negro Education* 55 (1986), 492.

85. As quoted in Platt, *E. Franklin Frazier Reconsidered*, 130.

— 7 —

Pitirim A. Sorokin: Sociological Prophet in a Priestly Land

Whether as a revolutionary youth in his Russian homeland, as immigrant in the United States, as refuge in exile, or as iconoclastic professor of sociology, his scholarly niche, Pitirim Sorokin spent most of his life as an itinerant stranger, a critical and marginalized outsider. An unresistant critic of conventional wisdom and an outspoken advocate of the unpopular or overlooked, it was his "deepest conviction that a supreme duty of a scholar is to 'tell the truth' as he sees it, regardless of any and all consequences."[1] Imprisoned three times by the Czarist regime for his revolutionary activities, sentenced to death by the Bolsheviks for his counterrevolutionary activities, suspected and surveiled by the FBI for alleged Communist sympathies, and outcast by the mainstream of American sociology for his critical blasphemy, the consequences turned out to be not insignificant.

Born a Komi peasant in the agricultural wilderness of the Vologda Province in northern Russia, Sorokin grew up with his widowed father, a talented and nomadic goldsmith, learning his father's craft of making and repairing icons. At age ten, he and his fourteen-year-old brother struck out on their own, fleeing one of their father's particularly violent bouts of alcoholic and hallucinatory depression. Three years later, while passing through a village which was holding entrance examinations to its advanced grade school, Sorokin, with no formal education (though he was a voracious reader), entered the competition and won a scholarship. So impressed were his teachers that upon his graduation at age fourteen they secured another scholarship for him at the Khrenovo Teachers' Seminary. At Khrenovo he quickly adjusted to the more urban environs, joined the Social Revolutionary party, and during the Christmas vacation of 1906 was arrested and imprisoned for his anti-Czarist activities. Kicked out of Khrenovo because of his imprisonment, he went underground as a revolutionary missionary. Once again he began traveling from town to town, this time organizing at factories and speaking at meetings under the pseudonym "Comrade Ivan." The following year he snuck a train to St. Petersburg. After two years of night school and a brief period at the Psycho-Neurological Institute, he gained entry to the University of St. Petersburg where, upon graduation, he was offered a position to prepare for professorship. Since sociology was not yet offered as an area of formal study, Sorokin specialized in criminal law and penology, a decision influenced by his own arrests and prison experience.[2]

Following the outbreak of the Russian Revolution and fall of the Czar in 1917, Sorokin was appointed secretary to Alexander Kerensky, Prime Minister of the new Provincial Government, and became one of the most outspoken critics of the Bolshevik faction. After the victory of the Bolsheviks, he was arrested in 1918 for attempting to foment a counterrevolutionary rebellion in the Arkhangelsk province and sentenced to death. Each day his wife would come to the prison dressed according to a secret code which would inform him whether he was to be one of the prisoners chosen to be taken from his cell and shot that evening.[3] Only after publishing a letter in *Pravda* in which he publicly withdrew from all political activities and memberships was he pardoned from execution by Lenin himself, who was reported to have once commented, "Who is that sociologist who always quotes his earlier works more than anyone else's?"[4]

Shortly after his exile from Russia in 1923, Edward Hayes and E. A. Ross invited Sorokin to do a series of lectures on the Russian revolution at the universities of Illinois and Wisconsin. This led to a six-year appointment at Minnesota from which he was offered Harvard's first chair in sociology and charged with establishing a new department there. This meteoric rise was due in large part to his early work; *Social Mobility*, which conceptualized stratification as pyramidal and helped establish mobility as a new field in sociology, and *Contemporary Sociological Theories*, recognized for its remarkable breadth and intelligence in presenting an overview of several recent important schools in sociology but with the glaring absence of any mention of the then virtually hegemonic Chicago school.

While Sorokin's early works were generally well-received and heralded as major contributions to American sociology, publication of his four-volume magnum opus, *Social and Cultural Dynamics,* between 1937 and 1941 marked the beginning of a long period of exile from the mainstream of American sociology. In it Sorokin presented his theory of social change, outlined his integralist philosophy and methodology, and prophesied the decline of contemporary Western sensate society.[5] *Dynamics* was vigorously criticized by mainstream sociologists as theoretically simplistic, statistically naive, unscientific and metaphysical, authoritarian, value-laden, and ideationally biased.[6] In part, Sorokin was only reaping what he had sown with his brusque manner and self-admitted "bull-headed personality," his appearance of arrogance, and the broadsides directed at American sociology and sociologists. He was a scathing and often merciless critic. A former student remarked, "It was as if, having reduced a city to rubble, one must pound the fragments to dust—and then sow the site with salt."[7] Even his friend, the philosopher of history Arnold Toynbee, gently critiqued Sorokin: "Woe to the critic who ventures to challenge the validity of Sorokin's tenets. . . . The one point in which Sorokin is in fact immoderate is his confidence that, within his own self-demarcated limits, he himself is 100 percent right and any opponent is 100 percent wrong."[8]

In the early 1940s, Sorokin began to argue that sociology, with its empirical methodology, was epistemologically inadequate and would remain so until it adopted his own integral philosophy and method. In his "Declaration of Independence of Social Sciences," he placed American sociology before the "Supreme Court of History" and gave it a grade of D, "representing neither complete failure nor satisfactory attainment" for its obsessed ambition to become a copy of the natural sciences. In 1956, he expanded and gave a more detailed critique in *Fads and Foibles in Modern Sociology and Related Sciences,* anticipating many of the points Mills would make two years later in his classic, *The Sociological Imagination.*[9] Sorokin castigated American sociology for its "testomania," "quantophrenia," and its many "new Columbuses," who like amnesiacs mistakenly claimed to have made a number of scientific discoveries for the first time in the whole history of sociology.[10]

With *Dynamics* and his criticisms of sociology Sorokin began to take on the role of sociological prophet at a time when mainstream sociology was firmly entrenched in a more priestly mode, having adorned itself with the scientific cloaks of natural scientific objectivity and value neutrality and preached the language of mathematics and empiricism.[11] He completed this transition when, at the end of World War II and marginalized in the new department of social relations at Harvard, he decided, "I would devote all my free time to the investigation of the means of preventing the imminent annihilation of the human race and of ways out of the deadly crisis."[12] This led to his establishment, with the assistance of the Midwestern pharmaceutical magnate and philanthropist Eli Lilly, of the Harvard Research Center in Creative Altruism, through which he undertook a series of investigations on the power of altruistic love.[13]

Unlike Sorokin's fellow sociologists, Lilly was intrigued with his efforts at social reconstruction and pledged his personal financial support even if the board of the Lilly Endowment would not.[14] The Lilly board was never as enthusiastic about Sorokin's work as Eli Lilly, and its secretary, G. Harold Duling, became particularly concerned when he learned that Sorokin was mentioned in *Counterattack* as one of the sponsors of an honor banquet for W.E.B. Du Bois.[15] Upon being informed of this, J. K. Lilly, Jr., Eli's nephew and one of the endowment's administrators, made a "special inquiry" into the matter and received a list of thirteen suspected communist organizations with which Sorokin had been somehow associated.[16]

Sorokin came under investigation by the FBI following a request, in July 1953, by the Boston office to interview him in connection with one of its ongoing Security Matter–C investigations. The request was denied following a review of Bureau files which revealed that Sorokin had been affiliated with Communist front activities and had sponsored affairs of such organizations.[17] As a result, the Boston office began an inquiry into Sorokin's activities and background. After reviewing its own files, Boston contacted several confidential informants familiar with the Communist Party in Boston and its efforts to infiltrate education in the Boston–Cambridge area.[18] The informants indicated that, to their knowledge, "PITIRIM ALEXANDROVITCH SOROKIN, Professor of Sociology at Harvard University, has never been a Communist Party member and has never been under the discipline of the Communist Party in the Greater Boston area." Synopses of several newspaper articles featuring Sorokin further support the informant's reports, including an early one entitled "Sees Soviet as Threat to West," in which he criticized "impotent sentimentalism and misdirected idealism in dealing with communism as the worst policy," and recommended that "each attack met by counter attack would efficiently answer communist gangsters and benefit the world."[19]

Nonetheless, at least initially, a much different picture was presented in the information concerning Sorokin's alleged Communist front associations. The same devotion to the pursuit of peace and altruism which had completed his marginalization and made his sociological credentials suspect was causing his loyalty to be questioned and subjecting him to the suspicions of the FBI. In December 1942, Sorokin and his wife Elena had been listed as members of the Executive Committee of the Massachusetts Committee of War Relief.[20] It is noted that according to the Fourth Report on Un-American Activities in California, "It should be understood that the Russian War Relief is, in every respect, a satellite front of the Communist Party and that it is not an organization similar to the American Red Cross."[21]

The Boston report continues with Sorokin's association with the National Council of American–Soviet Friendship. In November 1943, a confidential informant had made available one of its flyers advertising a "Salute to Our Russian Ally on her Twenty-Fifth Anniversary, . . . "to express the admiration of our culture for our gallant Soviet allies." Sorokin and his wife were listed as local sponsors. In a pamphlet purchased at a Communist Party meeting by a confidential informant, Sorokin himself was listed as signatory of a proposal circulated by the council that "the United States should immediately cease prosecution of its cold war and arrange immediately for a conference with the representatives of the Soviet Union looking towards a peaceful settlement of differences." Another pamphlet, purchased by a Boston FBI agent in November 1948, also listed Sorokin as a signatory of a council statement indicating that "such a venture will win the gratitude of the war weary millions [of Russia] and the fullest support of the American people."[22]

Much of the FBI's information on Sorokin's Communist front activities was listed in *Counterattack*, the same source from which the Lilly Endowment had acquired its information.[23] On May 1, 1951, three months after J. K. Lilly, Jr. had received his information, a confidential informant "of unknown reliability" made available a summary of those individuals, including Sorokin, who, according to *The Daily Worker*, had endorsed an appeal of the American Committee for Yugoslav Relief, a 10450 designee. The informant, who apparently had access to the files of *Counterattack*, also reported that in its fall 1948 issue Sorokin was listed as a member of the editorial board of *The Slavic American*, which had been cited by the *Guide to Subversive Organizations and Publications* as the official organ of the 10450-designated American Slav Congress.

Information from *Counterattack* also identified Sorokin as one of the sponsors of a "Conference to Defend the Bill of Rights," to be held July 16 and 17, 1949, which was being called by a group of distinguished scientists and professionals to discuss the situation of civil rights in the United States and the threat to its "traditional liberties of speech, press, pulpit and political advocacy."[24] Sorokin's sponsorship of the conference was confirmed by a Boston confidential informant who furnished the FBI a copy of a mimeographed letter, put out by the National Council of the Arts, Sciences and Professions, which announced the conference to its members and included a copy of the conference pamphlet where Sorokin's name was printed. The National Council had been identified by the *Guide* as a Communist front. In August 1949, Sorokin had signed a statement opposing passage of the European Arms Aid Bill, the Marshall Plan, and U.S. foreign policy in the Far East which had been issued by the Massachusetts branch of the council and sent to its Congressional representatives in Washington, D.C.

According to *Counterattack*, Sorokin was also among the signers of a statement attached to a December 1949 press release from the Committee for Peaceful Alternatives to the Atlantic Pact, calling for an international agreement to ban the use of atomic weapons. The *Guide* cited the committee as an organization formed to further the cause of Communists in the United States. In late March 1950, a confidential informant provided additional information on the committee, making available an announcement which stated that one of its objectives was to protest against the production and use of the hydrogen bomb while asserting, "War is not inevitable. The need for survival dictates the need of peaceful alternatives."[25] Sorokin was one of the signers listed in the announcement.

Counterattack noted that Sorokin, as reported in *The Daily Worker*, was a sponsor of the National Committee to Repeal the McCarran Act, which had grown out of an appeal by more than 1,900 leading Americans to President Truman and the Congress to defeat the act in fall 1950. *Counterattack* also indicated that he was listed as a signer of a statement against denaturalization sponsored by the American Committee for the Protection of Foreign Born, another 10450 designee, and as an endorser of the World Peace Appeal and a sponsor of the American Peace Crusade (APC).

The World Peace Appeal was launched by the World Peace Congress during its March 1950 meetings and characterized in the *Guide to Subversive Organizations and Publications* as having received the enthusiastic approval of every section of the international Communist hierarchy as well as the official endorsement of the Supreme Soviet of the U.S.S.R. The *Guide* cited the American Peace Crusade as an organization that "the Communists established as a new instrument for their 'peace' offensive in the United States." The FBI obtained a flyer with a statement issued by the Crusade, with Sorokin among the signers, calling for a peace pilgrimage to "show that the futile sacrifice of American lives in Korea is needless and that this country should negotiate peace with China."[26] He was also identified having endorsed an APC statement on a resolution offered by Senator Lyndon B. Johnson for an armistice in Korea. The *Harvard Crimson* reported that Sorokin had called for the United States to move away from its primarily military approach toward one of pacifist nonviolence and stated, "At the present moment in human history when we have man the killer at large, the paramount need of man is the decrease of militarism."[27]

While *Counterattack* was a major source of information concerning Sorokin's Communist front activities, it was not the only one. The FBI regularly kept track of local newspapers and learned from the *Harvard Crimson* that Sorokin was one of forty-six faculty members to sign a statement attacking the Mundt–Nixon Anti-Red Bill, declaring that while the bill was aimed at restricting Communists, "Its vague and loose phraseology, however, indicates that it threatens the expression of liberal and progressive thought. Its enactment would strike a serious blow at our cherished rights of free expression."[28]

On March 15, 1951, Sorokin had been identified as among those individuals who had signed a petition addressed to Governor Thomas Dewey of New York asking that he discontinue the liquidation procedures of the International Workers Order, a fraternal insurance organization and 10450 designee. Sorokin also joined 200 prominent individuals from throughout the United States in signing an amicus curia brief on behalf of the order to be presented before the New York State Appellate Court. In June, a confidential informant gave to the FBI a letter taken from the New York State Insurance Commission in which Sorokin excoriated its actions, stating, "The proposed compulsory dissolution of the International Workers Order is the rudest violation of the fundamental right of private property of several thousands of policy holders of this organization. Such a measure is identical with the Communist annihilation of private property. Such an act is not a reinforcement of Democratic order of free enterprise, based on private property, but a direct introduction of Communist measures in this great Democratic nation."[29]

The Boston report concludes with reference to a descriptive circular provided by a confidential informant in April 1953, which indicates that Sorokin was one of the sponsors of the Boston Committee of Americans for South African Resistance (BAFSAR). While the informant could not provide any additional information on BAFSAR, an article taken from the *Harvard Crimson* contained information that the organization had been recently formed to aid African men and women who were trying to achieve freedom through a campaign of nonviolent resistance against South African Jim Crow laws.

In early April 1954, copies of the report, along with a photo, were sent to Bureau headquarters, as well as to the offices in New York and Minnesota. When asked to recommend a course of action by Director, FBI, Boston replied that even though there was no evidence that either Sorokin or his wife were members of the Communist Party, and despite the fact that Sorokin had a reputation at Harvard as being strongly anti-Communist, his support of Communist front activities since 1942 should be clarified and recommended an interview. At the same time, since Sorokin had been identified by another informant as being able to provide information regarding another case at Harvard, Boston also suggested, "If this subject is cooperative, no affirmative steps will be taken during the initial interview to direct his activities, but a separate communication will be directed to the Bureau setting forth the results of the interview and requesting Bureau authority to recontact the subject as a potential security informant."[30]

At the end of April, Washington approved Boston's recommendation with the caution that since Sorokin was a professor at Harvard the interview "must be conducted in a most circumspect manner to insure that no embarrassment will result to the Bureau."[31] Boston was further instructed not to ask Sorokin about any of his colleagues during the interview, but that, "Should Sorokin prove to be cooperative, consideration will be given by the Bureau, based upon your recommendation, for subsequent interviews with him concerning his above mentioned colleagues [unidentifiable as their names are blacked out]."[32]

Sorokin was interviewed in his office at Harvard on May 25, 1954. Much of the report reads like a set of lecture notes and no doubt the agents must have felt somewhat like students sitting in one of his classes. Sorokin spent as much time presenting his analyses of the obstacles to world peace, Western policy, the decline of sensate culture, and the importance of nonviolent and altruistic responses to Russia and China as he did clarifying his relationship with the various Communist front organizations listed in his files.

After noting that two of his brothers had been killed by the Bolsheviks and making reference to his own imprisonment and condemnation, Sorokin began the interview with typical forthrightness, stating, "If the cause is good, I'll promote it even if its promotion is backed by the devil. If the cause is bad, I'll not aid in its promotion no matter who sponsors it."[33] The same applied to the actions of governments and it was for this reason that he could not sanction the use of antidemocratic means in the U.S. fight against totalitarianism. He further stated that in many countries throughout the world there were a considerable number of organizations and individuals fighting communism who, through their efforts, had begun to undermine the constitutional government in these nations. It was his estimation that these persons were more dangerous to the welfare of the world than the present Communist regime in the so-called "Iron Curtain" countries.

Sorokin continued that it was an axiom of sociological theory that governmental control increases in wartime, proof of which could be found in the number of restrictions imposed on the populations of the United States and Europe during World War II. Therefore, the more we armed the world, the more we helped totalitarianism in Russia and all the other countries of a similar nature. By maintaining a warlike attitude, as exhibited by the famous 1946 speeches of Truman and Churchill in Fulton, Missouri, and the pursuit of a policy of encirclement, the West was placing a terrific ideological weapon in the hands of the Soviet government.

In order to eliminate communism and the Communist Parties of the world, Sorokin felt a change of tactics was essential. Such a goal could only be achieved through the pursuit of world peace, which was also crucial if World War III was to be averted. According to Sorokin, "A real approach to peace would be understood by the Russian, Chinese and Indian people."[34] One of the best ways to pursue this was by the establishment of trade with both Russia and the nations of the Orient. Anticipating the policies of détente and "constructive engagement," it was his belief that once trade was established cultural relations and interconnections between the nations of the world would follow.

Sorokin also noted in passing that in his opinion the Pacific area (i.e., China, India, and other nations in the region) would become the next center of world civilization once it passed from the West, which was currently in ascendancy but also experiencing a degeneration of its sensate culture. For this reason it was important that the West attempt to win over these nations through constructive measures. He concluded this part of the interview by likening himself to the mythologic Russian character, Ivan the Fool, who sings funeral dirges at weddings and gay songs at funerals, indicating that while many persons might oppose his policies and actions, no sincere person could fight his objective of attaining world peace.

In the second part of the interview Sorokin's responses to the listing of Communist front activities with which he was associated are recorded. He had been invited to support the Boston Chapter of Russian War Relief by either the governor of Massachusetts or the late surgeon, Dr. Frank Lahey. He had attended four meetings and later helped out in clothing and food drives. He pointed out that most of the individuals he knew in the organization were "Beacon Hill Brahmins" (i.e., conservative and loyal Americans), and that there had been nothing in the Chapter's activities to indicate it had been infiltrated by the Communist Party.

Sorokin stated he had never participated in the activities of the National Council of American–Soviet Friendship nor could he recall whether he had given permission for his name to be placed on a list of local sponsors. However, he did remember signing the petition concerning a campaign for a peaceful settlement of differences between the United States and the U.S.S.R. He had done this deliberately and in the hope that others would realize that securing world peace was truly essential. He could not recall having dealt with the American Committee for Yugoslav Relief nor could he recollect that he was ever involved in any editorial capacity with the "Slavic American," though he had submitted an article to it in the late 1940s. He said he could not remember the identity of anyone from either organization who might have contacted him.

Sorokin did remember being contacted by telephone some time during 1948 and being asked to add his name to a list of Harvard faculty opposed to the Mundt–Nixon Bill. He permitted his name to be used since he opposed the bill as contrary to the best interests of the nation, but was unable to recall the identity of the person making the request. However, he professed no knowledge of the Civil Rights Congress, its activities, or any of its members. Sorokin stated that he never attended meetings of the Massachusetts Council of the Arts, Sciences and Professions, but did recall that, in 1947, a Harvard faculty member, whose name he could not recall, had contacted him for permission to use his name in connection with the "Conference to Defend the Bill of Rights." Since the Bill of Rights was the foundation of the American constitution, any conference dealing with its violation represented a force in attaining world peace and therefore he supported it. He also recalled, in 1950, joining thousands of leading American scientists, educators, businessmen, and politicians in calling on President Truman and Congress to defeat the McCarran Immigration and Nationality Act. He opposed the bill because he regarded it as undemocratic and a potentially valuable source of propaganda for the Soviet government. He also admitted having given permission to an unknown individual to use his name in connection with a statement issued by the American Committee for Protection of the Foreign Born against the denaturalization of foreign-born Americans found guilty of criminal or subversive practices. It was his belief that once granted, citizenship should not be repealed, no matter what the reason. He noted that he had been naturalized and that his American citizenship was one of his most prized possessions.

Sorokin also permitted his name to be used by the Committee for Peaceful Alternatives to the Atlantic Pact in connection with a plan calling for an international ban of atomic weapons, even though he knew nothing of the organization nor whether it was Communist inspired or controlled. He stated that initially he had gladly permitted the use of his name in connection with the activities of the World Peace Appeal, as they reflected his own aims. At a later date, upon learning of its Communist affiliations, he no longer allowed his name to be used. He also had allowed his name to be used by the American Peace Crusade, declaring, "Any appeal to peace is a good cause."[35]

Sorokin stated that he was well aware that the International Workers Order had been designated a subversive organization by the U.S. attorney general. But upon reading in 1951 that the state of New York had taken over its assets, he immediately thought, "Here is a policy which imitates the worst characteristic of the Soviet regime itself."[36] The trained observer could see in this process the beginnings of nationalization and socialization in the United States. Sorokin said he had no knowledge of any Communist affiliations of the Boston Committee of Americans for South African Resistance and could not recall the name of those individuals who had interested him in the movement. However, he commented, "I not only condemn the policies of Malan in South Africa and of all colonial powers—of Britain in Malay and South Africa, of France in Indo-China and Morocco—but I also say that besides being stupid they are singularly hopeless. They are going against invincible trends of history. These countries, after a few centuries of slumber are reawakening, and although Malan and others may slow them down, there is no one on earth who can stop them."[37]

At the end of the interview, Sorokin suggested that while his granting permission for use of his name to a number of organizations which have been Communist dominated or controlled might indicate he was pro-Communist, nothing could be further from the truth. While it might appear that the Communist front organizations had used him and others for many years, this was not the case, "Like the Communists, I long ago learned that one must change his tactics but never lose sight of the overall strategy designed to obtain a desired end."[38] By permitting the use of his name on various petitions he had in effect been initiating his own personal program to bring about a true and workable world peace. He had only acted as a proponent of such a peace, and he concluded somewhat plaintively, "Now because my theories are unpopular I suppose I'll be regarded as subversive."[39]

In fact, Sorokin was not regarded as subversive. In the cover memo accompanying the investigative report, SAC, Boston noted that Sorokin had been extremely friendly and cooperative during the interview and that his activities did not warrant a recommendation for his name to be placed on the Security Index. The memo also includes some additional remarks made by Sorokin which had not been recorded in the initial report. Sorokin had indicated that while he was aware that some Harvard undergraduates, graduate students, and instructors had formed a Communist Party cell, he did not know of any regularly appointed faculty member holding a professorial chair who was a member of the Communist Party. And he did not believe that a Party cell was still operating at Harvard.

Sorokin also made reference to the Russian Research Center. He indicated that even though he had firsthand knowledge of Russia, the Bolsheviks, and the Communist Party, he had never been asked to participate in its activities. He suggested that the Carnegie Institute, its sponsoring organization, had installed as director a man (Clyde Kluckhohn) whose chief claim to fame was that he knew absolutely nothing about Russia. He continued his critique, deprecating the work of the center as futile and valueless, and representing approximately a third-grade student's idea of Russian history. Sorokin's estimation of the Russian Research Center, though more strongly stated, was similar to that of the State Department, which had informed the FBI that it placed "a very, very low evaluation on its usefulness."[40]

Little additional information appears in Sorokin's file until June 1963, when SAC, Boston submitted a request to the Director, FBI to interview him in connection with another case.[41] However, it is clear that in the intervening years Sorokin had undergone a transformation in the eyes of the FBI from suspect to source. A confidential memo notes, "Subsequent to the initial interview, Sorokin has been contacted as a source on several occasions concerning other individuals of interest to the Boston office and has always been cooperative."[42] The request was approved on July 1, but Sorokin was not interviewed until September as he and his wife were on an extended vacation. The interview took place at his home in Winchester but all information which might indicate who was being investigated, what Sorokin was asked, or what he answered has been deleted. No other records of any previous or later interviews are included in his file.

It is a curious coincidence that Sorokin's transformation in the eyes of the FBI roughly parallels a similar reappreciation which was occurring in the sociological community. In April 1963, following a write-in campaign to place his name in nomination, he was elected president of the ASA by an overwhelming majority.[43] Yet while he may have softened his delivery with a somewhat more hopeful view of the future of the discipline, he did not compromise his critical stance toward sociology, reiterating in his presidential address themes developed in earlier works.[44] His reentry into the fold of American sociology from outcast to elder statesman was accompanied by two volumes dedicated to him and his work.[45]

Having been introduced to a new generation of sociologists, Sorokin was celebrated for the very activities that had earlier led to his sociological exile. Redefined as an icon of antiestablishment sentiments which had exploded among the younger generation, he was feted at the unsanctioned counterconvention held by student dissidents during the 1969 meetings of the American Sociological Association in San Francisco. The introduction to the "Counter-Convention Call," published by *The Insurgent Sociologist*, stated, "Modern scholarship is in deep crisis. The extent of intellectual prostitution to those who oppress and manipulate others may have already reached the point of no return. . . . A social science that serves to liberate people and not to oppress them cannot flourish in the present intellectual and career environment." The organizers saw a kindred spirit in Sorokin, many sporting the button "Sorokin Lives," and held a special symposium in his honor dedicated to discussing the issues he had addressed and illuminating the crises within the profession and American society.[46] As indicated earlier, the FBI saw in the counterconvention a subversive threat and placed it under surveillance, initiating yet another wave of investigations of a new generation of American sociologists.[47]

In many ways, Sorokin's investigation and questioning by the FBI must have reminded him of earlier interrogations in his life, first at the hands of the Czarist authorities and then the Bolsheviks. And though it is a bit difficult to believe he could not remember anyone who was associated with any of the front organizations about which he was asked, it is not surprising that he did not name any names. He was an experienced interrogee under much more threatening circumstances, and therefore probably more inclined to feign a lapse of memory than turn anyone in. It is much more difficult to know what to make of indications that Sorokin was himself an FBI informant. Since all files concerning his "cooperation" with the FBI have either been blacked out or withheld, it is impossible to know whether he provided any substantive information or just successfully maintained the friendly manner he had adopted during his own interrogation.

While Sorokin was somewhat plaintive that he would be regarded as a subversive because his ideas were unpopular, he could not have been totally surprised that he, along with so many others, was being investigated by the FBI. His own theories, especially as manifested in the "Basic Law of Fluctuation of Governmental Control" could have accounted for if not actually predicted it: "When a given organized group faces a grave emergency menacing its existence or its basic values, the governmental control over it tends to become more rigid and severe and tends to expand to embrace many social relationships of its members hitherto free from such control."[48]

It was on the basis of this law that during his interrogation by the FBI Sorokin argued that the aggressive anti-Communist and Cold War policy of the United States toward the Soviet Union was counter-productive, and not only strengthened the latter's totalitarian character but shored up its legitimacy in the eyes of the Russian people as well. However, as he also intimated, at the same time such a stance was undermining—perhaps even more dangerously so than the Communists themselves—the very democratic and constitutional freedoms and values of those countries whose individuals and organizations were vigorously pursuing these policies. While he was too sanguine to be more direct, clearly Sorokin must have been thinking of the McCarthyist hysteria and the activities of the FBI and could not resist tweaking his interrogators even as he was being interviewed.

NOTES

1. Pitirim A. Sorokin, "Sociology of My Mental Life," in *Pitirim A. Sorokin in Review*, ed. Phillip J. Allen (Durham: Duke University Press, 1963), 30.
2. For a more detailed account, see Pitirim A. Sorokin, *A Long Journey: The Autobiography of Pitirim Sorokin* (New Haven: College and University Press, 1963), as well as Sorokin, "Sociology of My Mental Life." More recently, see Barry Johnston, *Pitirim A. Sorokin: An Intellectual Biography* (Lawrence: University of Kansas Press, 1995), an excellent comprehensive intellectual biography. Joseph B. Ford, Michel P. Richard, and Palmer C. Talbutt, *Sorokin and Civilization: A Centennial Assessment* (New Brunswick, N.J.: Transaction, 1996), is a series of critical essays on Sorokin's work.
3. Carle C. Zimmerman, *Sorokin: The World's Greatest Sociologist* (Saskatoon: University of Saskatchewan Press, 1968), 20.
4. Ibid., 19–20. See also Johnston, *An Intellectual Biography*, 16–17.
5. According to Sorokin, for the last twenty-five centuries Western civilization had cycled through a variety of cultural forms. Each form was defined by the fundamental conception of reality which informed its epistemology and dominated all of its social institutions, norms, and values. Ideational defined reality as nonmaterial, Sensate as mainly material and sensory, and Idealistic as a kind of rational synthesis of the other two. Periods of each type were separated by crises and determined by operations of the Principle of Immanent Determinism, the inherent potentiality within each system as opposed to external forces, and the Principle of Limits, a kind of dialectic process which would shift momentum toward the opposite type as a civilization became increasingly dominated by its opposing form. Epistemologically and ontologically Sorokin argued that reality consists of spirit, mind, and body and therefore could only be known through a synthesis of intuition, reason, and the senses, or what he referred to as Integralism. He attempted to give some idea of what an integral sociology would look like in Pitirim A. Sorokin, *Sociocultural Causality, Space, and Time* (Durham: Duke University Press, 1943).
6. Johnston, *An Intellectual Biography*, 125.

7. Robin M. Williams, Jr., "Pitirim A. Sorokin: Master Sociologist and Prophet," in *Sociological Traditions from Generation to Generation*, ed. Robert K. Merton and Matilda White Riley (Norwood, N.J.: Ablex, 1980), 100.

8. Arnold J. Toynbee, "Sorokin's Philosophy of History," in *Pitirim A. Sorokin in Review*, ed. Phillip J. Allen (Durham: Duke University Press, 1963), 73.

9. In Sorokin, *A Long Journey*, 297, Sorokin notes the similarities between his and Mills's work, as well as the fact that even though Mills had earlier written him a personal letter indicating his full concurrence with Sorokin's points, Mills never acknowledged or cited him for his work.

10. Pitirim A. Sorokin, *Fads and Foibles in Modern Sociology and Related Sciences* (Chicago: Henry Regnery, 1956), 3. Among those singled out as examples of "new Columbuses" were Samuel Stouffer for his work *Studies in Social Psychology of World War II*, Clyde Kluckhohn's *Mirror of Man*, and Talcott Parsons and Edward Shils for their *Toward a General Theory of Action*. Sorokin also repeats accusations of plagiarism which he had previously leveled against Parsons in an unpublished manuscript, *Similarities and Dissimilarities between Two Social Systems*, some 200 copies of which he had distributed in mimeographed form. See Johnston, *An Intellectual Biography*, 226.

11. Johnston, *An Intellectual Biography*, 26. See also Lawrence T. Nichols, "Sorokin and American Sociology: The Dynamics of a Moral Career in Science," in *Sorokin and Civilization: A Centennial Assessment*, ed. Joseph B. Ford, Michel P. Richard, and Palmer C. Talbutt (New Brunswick, N.J.: Transaction, 1996). For an account of sociology's empiricist and scientistic development, see Robert Friedrichs, *A Sociology of Sociology* (New York: Free Press, 1970).

12. Sorokin, "Sociology of My Mental Life," 268.

13. See Pitirim A. Sorokin, *Explorations of Altruistic Love and Behavior: Symposium* (Boston: Beacon, 1950); Pitirim A. Sorokin, *Altruistic Love: A Study of American Good Neighbors and Christian Saints* (Boston: Beacon Press, 1950); Pitirim A. Sorokin, *The Ways and Power of Love* (Boston: Beacon Press, 1954).

14. Johnston, *An Intellectual Biography*, 182. The Lilly Endowment initially supported the establishment of the Harvard Center for Creative Altruism with a $100 thousand grant to be given in $20 thousand installments over five years. However, in 1957, it rejected another proposal to expand its support of the Center, offering at the behest of Eli Lilly only a $15 thousand terminal grant for completion of its activities.

15. Sorokin was listed as a sponsor of the Du Bois dinner in Letter No. 172 (February 9, 1951). Among those listed in the same letter were Albert Einstein, Thomas Mann, and Linus Pauling.

16. Johnston, *An Intellectual Biography*, 215–216.

17. Federal Bureau of Investigation, *Pitirim Alexandrovich Sorokin*, Bureau File 100-409199-1 (Washington, D.C.: FBI Freedom of Information–Privacy Acts Section).

18. Ibid.

19. This article appeared in the December 20, 1930 edition of the *Boston Herald*. Others were drawn from the *Boston Traveler* (December 22, 1948), the *Harvard Crimson* (May 11, 1951), and the *Boston Globe* (September 27, 1953). Interestingly, in the latest article, while Sorokin still notes the "endless horrors of human bestiality and a hurricane of death and destruction" that he observed in Russia under the Communist government, his attitude toward what would constitute an appropriate response has changed in accordance with his growing interests in altruism and social reconstruction, leading him to state, "Cruelty, hatred, violence and injustice never can and never will be able to create a mental, moral, or material millennium. The only way toward it is the royal road of all-giving creative love, not only preached but consistently practiced."

20. This listing appeared in the December 14 edition of the *Boston Globe*.

21. FBI, *Sorokin*, Bufile 100-409199-1.

22. Ibid.

23. Several of the same organizations were listed in both reports. These included the American Peace Crusade, the Civil Rights Congress, and the American Committee for Protection of Foreign Born. Johnston, *An Intellectual Biography*, 328.

24. FBI, *Sorokin*, Bufile 100-409199-1.

25. Ibid.

26. Ibid.

27. Ibid.

28. Ibid.

29. Ibid.

30. FBI, *Sorokin*, Bufile 100-409199-3.

31. Ibid.

32. FBI, *Sorokin*, Bufile 100-409199.

33. FBI, *Sorokin*, Bufile 100-409199-4.

34. FBI, *Sorokin*, Bufile 100-409199-3.

35. Ibid.

36. Ibid.

37. FBI, *Sorokin*, Bufile 100-409199-1.

38. FBI, *Sorokin*, Bufile 100-409199-4.

39. FBI, *Sorokin*, Bufile 100-409199-3.

40. FBI, *Sorokin*, Bufile 100-409199-15, 16.

41. In 1957, reference is made to an article that appeared in *Akahata*, an organ of the Japan Communist Party, in which it is reported that Sorokin had sent a letter to a Japanese middle school teacher indicating that he admired Japan's antibomb movement. There is also a copy of a letter which he wrote to Alexandra Tolstoy in which he indicates that he does not agree with her political activity for a number of reasons, including, "If the war breaks out between Russia and the USA the victims of this war would not be Eisenhower, Dulles and Khrushchev and the Polit Bureau but scores of millions of American and Russian people." FBI, *Sorokin*, Bufile 100-409199-6.

42. FBI, *Sorokin*, Bufile 100-409199-8.

43. Johnston, *An Intellectual Biography*, 247–252.

44. Pitirim Sorokin, "Sociology of Yesterday, Today and Tomorrow," *American Sociological Review* 30 (1965): 833–843.

45. Phillip J. Allen, ed. *Pitirim Sorokin in Review* (Durham: Duke University Press, 1963); Edward A. Tiryakian, ed., *Sociological Theory, Values, and Sociocultural Change: Essays in Honor of Pitirim A. Sorokin* (New York: Harper Torchbooks, 1963).

46. For an account of the symposium and its relation to Sorokin's character and work, see Edward A. Tiryakian, "Sociology's Dostoyevski: Pitirim A. Sorokin," *The World and I* 3 (1988): 569–581.

47. Federal Bureau of Investigation, *American Sociological Association*, Bureau File 100-455276-1-13 (Washington, D.C.: FBI Freedom of Information–Privacy Acts Section).

48. Pitirim A. Sorokin, *Society, Culture and Personality* (New York: Harper & Brothers, 1947), 466.

— 8 —

No One above Suspicion: Talcott Parsons under Surveillance

Few American sociologists have made as significant an impact on the discipline or been as controversially and contradictorily regarded as Talcott Parsons. At a memorial session sponsored by the American Sociological Association shortly following his death, former student and collaborator Jesse R. Pitts noted Talcott Parsons would probably "take his place among the very great of our discipline. . . . Yet, it is unlikely that any of these great men had to endure in their lifetime so much incomprehension, so much abuse."[1] Robin Williams, Jr., one of Parsons's early students, echoed these sentiments, suggesting, "Few sociologists of our time have been more subjected to stereotyping, to careless *ad hoc* readings, and to selectively distorted interpretations."[2]

Parsons was born in 1902 into an ascetic Protestant family. His father was a Congregational minister, and his mother a suffragist.[3] He grew up wanting to be a doctor, and, planning on a medical career, entered Amherst College in 1920 to study biology. However, in his junior year he became interested in the social sciences and, following graduation in 1924, traveled to England to spend a year at the London School of Economics. While there he took a seminar with Bronislaw Malinowski, whose functional view of culture made a lasting impression upon him. The following year Parsons moved to Heidelberg, where he first encountered the ideas of Max Weber, whose classic, *The Protestant Ethic and the Spirit of Capitalism*, he would later translate into English for an American audience.

Parsons returned to the United States, and after a year as an instructor of economics at Amherst, in 1927 accepted a similar position at Harvard. In 1931, he was appointed an instructor in the newly organized department of sociology, but got off to a difficult start, in large part because of the hostile relationship he had with its chairperson, Pitirim Sorokin. However, much to Sorokin's chagrin, Parsons quickly attracted the attention of several of the department's younger graduate students, and in 1937 published his first major work, *The Structure of Social Action*. An ambitious attempt to lay out the foundations for an integrated voluntaristic theory of action drawn from the works of Weber, Pareto, Marshall, and Durkheim, it marked the beginning of his rise to become American sociology's most prominent social theorist in the 1950s and 1960s, and assured his promotion to assistant professor, even against Sorokin's opposition.[4]

In 1942, Sorokin resigned as chairperson, and Parsons was appointed in his place. During the war, Parsons stayed on the home front, actively contributing to the effort through his service with the Office of Strategic Services.[5] He also came into contact with Freudian theory, undergoing psychoanalysis as a therapeutic response to the loss of his father, mother, and brother. Following the war, convinced of the necessity of interdisciplinary collaboration for the development of any significant social theory, Parsons reorganized the department of sociology into the department of social relations, incorporating anthropologist Clyde Kluckhohn and psychologists Henry Murray and Gordon Allport. Five years later, in 1951, Parsons published the fruits of this collaboration in *The Social System*, outlining the main tenets of his theory of "structural-functionalism."

It is for this theory that Parsons would become a household name within the discipline and has been both deified and demonized; characterized as an heir to Durkheim, Weber, and Pareto for his creation of a general theory of social systems and provision of a method for constructing a paradigm of normal social scientific research, and at the same time as a hegemonic agent of American imperialism and capitalist apologist for the status quo.[6] However, the last thing anyone, devotee and detractor alike, might imagine is that Talcott Parsons could have been conceived a threat to national security. And yet, at the height of his career, the Federal Bureau of Investigation launched an extensive investigation into Parsons's background and activities following accusations he was the leader of a Communist cell at Harvard University.

While it has been previously revealed that Parsons's defense of a younger member of his department accused of Communist affiliation (Robert Bellah), and his prominent support of Robert Oppenheimer during the McCarthy era, led officials at the State Department to consider withdrawing his passport, until recently the existence and details of any formal investigations directed toward him remained unknown.[7] According to the informant who identified Parsons and the group of indoctrinated professors of which he was said to be the leader, "The members of this group were very clever and were subtle enough not to advocate un-American doctrines in their classes, but that their beliefs were more evident in the smaller seminar classes."[8]

Robert Merton, then head of the sociology department at Columbia University, was identified by the informant as a likely member of this inner group who had probably been selected for his position by Parsons. As evidence, the informant provided the interviewing agent with a copy of Merton's book, *Theory and Social Structure*, claiming it contained information which sounded un-American to him because it stated, among other things, that there were no opportunities for young men in America.[9] The informant also suggested that not all of the professors were members of this inner circle and provided the FBI with the name of one he knew to be a loyal American.

There is a certain, though obviously unintentional, hilarity in these observations about academia which liken the typical "old boy" network of prominent professors and their select students to a Communist cell. Yet the analogy is not without merit. Such networks, though not generally covert, are not open to everyone, and have a significant influence on the employment potential of their members as well as the development of the discipline. Clearly, Merton was a member of Parsons's "cell"; the professor referred to by the informant most likely was not.

Three weeks later, in late April 1952, Hoover sent a memo to SAC, Boston, instructing him to interview the professor identified to the New York office and to develop additional information which might be used as the basis for initiating an investigation of Parsons.[10] On August 21, SAC, Boston advised Hoover of the investigation and interview in a detailed seventeen-page office memorandum "concerning possible Communist tendencies of Professor TALCOTT PARSONS of Harvard University."[11] The bulk of the memorandum is based on an interview with an informant who appears to be the social relations professor referred to earlier. He provided the Boston office with intimate knowledge concerning both the department of social relations and Parsons's activities. He indicated the department of social relations was an outgrowth of the department of sociology, which in its earlier days could be described as conservative and consisting of "loyal Americans of good character." However, he suggested, "Today, there is a decided left-wing tendency in the Department which has resulted from PARSONS' 'manipulations and machinations.' [DELETED] Professor SOROKIN hired TALCOTT PARSONS twenty years ago after the Economics Department at Harvard University had fired PARSONS for reasons unknown [DELETED] PARSONS responded to this act by having SOROKIN demoted when the opportunity came to reorganize the old department of sociology."[12]

The informant also claimed he had ascertained that matters of importance to the department were settled at nightly meetings called by Parsons, and that this was a known Communist Party technique since Parsons and his cohort knew busy professors would not be in a position to attend such hastily called evening meetings. He further suggested Parsons played a leading role in the group of left-wingers in the social relations department, but that he was a very devious individual and careful cover-up man who only rarely would take a public stand on social questions.[13]

Finally, the informant noted that two of the department of social relations's sections, the Russian Research Center and Social Relations Laboratory, had direct contact with the federal government and had done secret and/or classified work for several of its agencies. He stated that the Russian Research Center was gaining significant influence with the State Department and would "at a future time be in a position to dictate certain aspects of American foreign policy."[14] This particularly concerned him, since Parsons, through his position in the department, would be able to influence the actions of its director, Clyde Kluckhohn.

In conclusion, the memorandum lists several other reasons given by the informant for believing Parsons adhered to the Communist Party line. While several have been blacked out, those left include he was the leader at Harvard in the opposition to the University of California teachers loyalty oath, he was privy to and a leader of the defense in the Alger Hiss trial, and in 1936 or 1937 he had worn a button of the Young Communist League–sponsored Sons of Future Wars. The Boston agent who authored the memorandum wrote to Hoover, "The basic question at hand appears to be whether the Bureau has a basis for initiating a security type investigation on TALCOTT PARSONS. While admittedly any Communist Party membership of PARSONS and others of his group now at Harvard would be exceedingly difficult to prove, the Boston Division feels that a security type investigation on PARSONS [DELETED] is warranted at the time, [DELETED]."[15]

On October 27, 1952, Hoover granted Boston authorization to initiate a "security-type" investigation of Parsons. He instructed Boston to give particular scrutiny to Parsons's association with the

Russian Research Center and any access he might have to secret government work through it.[16] Five months later, on March 19, 1953, Boston produced a twenty-five-page report detailing the results of the investigation to date.[17] The report begins with a thorough examination of Parsons's background, listing birth data, citizenship, education, academic honors, published works, marital status, employment record, residences from 1920 to date, and the status of his health. Section I indicates that during the course of the background check an agent was sent to Amherst, Massachusetts to investigate Parsons's college days there. It appears the agent contacted an administrative secretary or perhaps registrar who made Parsons's records available but could not provide derogatory information concerning him. Another member of the Amherst community made similar statements. The chief of police was also contacted and stated he had no record concerning Parsons in his files. However, a check with the Massachusetts Board of Probation, a central repository for all arrest records in the state, resulted in the identification of a criminal record consisting of five traffic violations, including failure to stop while entering a through street, $5 expenses, and proceeding at a speed greater than reasonable or proper, $10 fine.

Section II summarizes inquiries into Parsons's activities as described by an undeterminable number of informants. The information in this section is largely a recapitulation of that contained in the earlier Boston memorandum which served as a justification for initiating the investigation, though with much more detail. In this account, it is stated, "[DELETED] the group headed by TALCOTT PARSONS, which now runs the Department of Social Relations at Harvard, commencing approximately in 1936, [DELETED] to be a Communist Party cell at Harvard University. [DELETED] these pro-Communist groups favored a Communist or Socialist approach to sociological problems and cast aside 'the American and scientific approach' advanced by American sociologists at Harvard and other institutions of learning."[18] This is another rather amusing claim, given that Parsons has often been seen as a paragon of the "American and scientific approach," and charged with scientism by his critics.

It is further noted it was in his capacity as president of the American Sociological Society that Parsons was instrumental in passing several motions censuring the University of California for requesting its faculty take a loyalty oath. With regard to the Alger Hiss trial, it is alleged Parsons instigated the appearance of Dr. Henry Murray, Professor of Clinical Psychology at Harvard, as an expert witness for the defense. Murray was used in an attempt to discredit the testimony of Whitaker Chambers by bolstering the defense claim that a series of translations of fairy tales made by Chambers several years previous represented a diseased mind. It is also reported that one informant contacted was unable to provide evidence Parsons had been or was affiliated with the Communist Party nor was the informant able to cite a particular instance in which Parsons's activities reflected Communist Party propaganda.

In Section III, several other presumably suspicious activities, not previously mentioned, are listed. The first concerns a four-page flyer issued by the Cambridge Conference on War Time Problems. The flyer announced a meeting would be held on April 30, 1944, to discuss "immediate home front problems which affect the welfare of the community and nation," in order that "individuals and groups of varied interest can meet together and exchange ideas on working out democratic solutions to our common interests."[19] Parsons was listed among the organization's sponsors, but the FBI was unable to determine the extent of his participation in the organization, or even its exact nature.

Another informant identified Parsons as a member of the Educator's Committee of the American Committee for Spanish Freedom (ACSF). While the informant could provide no other detail concerning Parsons's activities in this organization, it was noted the ACSF was among those organizations cited by the U.S. Attorney General as falling under the purview of Executive Order 9835. Reference is also made to the Association of Cambridge Scientists and the Progressive Citizens of America. The latter was identified by the California Committee on Un-American Activities as a "new and broader Communist front for the entire United States, formed in 1946 at the direction of Communist Steering Committees from the Communist dominated National Citizens Political Action Committee and the Independent Citizens Committee of the Arts, Sciences and Professions."[20] All other information is blocked out, so it is impossible to determine why these items were included or what Parsons's association with them might have been, if any.

Perhaps the most serious allegation concerned the claim by an informant that Talcott Parsons had served as one of the faculty advisors of the John Reed Club at Harvard. In the HUAC *Guide to Subversive Organizations and Publications*, the John Reed Club was identified as being "among the organizations created or controlled by the Communist Party or part of a united front with the Party, which supported the First U.S. Congress against war."[21] The report concludes with a detailed physical description of Parsons, indicating his build was "stocky," and his hair "brown, straight, balding." No scars and marks are noted. However, under peculiarities it is remarked, "Usually wears small mustache." Obviously, in addition to contacting several informants, at some point during the investigation Parsons must have also been placed under personal surveillance.

Attached to the report is an appendix listing administrative details and leads. It begins with a note that an informant from Amherst College reported Parsons had been among the Commencement Day speakers for the class of 1924 and that several members of the podium party, including Charles Evans Hughes, Supreme Court justice and one-time Republican presidential candidate, had shown some "slight amazement at the proposals expounded by TALCOTT PARSONS to effect social and economic changes in the world and U.S."[22] While the informant could not recall whether these proposals were communistic or socialistic, she did remember they caused some furor at the time of their delivery. Several requests for specific investigations from offices in Chicago, Denver, New York, Philadelphia, Boston, and Los Angeles are also listed.

Two months later, reports of these investigations began to filter in. The first came from the Chicago office on May 18, 1953.[23] Several persons were contacted at the University of Chicago, but no one was able to locate records of employment for Parsons, especially dating back to 1937. However, a search of Chicago FBI files led to identification of information regarding his publication of two articles in the *Bulletin of Atomic Scientists* in 1946. The first concerned national science legislation, and the second the Association of Cambridge Scientists' efforts to explore possibilities for cooperative research by social and physical scientists in atomic energy. It was also noted the journal's sponsor, the Atomic Scientists of Chicago, showed no evidence of having been infiltrated by the Communist Party.

On June 11, 1953, Los Angeles sent in a summary of an interview with an acquaintance of Parsons. The acquaintance reported first meeting Parsons in 1939 or 1940, when he had enrolled at Harvard University as a graduate student, and having had only occasional contact with him at sociology conventions since then. He also advised the FBI he recalled Parsons was strongly anti-Nazi before and during World War II, and may have associated himself with organizations which advocated the anti-Nazi principle. He further related he did not know of any "left wing" organizations to which Parsons had ever belonged and noted Parsons had written in some of his books that he was not in accord with Marxism. On a more personal note, the acquaintance claimed Parsons

> was constantly striving to advance himself into the office positions of the commercial psychological [sic] societies, of which he was a member, because he was very ambitious for personal recognition. The subject was known, on occasion, to advocate ideas and to join organizations, not because he was in full accord with their principles but because he believed these would eventually be to his advantage. The subject was not a natural

leader, in that he was very unimpressive and commanded very little attention to himself in that way. He was extremely successful in being named or elected to office and leadership positions in the societies and organizations more through his political manipulations than as a result of a pleasing personality.[24]

FBI offices from around the country continued to contact and interview acquaintances and colleagues identified by Boston as possibly being able to offer pertinent information to the investigation of Parsons. While reports from Albany and Detroit are blacked out, a September 18, 1953, report from New Orleans indicates the informant knew nothing of any subversive tendencies Parsons may have had.[25] A September 24 report from San Antonio resulted in a similar response, with the informants advising they had no reason to question Parsons's loyalty. One stated even more strongly he believed Parsons to be a loyal American and that he had never had any reason to doubt Parsons's reliability at any time.[26] The same sentiments were repeated in the report from Mobile.[27] New York reported Parsons had been employed at Columbia during the summers of 1933 and 1935.[28]

On July 9, 1953, an agent called the secretary at the department of social relations and discovered Parsons was planning to leave for Europe in the middle of August. Boston contacted the Passport Division of the State Department and the FBI's Washington office requesting information concerning the trip, the length of his stay, and address of his residence in England. On October 21, Boston informed Director, FBI that Parsons was teaching at Cambridge in England and intended to be there for the entire 1953–1954 academic year.[29] Parsons had been invited by Cambridge University to take up its Visiting Chair in Social Theory and deliver its annual Marshall Lectures.

Parsons's travel abroad led to the initiation of an international inquiry to supplement that already occurring within the United States. On November 23, Hoover sent copies of reports on the investigation and Parsons's overseas activities to Mr. Dennis A. Flinn, Director of the Office of Security for the Department of State, and copied the Director of the Central Intelligence Agency. No formal investigation was requested at the time, but he did ask to be informed should any information concerning the "subject's activities while outside the United States" come to their attention.[30] Hoover sent a similar memo, with reports attached, stamped "SECRET–AIR COURIER," to the FBI's legal attaché at the American Embassy in London, and requested he verify Parsons's employment and residence.[31]

As inquiries began overseas, a November 19 memo from Director, FBI instructed SAC, Boston to review the investigation and submit his recommendations as to whether or not Parsons should be considered for placement on the Security Index. A note attached to the memo suggests, "Allegations of substantial subversive activities made by persons of unknown reliability have not been supported by extensive investigation."[32] However, slightly less than a month later, the investigation appears to have been rejuvenated by further allegations. Under the "Leads" section of the Administrative Page of a December 29 Boston office case report, the Chicago Division is instructed to "obtain [DELETED] regarding the identity of former Young Communist League members at Harvard University during the middle 1930's, particularly whether TALCOTT PARSONS, Professor of Sociology at Harvard, was at that time affiliated in any way with the Young Communist League."[33] The New Haven division was instructed to make similar inquiries.

Taking into account these developments, Boston responded to the Director's request for recommendations concerning the Security Index: "Based on the results of investigation conducted thus far, but lacking the results of investigation to be conducted by the Chicago and New Haven Divisions, particularly in connection with the allegations made concerning PARSONS' activities in the Young Communist League at Harvard during the middle 1930's, Boston feels that PARSONS' name should not be considered for inclusion on the Security Index as of this time."[34] Boston qualified this recommendation by suggesting that if either Chicago or New Haven were able to identify Parsons as a member of the Communist Party or Young Communist League they would reverse their position and request placement on the Index.

The investigation continued into the new year, and its second year. Informants familiar with Communist Party activities in Boston during the 1930s stated that Parsons was not known to be associated with it. One informant did surface suggesting he "doubted the loyalty of PARSONS inasmuch as PARSONS had been closely associated with a group of graduate students and professors at Harvard who branded as fascist any individual who did not agree with their way of thinking on social and economic problems confronting this country and who espoused a propaganda line which closely approximated the Communist Party propaganda line during the 1930's and 1940's."[35]

During the entire two-year period, Parsons remained ignorant of the investigation and allegations concerning his activities. However, in early February 1954, Samuel Stouffer, his friend and colleague from the department of social relations, contacted him in England and informed him that he, Stouffer, had been denied access to classified documents by the Eastern Industrial Security Board. He advised Parsons his name had also been mentioned in a "Statement of

Reasons" justifying the denial, and in which Parsons was reported to be a member of the Communist Party.[36]

On February 23, Parsons delivered a sworn affidavit supporting Stouffer to the Eastern Industrial Security Board, in care of the American Embassy in London, stating he had "the highest respect for him as a patriotic American and a scholar."[37] He also denied the accusation made against himself and remarked, "This allegation is so preposterous that I cannot understand how any reasonable person could come to the conclusion that I was a member of the Communist Party or ever had been. . . . My political opinions have always been in support of free democracy and opposed to totalitarianism of any sort whether of the left or of the right. . . . It could not fail to be evident to one of my profession that freedom for the scientific study of social problems was drastically curtailed under any totalitarian system."[38] The legal attaché in London acquired a copy of the affidavit and forwarded it to the Director, FBI, on March 11.

At about the same time, Parsons had applied for work with UNESCO. In response to his application, the International Organizations Employees Board of the U.S. Civil Service Commission was delegated to make a loyalty determination, and on February 19, 1954, sent a memo formally requesting the Director, FBI, conduct a loyalty investigation. This investigation was immediately delegated to the FBI's Employee Security Section with a ninety-day deadline. It was to be carried out concurrently with the security investigation already under way.[39]

The Employees Board also sent an interrogatory to Parsons. On May 17, 1954, Parsons traveled to the American Embassy in London and provided sworn testimony in response to it in the presence of Vice-Consul Roland C. Shaw. The interrogatory was made available to the Boston office through an informant and excerpts were included in a report, five copies of which were forwarded to the Director, FBI on July 29, 1954.[40] In the interrogatory, each of the allegations made against Parsons during the course of the security investigation was listed and he was given an opportunity to reply to them one by one.

In response to the allegation that he had been a participant in the Communist Party cell at Harvard, Parsons stated, "I was never in any way affiliated with that cell, indeed I did not know of its existence. I did, however, know as individuals a few persons who have subsequently been identified as its members." These included Granville Hicks, a fellow member of the staff of Adams House, and Daniel Boorstin, with whom he served for one year on the Committee on Concentration in Social Science.[41]

To questions raised concerning his association with the John Reed Club of Harvard, Parsons replied, "May I repeat, I did not at any time sympathize with the political opinions held by the members of the club, but accepted this sponsorship only because I believed in their right to free speech and discussion. . . . I knew the club to be communist-sponsored, as I have stated. Knowing what I now do of the abuses which the Communist-front organizations have consistently made of the privileges of free speech I would not today accept sponsorship of such an organization. But having done so in 1945 was, I think, a different matter."[42] Parsons denied allegations he had been a member of the Educational Committee of the American Committee for Spanish Freedom.[43]

Parsons was also alleged to have been associated with the National Council of the Arts, Sciences and Professions, which HUAC had designated as a Communist front. In response to the claim he had received an invitation to attend one of its meetings, he stated, "I do recollect that in 1948 I received an invitation to attend a meeting in New York of the National Council of the Arts, Sciences and Professions. I remember positively, however, that, knowing it was Communist-sponsored, I declined the invitation and cannot see how I could be held responsible for the fact that some person, unknown to me, sent it to me. I never had anything to do with that organization."[44]

The interrogatory informed Parsons of several of the other allegations intimating he had been a Communist sympathizer. Parsons indicated he had "no memory of ever having worn a button of an organization known as the Sons of Future Wars, or having any other association with it though I remember vaguely that there was some such organization."[45] He affirmed that, like a majority of academic people in the United States, he had opposed the California loyalty oath as bad public policy. He had introduced a resolution opposing the oath at the 1950 American Sociological Society meetings in Denver. However, he noted it was a matter of public record the oath had been declared unconstitutional by the Supreme Court, and stated,

> I never made any secret of my conviction on this issue, that to require a special loyalty oath of teachers was bad public policy. The only sense, however, in which I was a "leader" of this opposition was that at a meeting of the American Sociological Society, in Denver in 1950, I introduced a resolution to the society, which was passed by a large majority, deploring the action of the California Regents. . . . This and my other actions in connection with the California oath are, in my opinion, entirely within the rights of a loyal American citizen and have nothing to do with sympathy for Communism.[46]

Parsons also denied any active role in the Alger Hiss case, indicating, "I do not remember any public ovation for Dr. MURRAY after his testimony in the HISS case, and I certainly do not remember leading any 'cheering section'"[47] He did recognize Murray as a professional colleague and friend with whom he had carried out a significant amount of professional collaboration and defended Murray's testimony as having been given in good faith.

Parsons could not remember having signed a petition in 1939 calling on the president to lift the embargo on loyalist Spain, but did admit it was possible. However, he did not see why such an action would be evidence of Communist sympathy, explaining, "As between Franco and the Loyalists, in the situation before the late world war, I favored the Loyalists, because Hitler and Mussolini had intervened on the Franco side. I knew of course that Soviet Russia had aided the Loyalists, but I considered that to be the lesser evil, just as after 1941 I considered our own alliance with the Russians preferable to a victory for Hitler."[48]

Perhaps the most fantastic claim in support of Parsons's alleged Communist sympathy was that in 1949, at a party in his home, his son had recited Marx's *Communist Manifesto* from memory. His son would only have been a high school student at the time. While Parsons indicated that his son was "unusually intelligent and intellectually alert," and might well have read the *Manifesto*, he also suggested, "That he had memorized the whole thing and repeated it I think incredible." He continued,

> I do not remember suggesting he should read the Communist Manifesto but I would not have opposed his doing so. It seems to me that young people should be informed about the world they live in and make up their own minds about its problems. This does not mean that they agree with or are "influenced by" everything they read. I have read extensively in the works of Marx—it has been my professional obligation to do so—but I am in fundamental disagreement with Marxian theory. I have also assigned the works of Marx, and of course of many anti-Marxists, to my students, because if they are to understand the history of Western social and economic thought they must know about the ideas of Marx. A highly intelligent fifteen-year-old is certainly mature enough to begin this process.[49]

Finally, in order to complete the interrogatory, Parsons was asked to explain where his sympathies lay in the ideological conflict between the United States and the Soviet Union. He responded that they were "unequivocally on the side of the United States," and indicated that he was puzzled as to how any fair-minded person could think otherwise:

> I am strongly opposed to Soviet Communism and its influence in the United States and elsewhere for four main reasons. First, the Communist Party advocates and works for revolution by violence and refuses to accept the

legal procedures of Constitutional Democracy as it is practiced in the United States and other countries like England. Second, it works by conspiratorial methods which are incompatible with the requirement of a democracy that differences of political opinion, which we treat as legitimate within a considerable range, should be openly threshed out before the forum of public opinion and decided by constitutional processes. Third, the Communist Party in the United States is known to be controlled by the Russian Party and not to be an independent movement of free Americans. The fourth reason is that I do not like the Communist ideal and where they have gained ascendancy, their practice, of what a society should be. Above all I abhor their ruthless suppression of the freedom of the individual.[50]

Parsons concluded his sworn statement by indicating, "I subscribe to these views, which I understand to be taken for granted by all loyal American citizens, without reservation."[51]

Along with copies of the excerpts from the interrogatory, SAC, Boston sent forth a memo to the Director indicating that since he appeared to have provided a straightforward account of his associations with other individuals known to him in connection with the Communist Party and other related Communist front organizations, and since the investigation had failed to develop proof of the allegations made against him, that the case should be closed.[52] And, on July 29, 1954, the security investigation that had been initiated by the FBI two years earlier was closed.

The UNESCO loyalty investigation, being overseen by the International Organizations Employees Loyalty Board of the U.S. Civil Service Commission, several months beyond its ninety-day deadline was also drawing to an end. The FBI's Employee Security Section had completed its portion of this investigation, largely retracing already tread grounds and summarizing information garnered from the security investigation. No additional information was uncovered.

Under the authority of Director, FBI, the Bureau had also requested the assistance of both the Central Intelligence Agency and the State Department in investigating Parsons's activities overseas.[53] The State Department had carried out inquires in Austria and France, Sweden and Switzerland, England and Norway, and Germany.[54] Documents indicate that neither agency turned up any derogatory information. On July 23, Hoover had sent a final memo to Kimbell Johnson, Chief of the Investigations Division of the Civil Service Commission, indicating he was enclosing the last report of the State Department's overseas investigation and requested the Bureau be advised of the "ultimate disposition which is made of this case."[55] Almost six months later, on January 19, 1955, a memo was forwarded to Hoover indicating that the International Organizations Employees Loyalty Board had made a favorable loyalty determination and forwarded it to UNESCO.[56]

Even though both investigations were completed in 1955 in Parsons's favor and he was never placed on the Security Index, this was not the end of FBI scrutiny of his activities. In September of the same year, a report entitled "Talcott Parsons Fund for the Republic" indicated, according to its annual report, the fund had supported a project under the leadership of Samuel Stouffer which resulted in the book, *Communism, Conformity, and Civil Liberties*. In the book Stouffer acknowledged the assistance of Parsons. The report presented a synopsis of Parsons's background, including a summary of allegations raised against him and his responses from the previous investigations.[57] In a section headed "RELATIONS WITH THE FBI," the report indicated that an earlier letter had advised, "It is believed an interview with Parsons, whose name appears on the proscribed list of those Harvard University professors whom Boston Agents are forbidden to contact and interview, would develop no worthwhile additional information and noted that the possibility of developing deeper antagonisms to the Bureau is enhanced."[58]

In April 1956, the legal attaché in London sent a memo to Director, FBI, informing him the Department of State had renewed Parsons's passport.[59] The memo, titled "Talcott Parsons Security Matter–C," and which mentions the decision was based upon favorable results of earlier investigations into his loyalty, shows that although the original investigation was officially closed, the FBI continued to maintain their file on him.

Several years later, at the end of December 1961, an "URGENT TELETYPE" from Director, FBI was sent instructing SAC, Boston to interview Parsons concerning the loyalty of an unidentifiable appointee.[60] Once again, the 1952–1954 security investigation was mentioned, along with allegations of Parsons's Communist sympathies and failure to produce any evidence in support of them. Seven years later, in February 1968, the FBI received a request from Mrs. Mildred Stegall of the White House staff for a name check concerning some individuals, including Parsons, who would be attending a Medal of Science presentation to be held at the White House. On February 14, the FBI delivered a classified letter, stamped "SECRET," to Mrs. Stegall (with the Attorney General copied), including several enclosures, one of which pertained to Parsons.[61] The Parsons' enclosure consisted of a brief summary of earlier security and loyalty investigations, noting allegations had been unsubstantiated and that it had been determined Parsons was a loyal American. It also included one previously unreported piece of information. Parsons had been among sponsors of a full-page advertisement placed in the *Harvard Crimson* (May 16, 1967) by department of social relations members protesting the Vietnam War and demanding immediate cessation to the bombing.[62]

Parsons's case illustrates several of the more pernicious aspects of the FBI's widespread surveillance activities. For example, it reveals the power of a few anonymous informants, acting on whatever personal motives, to bring on the full force of an FBI investigation on the basis of ridiculous charges. Once begun, Parsons's seeming "neutrality" and/or any action contrary to a Communist stance could be explained away as an example of his "subtlety" and "deviousness." Most disturbing is that many of the informants were close enough to employ personal anecdotes in their charges (i.e., his son's alleged recitation of the *Communist Manifesto*). Obviously, many were also colleagues and fellow sociologists. And, as is the nature of bureaucracy, once set in motion it could only slowly and methodically grind out its task until its inertia was eventually exhausted and Parsons cleared. Once collected, the data could not be relinquished, the taint of suspicion never entirely removed.

Parsons himself attempted to diagnose the source of the red hysteria and McCarthyist movement in an article published after he would have become aware of the allegations and investigation of his own activities.[63] He argued that it was not the result of political reaction or neo-fascism. He suggested it could be understood as a symptom of structural strains accompanying a major transformation in American society from isolated nation to international leader, the impact of growing industrialization, and a free-enterprise economy. Such changes required a stronger commitment to the national community. As a result, those segments of the society with more individualistic and critical traditions (i.e., liberal politicians and academics) came under a suspicion clothed in the garb of loyalty oaths and anti-Communism.

Perhaps the most difficult question to answer is what influence this episode had upon Parsons's scholarship. It might be tempting to say none. After all, Parsons was unyielding in his support of Stouffer, writing, "I am in it with you to the death,"[64] and of Bellah and Oppenheimer as well. And yet such a claim would defy the fundamental tenets of the sociology of knowledge. One possibility that immediately comes to mind is Parsons's treatment of Marx. Numerous sociologists have noted the relative lack of attention Parsons afforded Marx in his work, even though Marx is generally regarded as one of the major contributors to the classical tradition along with Weber and Durkheim, both of whom Parsons gave extensive attention throughout his career. Mark Gould suggests that this was because Parsons mistakenly characterized Marx as a utilitarian theorist (not a voluntarist) and therefore felt his theory was obsolete.[65] Robertson and Turner suggest that Parsons did not write against any particular framework of analysis and therefore presumably did not feel a need to take Marx into account in any systematic or concerted fashion.[66]

Ellen Schrecker has noted the chilling effect that McCarthyism had on the nation's colleges and universities, resulting in the marginalization of Marxism and disappearance of criticism of the status quo. In addition, faculty throughout the academy pruned their syllabi and avoided controversy.[67] Sociology was no exception. Might not Parsons have been subject to these influences, consciously or unconsciously? Staff researchers at the Russian Research Center were so concerned about the possibility of misinterpretation of their activities that even before going into Communist bookstores to purchase materials required for their work they sought "prior understanding" with the FBI.[68] Parsons was certainly politically sensitive enough to recognize this danger, and following the investigation had good reason to be concerned.

Parsons's case also offers an instructive lesson regarding the definitive importance of sociohistorical context. In a climate of anti-Communist fear and paranoia, accusations and characterizations of an apparent conservative member or critic of the academy and two or three disgruntled colleagues or acquaintances were enough to set the security bureaucracy in motion. Once the suspicion that Parsons was a Communist was raised, it functioned in an almost paradigmatic fashion. Acts of political liberalism and old-boy networking were seen as suspect, and anomalous behavior was ignored or explained away. The ultimate irony is that only a decade later, within the context of national and international civil unrest and student protests and the rise of critical sociology, Parsons was subjected to a much different paradigm, that of conservative champion of the status quo. The very political liberalism and activities that led to accusations of Communist sympathy were now ignored.

Parsons never made public mention of his own case. And, as he indicated in his initial affidavit, to suggest he was a Communist was indeed preposterous. It is particularly ironic given more recent allegations that during the summer of 1948 Parsons assisted Army intelligence officers and the State Department in attempts to bring suspected Nazi collaborators into the country as anti-Communist Soviet experts.[69] It is also difficult not to recognize the incongruity of the commitment to democratic values on which he based the anti-Communist assurances of his interrogatory, and the threat to those selfsame values posed by the inquisition to which he and so many others were being subjected.

NOTES

1. Jesse R. Pitts, "Talcott Parsons: The Sociologist as the Last Puritan," *American Sociologist* 15 (1980): 62.

2. Robin M. Williams, Jr., "Talcott Parsons: The Stereotypes and the Realities," *American Sociologist* 15 (1980): 66.

3. Several biographical sketches are available which broadly outline the details of Parsons's life and work. See Peter Hamilton, *Talcott Parsons* (New York: Tavistock and Horwood, 1983); Pat N. Lackey, *Invitation to Talcott Parsons' Theory* (Houston: Cap and Gown, 1987); Martin Martel, "Talcott Parsons," in *International Encyclopedia of Social Sciences* vol. 18, ed. David L. Sills (New York: Free Press, 1979); Roland Robertson and Bryan S. Turner, *Talcott Parsons: Theorist of Modernity* (London: Sage, 1991).

4. Sorokin would later characterize the work as "full of sham scientific slang devoid of clear meaning, precision and elementary elegance." See Pitirim A. Sorokin, *Sociological Theories of Today* (New York: Harper and Row, 1966), 56. Even Parsons's father found the work hard going and inquired if his son's lectures were similar to how he wrote. See Hamilton, *Talcott Parsons*, 39.

5. During the war Parsons delivered several radio addresses urging Americans to abandon their isolationism and join the fight against Fascism, and also wrote several articles analyzing and critiquing National Socialist Germany's social system. These works are now available in Uta Gerhardt, ed., *Talcott Parsons on National Socialism* (New York: Aldine de Gruyter, 1993). Contrary to his often-cited reputation as a verbose and jargonistic scholar lost in the abstraction of grand theory, the picture that emerges from this collection is Parsons the political activist, applied social analyst, and practical policy advisor presenting his arguments with remarkable clarity and forcefulness.

6. See Hamilton, *Talcott Parsons*, 16–18; Martin Martel, "Talcott Parsons," 609; Robertson and Turner, *Theorist of Modernity*, 9–11.

7. Pitts, "Last Puritan," 63; Hamilton, *Talcott Parsons*, 44–45; and Ellen Schrecker, *No Ivory Tower: McCarthyism and the Universities* (New York: Oxford University Press, 1986), 262–263. Sigmund Diamond has also obtained documentation of Parsons's case through the Freedom of Information Act and makes reference to it in his work, *Compromised Campus: The Collaboration of Universities with the Intelligence Community, 1945–1955* (New York: Oxford University Press, 1992). Jens Kaalhauge Nielsen, "The Political Orientation of Talcott Parsons: The Second World War and Its Aftermath," in Robertson and Turner, *Theorist of Modernity*, also refers to the investigation in his discussion of Parsons's political orientation, using documentation obtained from the Parsons collection at the Harvard University Archives.

8. Federal Bureau of Investigation, *Talcott Parsons*, Bureau File 100-390459-2 (Washington, D.C.: FBI Freedom of Information–Privacy Acts Section).

9. Ibid.

10. Ibid.

11. FBI, *Parsons*, Bufile 100-390459-3.

12. Ibid. Parsons has stated he chose to leave economics and enter sociology because of his developing intellectual directions. See Talcott Par-

sons, "On Building Social System Theory: A Personal History," in *Social Systems and the Evolution of Action Theory* (New York: Free Press, 1977), 32–33. No evidence has ever surfaced that he was fired. However, according to Barry Johnston, "Sorokin and Parsons at Harvard: Institutional Conflict and the Rise of a Hegemonic Tradition," *Journal of the History of Behavioral Sciences* 22 (1986): 107–127, he did lead the charge to replace Sorokin as chairperson of sociology in 1944.

13. FBI, *Parsons*, Bufile 100-390459-3.

14. Ibid. The Russian Research Center was formed through the collaboration of Harvard University, the Carnegie Foundation, and the U.S. intelligence community. Diamond, *Compromised Campus*, provides a detailed and fully documented account of its creation and early operations, including Parsons's active participation as one of the founding members of its executive committee. The FBI also compiled several hundred pages of information on the Center in its files. Federal Bureau of Investigation, *Russian Research Center*, Bureau File 100-360557 (Washington, D.C.: FBI Freedom of Information–Privacy Acts Section).

15. FBI, *Parsons*, Bufile 100-390459-3.

16. Ibid.

17. FBI, *Parsons*, Bufile 100-390459-7.

18. Ibid.

19. Ibid.

20. Ibid.

21. Ibid.

22. Ibid.

23. FBI, *Parsons*, Bufile 100-390459-12.

24. FBI, *Parsons*, Bufile 100-390459-14.

25. FBI, *Parsons*, Bufile 100-390459-25.

26. FBI, *Parsons*, Bufile 100-390459-26.

27. FBI, *Parsons*, Bufile 100-390459-27.

28. FBI, *Parsons*, Bufile 100-390459-28.

29. FBI, *Parsons*, Bufile 100-390459-30.

30. FBI, *Parsons*, Bufile 100-390459-32.

31. FBI, *Parsons*, Bufile 100-390459-30, 35.

32. FBI, *Parsons*, Bufile 100-390459-32.

33. FBI, *Parsons*, Bufile 100-390459-35.

34. FBI, *Parsons*, Bufile 100-390459-36.

35. Ibid.

36. FBI, *Parsons*, Bufile 100-390459-42.

37. Ibid.

38. Federal Bureau of Investigation, *Talcott Parsons*, Bureau File 138-2572-28 (Washington, D.C.: FBI Freedom of Information Acts–Privacy Section).

39. FBI, *Parsons*, Bufile 138-2572-1.

40. FBI, *Parsons*, Bufile 100-390459-46.

41. FBI, *Parsons*, Bufile 138-2572-28.

42. Ibid.

43. Ibid.

44. Ibid.

45. Ibid.
46. Ibid.
47. FBI, *Parsons*, Bufile 100-390459-46.
48. FBI, *Parsons*, Bufile 138-2572-28.
49. Ibid.
50. Ibid.
51. Ibid.
52. FBI, *Parsons*, Bufile 100-390459-46.
53. FBI, *Parsons*, Bufile 138-2572-1, 15.
54. FBI, *Parsons*, Bufile 138-2572-26, 27, 28, 29. The FBI removed CIA and State Department materials from information they released and forwarded them to each for review. The CIA responded that they have determined all of its information must be withheld in entirety on the basis of FOIA exemption (b)(3), which "applies to the Director's statutory obligations to protect from disclosure intelligence sources and methods, as well as the organizations, functions, names, official titles, salaries or numbers of personnel employed by the Agency, in accord with the National Security Act of 1947 and the CIA Act of 1949, respectively."
55. FBI, *Parsons*, Bufile 138-2572-29.
56. FBI, *Parsons*, Bufile 138-2572-30.
57. FBI, *Parsons*, Bufile 100-390459-49.
58. Ibid.
59. FBI, *Parsons*, Bufile 100-390459-50.
60. FBI, *Parsons*, Bufile 100-390459-54.
61. FBI, *Parsons*, Bufile 100-390459-57.
62. Ibid.
63. Talcott Parsons, "'McCarthyism' and American Social Tension: A Sociologist's View," *Yale Review* 44 (1954): 226–245.
64. As quoted in Nielsen, "Political Orientation," 228.
65. Mark Gould, "Parsons versus Marx: 'An Earnest Warning . . .'," *Sociological Inquiry* 51 (1981): 197–218.
66. Robertson and Turner, *Theorist of Modernity,* 256.
67. Schrecker, *No Ivory Tower*, 339.
68. Diamond, *Compromised Campus*, 69.
69. Nielsen, "The Political Orientation of Talcott Parsons, 224.

— 9 —

Testing a Concept: Herbert Blumer's Loyalty

Best known for his development of symbolic interactionism, Herbert Blumer, like Parsons, was a center of controversy throughout his career.[1] As structural functionalism emerged in the 1950s, he became the spokesman for a small group of dissidents and has been recognized as "the single mid-century sociologist who could rival Talcott Parsons in his significance for the development of social theory."[2] Blumer was a persistent critic of logical empiricism, with its dualistic assumptions concerning the separation of subject and object, knower and known, mind and action, and structure and process, that was coming to dominate social science in the 1940s and 1950s. He used his positions as President of the Society for the Study of Social Problems in 1954, and of the American Sociological Association in 1955, as a bully pulpit to warn against the blind importation into the social sciences of research methods proved successful in the natural sciences.[3]

Like George Herbert Mead, with whom he studied and on whose works he relied heavily in developing his own position, Blumer left behind the eighteenth century Cartesian logic of separation and challenged sociologists to rethink their reified methodologies designed to measure a world "out there."[4] Blumer rejected any theory or method not grounded, as was his own symbolic interactionism, in the fundamental recognition that social reality is an ongoing, emergent process and that human beings, collectively and individually, act on the basis of the meanings they attribute to the objects and experiences that make up their world. A methodological muckraker, he was fond of "testing a concept" to see if it could actually take account of the phenomena it was claimed to describe. This led to his embroilment in several vitriolic controversies, including one episode in which he subjected *The American Soldier* to such a critique, provoking its author, Samuel Stouffer, to remark that Blumer was "the gravedigger of American sociology."[5] Even today, Blumer's legacy remains the subject of debate, misunderstandings, and myths and has largely set the tone and provided the outline for the quantitative versus qualitative debate that has over the years continued to smolder within the discipline.[6]

Born and raised in Missouri, Blumer dropped out of high school when a fire in his father's business forced him to help support the family as a typist. Not only was he proud of his typing speed, but also his tremendous strength, once boasting that during World War I as a tent raiser for the Army he could pound in the stakes of its huge tents with a single arm.[7] Following World War I, and after a year of self-study, he passed the entrance exam to the University of Missouri. He received his B.A. in 1921, and his M.A. the following year. In 1922, Blumer was appointed an instructor at Missouri and taught there until 1925, when he enrolled in the Ph.D. program at Chicago while on leave from Missouri following Ku Klux Klan criticism of one of his lectures.[8] During this period he also played professional football with the Chicago Cardinals and in 1928 he completed his Ph.D. and was offered an appointment at the University of Chicago. As a sociologist Blumer sported a wide berth of interests, including the cinema, collective behavior, drug use, fashion, industrialization and labor relations, morale, race relations, and, of course, his own symbolic interactionism.[9]

Blumer came under FBI investigation while he was President of the ASA and had applied, in February 1956, to attend a three-day UNESCO conference on social science terminology to be held that May in Paris. He had been previously subject to a confidential investigation by the Federal Works Agency in June 1943, prior to his appointment as Principal Liaison Officer to the Office of War Information, where he served for one year. That had been a routine investigation in which William Fielding Ogburn, by then chair of the department of sociology at the University of Chicago, and Elizabeth Dunphy, a university stenographer, indicated that his performance at Chicago had been excellent. Charles E. Merriam, professor emeritus, and Robert Redfield, Dean, had vouched for his character, reputation, integrity, and patriotism.

On February 21, 1956, under the provisions of Executive Order 10422, Director, FBI issued a memo instructing that a Full Field Investigation be launched, with the Chicago office to set forth the basis and San Francisco to compile a personal history.[10] Several leads were listed and additional copies and requests for assistance were forwarded to field offices in Baltimore, Honolulu, Kansas City, Los Angeles, Omaha, Pittsburgh, New York, St. Louis, and Washington, D.C. The memo indicated, "Office indices and credit and criminal records should be checked concerning captioned individual's relatives who reside in the area covered by your field division." It concluded by cautioning that, "This case must be assigned to Agents experienced in Security of Government Employees and applicant-type investigations and must receive immediate and efficient handling," that all reports should be referred to the Employees Security Section, and that the Bureau deadline, March 13, must be met without fail. Also on February 21, Hoover sent a confidential correspondence to Dennis Flinn, Director of the Office of Security at the Department of State, requesting that he conduct the necessary investigation abroad in accordance with Executive Order 10422, and requesting that "in the event information is received reflecting adversely on applicant's loyalty, please incorporate this data in a signed statement and furnish five copies of your report to this Bureau."[11] He also copied in Kimbell Johnson, Chief of the Investigations Division at the U.S. Civil Service Commission, whose office would ultimately be responsible for disseminating the results of the investigation.

Three weeks later, on March 12, in a forty-plus-page report laying out the basis for the investigation, Chicago noted that a reliable informant had advised, in 1941, that Blumer's name, along with that of Burgess, was on file in the offices of the United Spanish Aid Committee, which maintained offices with the Veterans of the Abraham Lincoln Brigade, 203 North Wabash Avenue, Chicago, Illinois. According to the informant, these names were under the heading, "Chicago Sponsors of the Teachers Committee of the Spanish Refugee Relief Committee."[12] In addition, Chicago identified testimony from a special report of the Seditious Activities Investigation Commission of the State of Illinois, "Investigation of the University of Chicago and Roosevelt College, 1949," in which the typed signatures of several Chicago faculty were appended to a letter which appealed for support and endorsed the activities of the American League for Peace and Democracy. A copy of the testimony, referred to as "Exhibit B," noted that Blumer's name was included among the signers.[13]

Chicago had also unearthed a transcript from the public hearings of the U.S. Senate Judiciary Subcommittee to Investigate the Administration of the Internal Security Act and Other Internal Security Laws in which Subcommittee Counsel Robert Morris introduced an article from the July 17, 1952, issue of the *Daily Worker* headlined, "41 Professors at Chicago University Urge Big Four Parley on Germany." The article indicated that the previous day an open letter to President Truman had been released at the university by the Faculty–Graduate Committee for Peace urging that the United States explore every means possible to reach an agreement with the Soviet Union for the establishment of a neutral postwar Germany. Blumer was listed among the signers of the letter.[14]

This was not the only time that the FBI had identified Blumer's name among the pages of the *Daily Worker*. Records released to the FBI by the Civil Service Commission and a report from SAC, New York reflect that on July 3, 1950, an article entitled, "CP Warns of Plan to Blitz Mundt Bill Thru Congress," noted, "Chicago clergymen, professors, authors, labor leaders, Negro leaders, scientists and others joined yesterday in a telegram to Sen. Scott Lucas urging him to prevent any action on the Mundt police-state bill. The message was made public by the Chicago chapter of the NATIONAL COMMITTEE TO DEFEAT THE MUNDT–FERGUSON BILL."[15] Blumer was listed as a signer of the telegram and the National Committee was cited in the HUAC *Guidebook* as a registered lobbying organization which had "carried out the objectives of the Communist Party in its fight against anti-subversive legislation." Another article appearing on March 5, 1951, "90 on Faculty of Chicago U. Urge Recognition of China," indicated that Blumer had been among the signers of an open letter addressed to President Truman urging him to recognize the People's Republic of China and to seek talks with China.

Chicago obtained information concerning Blumer's education from the Registrar's office at the University of Chicago, including the dates of his degrees and the title of his Ph.D. thesis, "Method in Social Psychology." Employment information was acquired from the offices of the comptroller and the vice-president indicating that Blumer had resigned his position at Chicago on September 30, 1952, in order to accept the chair of the department of sociology at the University of California. Two interviewees suggested that Blumer's decision to accept the position in California had been influenced by the health of his wife. An assistant to the vice-president of the university made available records listing Blumer's residence on South Shore Drive in 1949, and his dates of promotion to associate professor on October 1, 1931, and full professor July 1, 1947. It was also noted that Blumer had been the plaintiff in a divorce action in 1938.

Several colleagues and associates from the department of sociology and throughout the university were interviewed and without exception praised Blumer, indicating that he was "brilliant," a "top man," whose "reputation is excellent among those engaged in the sociological field in the United States," and who "sees the human issues of our time, but he sees them in the light of the most dedicated conception of the nature of man." He was characterized as a man who "was not a 'joiner' and did not tend to identify himself with the political or other movements of the day," but rather was a sociologist who "regarded it as his duty to be an impartial observer and not a participant."[16]

Chicago agents also visited the regional office of National War Labor Board (NWLB) and the Joint Electrical Arbitration Board (JEAB). Blumer had served as chairperson and public representative for a three-person panel in the disputes section of the NWLB from 1943–1945. From 1948 to 1952, he had helped to establish and administrate a seniority system for the JEAB. Both offices reported nothing but "the highest respect and admiration for Dr. BLUMER."

On March 22, 1956, Chicago forwarded an additional report detailing three more bits of information.[17] A November 12, 1942, article in the morning edition of the *Washington Times-Herald* reported that Blumer had attended the funeral of Dr. Ben Reitman. Reitman was described in the article as a "nonaggressive, philosophical anarchist." A heavily blacked out passage from the report indicated that an informant had stated, "[DELETED] to a certain extent at least the applicant was in sympathy with the Socialist theory of government. [DELETED] as a sociologist the applicant undoubtedly studied the writings of KARL MARX as well as other social philosophers but [DELETED] had never expressed any sympathy for this theory."[18] Finally, another informant stated that while he rated Blumer's integrity and character highly, "he apparently overrated his own importance," and believed this trait, "was actually an inverted inferiority complex resulting from an unhappy childhood due to overbearing parents."[19] Two of the things that Blumer was reported to have exaggerated in an effort to build up his own ego were that he was an All American in football and that he could have been a Rhodes scholar.[20] It was also reported that Blumer had undergone psychoanalysis for about one year (1939 to 1940) in an "attempt to understand himself better and perhaps overcome his inferiority complexes."[21] The informant could not provide the identity of Blumer's therapist.

In fulfilling its charge, San Francisco obtained much of the personal history data on Blumer from the biographic files of the President's Office at the University of California, Berkeley, where he had been employed as a professor of sociology and social institutions, beginning July 1, 1952.[22] Agents visited the president's and the comptroller's office, where unidentifiable sources made available Blumer's personnel and employment records. Nothing of an "unfavorable nature" was revealed and both offices recommended him as a man of "excellent character, loyalty, reputation and ability." Blumer's neighbors in Orinda, California, were also interviewed. One indicated that the Blumers were "good parents who are interested in their own family but who participate in activities which benefit both themselves and their neighbors." Another stated what had impressed her most during the short time she had known Blumer was the fact "he apparently is absolutely free of any prejudice whatsoever concerning the race, color or religion of any individual." Credit and criminal records were also reviewed at Walnut Creek, the Contra Costa County Sheriff's office at Martinez, the police station at Berkeley, and the Credit Bureau of the Greater East Bay in Oakland, where Blumer was reported as one who "makes payments as agreed."[23]

In compiling its personal history, San Francisco had also identified several past positions and visiting appointments Blumer had held and field offices in each of these locations were instructed to carry out investigations.[24] Kansas City, assigned to investigate Blumer's time at the University of Missouri, ascertained from the admissions office that he had enrolled in the College of Arts and Sciences from January 1918 to June 1922.[25] Additional investigation indicated he was granted a scholarship in January 1922, appointed assistant in sociology on June 26, 1922, and instructor the following May. No derogatory information was uncovered and faculty and staff interviewed at the university attested to his character and loyalty and remarked that he was mainly remembered for his athletic prowess and skill as a football player. One person did recall that Blumer had "circulated a questionnaire in regard to sex habits of students that was quite controversial at the time."

In 1936, during the fall semester, Blumer was a visiting associate professor of sociology at the University of Michigan in Ann Arbor. Detroit was assigned the investigation and agents contacted the alumni office and the department of sociology.[26] He was said to be "above reproach" and inquires at the Ann Arbor credit bureau, police department, and traffic bureau failed to turn up any records.

Blumer had also held visiting positions at the University of Hawaii from February to August 1939 and again in 1950–1951, and the University of Iowa from January to March 1943. Honolulu carried out the Hawaii investigation and discovered that a confidential informant from another government agency reported on June 24, 1939, Blumer had delivered a lecture at the Honolulu Y.M.C.A., entitled "Race Prejudice," to the Inter-Professional Association.[27] In interviews with colleagues and associates, Blumer was once again characterized as "brilliant," a "top man," and "a learned person in his field of sociology and [who] has also done extremely well in the field of arbitration, having worked with a couple of large strikes on the U.S. Mainland as an arbitrator." The Omaha office, assigned to carry out the Iowa investigation determined that Blumer had been employed as a guest lecturer and no unfavorable or disloyal information was uncovered at the university, credit bureau or police station, though one interviewee stated that he was, "cynical and outspoken in all matters of discussion."[28]

Additional investigations were carried out by St. Louis, Pittsburgh, Birmingham, Memphis, Mobile, Miami and Los Angeles. St. Louis was brought into the investigation because that was where Blumer had been born on March 7, 1900.[29] An examination of consolidated high school records on microfilm indicated he had attended McKinley High School from September 2, 1913 to January 1915. The files of the St. Louis police department and the local credit bureau contained no information on his parents Richard George and Margaret Marshall Blumer. St. Louis did note that there was a discrepancy between Blumer's actual birth date and that listed in his military records, March 7, 1899. Blumer was inducted into the U.S. Army on October 1, 1918, and immediately transferred to the Student Army Training Corp. He had no active duty while with the army and was honorably discharged three months later, as a private.

Pittsburgh and Birmingham were asked to investigate Blumer's employment as Chairman of the Board of Arbitration for the United States Steel Corporation and the United Steel Workers of America from 1945 to 1947.[30] At both locations he was reported to be highly intelligent, thoroughly loyal, and generally well regarded. Mobile, Memphis, and Miami were brought into the investigation to inquire into Blumer's service as Administrative Head of the Joint Electrical Arbitration Board from 1948 to 1952.[31] Several persons were interviewed by the three offices, including his former professor and longtime friend Ernest Burgess, who was then residing in Palm Beach, Florida. All reported Blumer to be honorable and respectable with no sympathy for communism and of considerable administrative ability.

On March 2, 1956, the field office in Baltimore sent an airtel to the Washington D.C. office indicating that the search it had requested of G-2 military intelligence records at Fort Holabird in Maryland had turned up a reference to Blumer in the files of Saul Padover.[32] Since the file was charged out to San Francisco, an agent there was sent to review it and determined that it contained no information Blumer was acquainted with Padover.[33] However, Leo Calvin Rosten (also known as Leonard Q. Ross and L. Rosenberg) was reported as being well acquainted with Padover and that "members of ROSTEN's advisory Board for the Motion Pictures Research Project were: ROBERT S. LYND, a members [*sic*] of numerous Communist front organizations; HERBERT BLUMER and LOUIS WIRTH, both of whom endorsed a letter from the American League Against War and Fascism in 1937 urging members of the University of Chicago faculty to attend and support financially a People's congress [sic] for Democracy and Peace."[34] In the preface to his book, Rosten acknowledged Blumer, who he probably first met while a student at Chicago, Wirth, and Lasswell. At the invitation of the Motion Picture Research Council, Blumer had earlier carried out his own study, *Movies and Conduct*, of the influence of motion pictures on the lives of youth.[35]

On March 23, ten days after the Bureau deadline, Hoover transmitted three copies of the reports covering the investigation on Blumer to Kimbell Johnson, to be disseminated to the appropriate offices in accordance with the established United Nations Loyalty Program procedures established under Executive Order 10422.[36] He also indicated that "this Bureau is conducting a small amount of additional investigation which will be made available upon receipt." Not all of the leads had been adequately investigated and the results of the overseas investigations were yet to be received.

On May 22, Dennis Flinn sent Hoover the final results of the overseas investigation. Inquiries had been conducted in Jamaica, Germany, and France.[37] Blumer had traveled to St. Andrews in January 1954 to deliver some lectures at the University College of the British West Indies. Hugh W. Springer, the registrar, reported that Blumer's stay was "singularly uneventful, there was no gossip of any sort, and Mr. BLUMER was impressive to the students who attended the lectures." Blumer's closest associate during the visit was D. J. Matthews, a former pupil from the University of Chicago. The records of the Consulate General, the local police, and a controlled local source were also checked, with negative results.

The Security Office in Bonn carried out the German investigation and determined that Blumer had visited Germany in 1934, as a representative of the University of Chicago on a special tour arranged by the Amerika Institut.[38] Though not mentioned in the German report, Blumer had also visited in 1932, during a year spent traveling and studying in France, England, Austria, Switzerland, Germany, Spain, and Morocco on a Social Science Council Fellowship. He spent at least one month in Paris, but the investigation, including inquiries with the Paris Legal Police and the Political Division of the U.S. Embassy, failed to turn up any information except that he had lived on the Avenue de La Bourdonnais and the rue Hsyumans.[39]

On June 1, with the results of the foreign investigation in all other leads followed up, and all remaining reports forwarded to the Civil Service Commission, Hoover sent notice to Kimbell Johnson that the FBI's additional investigation was complete and requested notification of the final determination made on the case.[40] On June 14, the Executive Secretary of the International Organizations Employees Loyalty Board of the Civil Service Commission informed the FBI that a favorable loyalty determination had been made and forwarded to UNESCO.[41]

Two years later, on February 4, 1958, Hoover sent Johnson another memo with an additional piece of information to be placed in Blumer's loyalty file.[42] He indicated that in an Identification Data Form that had been recently submitted under Executive Order 10459, Blumer had listed his membership in the Consumers Research Union. While it was not known whether the Consumers Research Union was identical to the Consumers' Union of the United States, Inc., it was noted that the latter had been cited as a Communist front by the California Committee on Un-American Activities. It was also noted in Blumer's file that he belonged to the American Association of University Professors and the American Civil Liberties Union.[43]

Unlike Parsons, Blumer never made any published attempt to explain McCarthyism, nor is there any record that he ever commented on his own loyalty investigation. However, it is likely that he would have critiqued Parsons's explanation of structural strain and proposed his own based on his symbolic interactionism. From a symbolic interactionist perspective, McCarthyism would have to be approached as a social situation consisting of the joint action emerging from the various intersecting lines of action of the individuals and collectivities involved; that is, the President of the United States and the Executive Orders issued from his office, the House Un-American Activities Committee and its legislative activities, the FBI including Hoover and his Special Agents as the main investigative body, as well as those individuals acting as informants or subject to investigation. Such an explanation would have required examination of the concrete definitions of the situations and responses of these individuals and collectivities. Blumer might also have tested the federal government's concept of loyalty and critiqued the FBI's methodology for investigating it. What exactly was loyalty, and were the indicators employed by the FBI, such as the appearance of one's name in the *Daily Worker*, membership in organizations listed in the HUAC Report on Subversive Organizations, association with suspected Communist sympathizers, or signing public petitions, reliable measures of it?

Blumer did write on morale and its relation to loyalty.[44] He was philosophically opposed to the restriction of discourse that loyalty investigations and the FBI's activities represented. Not only was his sympathetic recognition of the importance of the actor's viewpoint, imbedded within the symbolic interactionist perspective, profoundly democratic, he also believed that the quality of public discourse and opinion rested on the openness of such debate and the availabilities of the means by which it might transpire.[45] He was opposed to censorship and held, "If certain of the contending views are barred from gaining presentation to the disinterested public or suffer some discrimination as to the possibility of being argued before them, then, correspondingly, there is interference with effective public discussion."[46]

NOTES

1. Herbert Blumer, *Symbolic Interactionism: Perspective and Method* (Engelwood Cliffs, N.J.: Prentice-Hall, 1969).
2. Gary Allan Fine, "Editor's Introduction," *Symbolic Interaction* 11 (1988), i–ii. See also Tamotsu Shibutani, "Herbert Blumer's Contribution to Twentieth Century Sociology," *Symbolic Interaction* 11 (1988): 25. The Spring 1988 issue of *Symbolic Interaction* is devoted to Blumer's legacy and offers a broad range of biographical, evaluative, and critical materials.
3. Herbert Blumer, "Sociological Analysis and the Variable," *American Sociological Review* 21 (1956): 685–691.
4. David Wellman, "The Politics of Herbert Blumer's Sociological Method," *Symbolic Interaction* 11 (1988): 60.
5. Howard Becker, "Herbert Blumer's Conceptual Impact," *Symbolic Interaction* 11 (1988): 15; Shibutani, "Herbert Blumer's Contribution," 27.
6. See David R. Maines, "Myth, Text, and Interactionist Complicity in the Neglect of Blumer's Macrosociology," *Symbolic Interaction* 11 (1988): 43–57; Thomas J. Morrione, "Herbert G. Blumer (1900–1987): A Legacy of Concepts, Criticisms and Contributions," *Symbolic Interaction* 11 (1988): 1–12; Sheldon Stryker, "Substance and Style: An Appraisal of the Sociological Legacy of Herbert Blumer," *Symbolic Interaction* 11 (1988): 33–42; and Charles W. Tucker, "Herbert Blumer: A Pilgrimage with Pragmatism," *Symbolic Interaction* 11 (1988): 99–124.
7. Jacqueline P. Wiseman, "In Memoriam: Herbert Blumer (1900–1987)," *Journal of Contemporary Ethnography* 16 (1987): 243.
8. Martyn Hammersley, *The Dilemma of Qualitative Method: Herbert Blumer and the Chicago Tradition* (London: Routledge, 1989), 86.
9. For an extensive bibliography of Blumer's work see Stanford M. Lyman and Arthur J. Vidich, *Social Order and the Public Philosophy: An Analysis and Interpretation of the Work of Herbert Blumer* (Fayetteville: University of Arkansas Press, 1988).
10. Federal Bureau of Investigation, *Herbert Blumer*, Bureau File 138-3450-1 (Washington, D.C.: FBI Freedom of Information–Privacy Acts Section).
11. FBI, *Blumer*, Bufile 138-3450-3.
12. FBI, *Blumer*, Bufile 138-3450-18.
13. Ibid.
14. Ibid.
15. FBI, *Blumer*, Bufile 138-3450-1. For the New York report see Bufile 138-3450-20.
16. Ibid.

17. FBI, *Blumer*, Bufile 138-3450-43.
18. Ibid.
19. Ibid.
20. Blumer played professional football for the Chicago Cardinals from 1925 to 1930, and again in 1933. At the time players played both offense and defense and Blumer's positions included offensive and defensive end, offensive and defensive guard, offensive and defensive tackle, and center. He scored two touchdowns during his career, both in 1925. Wiseman, "In Memoriam," 284, makes reference to his selection as All American guard in 1928. However, "All American" is a college designation, the pros used "All Pro" or "All League." There is no listing of Blumer under either of these designations for the year 1928 or the other years he played professional football. He was captain of his collegiate team at the University of Missouri in 1922, and noted to be one of the two best players on the team that year. See Walter Camp, ed. *Official Intercollegiate Football Guide* (New York: American Sports Publishing, 1922), 185.
21. FBI, *Blumer*, Bufile 138-3450-43.
22. FBI, *Blumer*, Bufile 138-3450-28.
23. Ibid.
24. FBI, *Blumer*, Bufile 138-3450-15.
25. FBI, *Blumer*, Bufile 138-3450-34.
26. FBI, *Blumer*, Bufile 138-3450-30.
27. FBI, *Blumer*, Bufile 138-3450-14.
28. FBI, *Blumer*, Bufile 138-3450-15.
29. FBI, *Blumer*, Bufile 138-3450-26.
30. FBI, *Blumer*, Bufile 138-3450-23, 24.
31. FBI, *Blumer*, Bufile 138-3450-17, 21, 25.
32. FBI, *Blumer*, Bufile 138-3450-15.
33. FBI, *Blumer*, Bufile 138-3450-36.
34. Ibid.
35. Leo C. Rosten, *Hollywood: The Movie Colony, the Movie Makers* (New York: Harcourt Brace, 1941); Herbert Blumer, *Movies and Conduct* (New York: Macmillan, 1933).
36. FBI, *Blumer*, Bufile 138-3450-18.
37. FBI, *Blumer*, Bufile 138-3450-56.
38. FBI, *Blumer*, Bufile 138-3450-55.
39. FBI, *Blumer*, Bufile 138-3450-58.
40. Ibid.
41. FBI, *Blumer*, Bufile 138-3450-54.
42. FBI, *Blumer*, Bufile 138-3450-59.
43. FBI, *Blumer*, Bufile 138-3450-1.
44. Herbert Blumer, "On Morale," in *American Society in Wartime*, ed. William F. Ogburn (Chicago: University of Chicago Press, 1943).
45. Wellman, "Blumer's Sociological Method," 62; Lyman and Vidich, *Social Order*, 44–52.
46. Herbert Blumer, "Collective Behavior," in *Principles of Sociology*, 3d ed., ed. Alfred McClung Lee (New York: Barnes and Noble): 93.

— 10 —

Samuel Stouffer: Patriot and Practitioner

Samuel Stouffer was a sociological practitioner engrossed in the mission of making sociology a science, and a patriot with an unabashed love for his country.[1] In his enthusiasm for social research he would often become so caught up hovering over the "machine" in anticipation of the results of yet another run that he would miss appointments, forget dinner with his wife, and neglect the subtleties of personal appearance. A chain-smoker, students would watch in class hypnotized as the ash hanging precariously from the end of his cigarette would slowly grow and grow until a sudden gesture would cause it to drop onto his already well-dusted jacket.[2] He was an interesting and exciting teacher, always deeply concerned about the quality of his lectures and frequently worried lest he waste some "200 hours of people time" in a single lecture. Remarked one student, "Sam was one of the most stimulating and disheveled professors that ever existed."[3] Through his enthusiasms, he was, with Paul Lazarsfeld, at the forefront of the introduction of statistical analysis and survey research methods in the discipline and pioneered the pursuit of an entrepreneurial applied research which was regarded by many as the future salvation of sociology, although others saw it as the selling out of its soul.[4]

Throughout his career Stouffer regularly put his patriotism into practice by offering his sociological services to the military and working with the government. A virtual incarnation of the quantitative and scientistic mainstream that was increasingly coming to dominate the field, he was uncomfortable with the critical vision of sociology championed by the likes of Robert Lynd and C. Wright Mills. As a consulting editor to John Wiley and Sons, he included comments in his preface to a text on social problems which seem to serve as an apology not only for the critical perspective of its authors, but also for that of the discipline as a whole: "The authors love America and American institutions. But as social scientists they know that in any society there are tensions, generated often by the very ideals which are most basic and most honored in that society. America is, of course, not an exception. And the authors pull no punches in showing in detail wherein it is so."[5] There is therefore a certain irony in the fact that as Stouffer began supervision of a national survey which would include investigation of public opinion on public attitudes concerning J. Edgar Hoover and the activities of the FBI, the FBI in turn was conducting its own investigation of his loyalty and alleged associations with Communists and Communist front organizations.

Stouffer was born at the turn of the century in the American heartland, in Sac City, a small town in Iowa. He grew up there, received his bachelor's from Morningside College in Sioux City, Iowa, and then went on to Harvard where he earned a masters degree in English. He returned to work as an editor for his father's newspaper, the Sac City *Sun*, from 1923 to 1926, and then left to attend the University of Chicago where he received his Ph.D. in Sociology in 1930.[6]

Stouffer arrived at Chicago at about the same time Ogburn, a "vehemently scientistic sociologist," became chairperson.[7] Stouffer was Ogburn's best student, and the most distinguished representative of the often neglected quantitative tradition in Chicago. Not surprisingly, through his dissertation he joined the department's ongoing debate over the use and value of quantitative versus qualitative methods, weighing in on the side of Ogburn in championing the survey versus the case study against Wirth, Hughes, and Blumer.[8] After serving as an instructor at Chicago for one year following his Ph.D., he obtained a position as an assistant professor at Wisconsin. Prior to going to Wisconsin, he received one of the first social science research fellowships to study abroad and acquired additional quantitative training and was exposed to the English intellectual tradition of statistics while working for a year at the University of London.[9] In 1934, he took a leave of absence from Wisconsin to serve as a staff member on the Central Statistical Board in Washington, D.C.

Stouffer returned to Chicago, as a full professor, in 1935, and later played a significant role in Gunnar Myrdal's study of race relations, *An American Dilemma*, overseeing its completion when Myrdal was detained in Europe by the war.[10] In 1941, Stouffer took leave from

Chicago to join the war effort as Director of Professorial Staff for the Research Branch of the War Department's Information and Education Division. In August 1942, he was appointed Chief Social Science Analyst of the Morale Division and charged with providing the military command staff with social scientific information which would help maintain morale and increase fighting efficiency.

Stouffer was an ardent champion of applied research, not only on practical grounds for the developments in technique and theory that it might facilitate, but for pecuniary reasons as well, arguing, "If social science is to be taken seriously and receive large financial support its 'engineering' applications must visibly pay off."[11] During the next five years he was able to combine his interests as sociological practitioner and patriot, directing the military's social scientific equivalent of the Manhattan Project and organizing several hundred attitude surveys of more than half a million American soldiers. Though many of the surveys requested by the command staff were as trivial as asking whether soldiers preferred Pepsi or Coke, research findings also led to the creation of a point system for repatriating soldiers from Europe and recommendations for the establishment of the G.I. Bill.[12]

Following the end of the war, the Carnegie Corporation gave Stouffer a grant to publish a summary of the Research Branch's findings under the title of his now classic study, *The American Soldier*. The book was introduced to the public through a massive publicity campaign, unprecedented in sociology, as reflecting the core paradigm of the modern social scientific method and certifying the birth of a new social science: "These volumes . . . represent one of the most elaborate applications ever made of the new methods of objective study which are revolutionizing social science research and taking the study of man out of the realm of guesswork and conjecture. . . . For the first time on such a scale an attempt was made to direct human behavior on a basis of scientific evidence, and the results suggest the opening of a new epoch in social studies and in social management."[13]

The study was similarly heralded by the discipline, especially in its major professional journals, though there were some voices of dissent.[14] Nathan Glazer criticized it for its misplaced scientistic pretensions and "overpowering obsession with the physical sciences and their great achievement."[15] Robert Lynd and Alfred McClung Lee raised more fundamental questions concerning the dangers of applied sociology, its social engineering implications, and who it would serve, questions which have continued to challenge the discipline ever since: "If managerial problems for industry and the military are to continue to dominate the research of leading social psychologists and sociologists, the value orientation of the managerial technician rather than the value orientation of the social science educator will dominate what evolves and is called social science. The emphasis can thus shift from service to citizens in a democracy to service for those who temporarily control and who wish to continue to control segments of our society."[16] While Stouffer was not unaware of the potential pitfalls of applied research, he clearly felt the benefits were much more significant than the risks.

Following the war, Parsons offered Stouffer an appointment at Harvard. Having reorganized the department a few years earlier, Parsons was looking for someone to direct the new Social Relations Laboratory, and who better than the man who had just finished directing arguably the largest social scientific project ever undertaken. Stouffer became a major partner with Parsons in a joint stewardship of the department based on a common faith that both theory and empirical investigation were necessary for scientific progress.[17] The two became deep and loyal friends, as evidenced by Parsons's unqualified support when Stouffer's national loyalty was being questioned by the FBI.[18]

Stouffer was first investigated by the FBI in September 1936, when the attorney general sent a memo to Hoover requesting a confidential check-up on several individuals in order to obtain "a general impression as to their standing, stability, and aptitude for cooperation."[19] A "brief and very discreet investigation" carried out at the University of Chicago indicated that Stouffer had returned to the university after only four years, as an unusually young full professor, jumping the ranks of assistant and associate professor, and at a much higher salary than ordinarily paid in that position. In the investigative report Stouffer was characterized as "very brilliant, dependable, possesses complete integrity, is an individual of highest character. . . . Is considered very cooperative on anything for which he is equipped."[20] There is no indication for what Stouffer was being considered.

There is no record of any kind of FBI investigation of Stouffer at the time he was appointed Director of Professional Staff for the Army research. Executive Order 9835 had not yet been signed by Truman, and Stouffer had already been vetted. However, in April 1952, when being considered for a position as a consultant with the Air Force's Civilian Personnel Branch, it was noted that, in accordance with requirements of 9835, Stouffer was not to be appointed until a preliminary inquiry "sufficiently complete to resolve the question of loyalty" was undertaken. A month later, in the memo charging Boston with the investigation, Director, FBI cautioned, "Inasmuch as this is a 'sensitive' loyalty form it is imperative that the Bureau deadline be met. This investigation should be assigned to a mature experienced agent and should be conducted in a discreet circumspect manner."[21]

A check of Bureau files turned up three leads, one of which is completely blacked out. A report which had been sent in by Boston several years earlier, in 1947, indicated that during his second year at Harvard Stouffer had been one of the faculty sponsors of the Students Association for Natural and Social Sciences (SANSS). An informant had advised that SANSS was actually under the umbrella of, and served as a recruiting ground for, the American Association of Scientific Workers. The AASW had been cited by the California Committee on Un-American Activities as included among Communist fronts reported at the Win the Peace Conference held in Washington, D.C., April 5 through 7, 1946.[22] Prior to that, in 1943, Chicago had sent in a report which reflected that Stouffer had been listed as an acquaintance by Charles Florant, whose name had reportedly appeared among records of the White Collar Branch of the Communist Party of the District of Columbia.

For its part of the preliminary inquiry, in early June 1952, the Chicago office once again made inquiries at the University of Chicago and turned up roughly the same information obtained in 1936. An unidentifiable professor of sociology noted that Stouffer was now considered to be an outstanding sociologist and that his mind "is principally the mind of a scientist who is interested in research and has no interests in any disloyal philosophy such as Communism."[23] Former neighbors confirmed this assessment and a check with the local headquarters of G-2, the Office of Naval Intelligence, and the security unit of the Chicago police department turned up no negative information.[24]

Since Stouffer was at Harvard, Boston provided a more detailed report with some additional disclosures of possible Communist affiliations.[25] A search of its files determined that Stouffer had been listed as a faculty member of a "School of Political Action Techniques" (so was Pete Seeger) sponsored by the Massachusetts Citizens Political Action Committee in September 1946. The purpose of the school was to train citizens for winning the 1946 elections and in successful campaigning year round. Though the committee stated that it was independent and nonpartisan, a confidential informant had reported that the committee was under Communist influence and leadership. In October 1946, informants had also reported that Stouffer had led a panel on public opinion and the political aspects of atomic energy at a conference jointly sponsored by Harvard and MIT and attended by nine Russian scientists.

As part of its preliminary inquiry, Boston obtained Stouffer's academic record from the registrar of the Harvard Graduate School of Arts & Sciences and his employment record from the Office of the President and Fellows. Several members of the department of social relations were interviewed, including one who stated that he regarded Stouffer as having an "enlightened awareness of Communism," and another who indicated Stouffer had worked in several different capacities for the government and had access to top-secret material. However, he considered him to be a "firm believer in the American principles of democracy."[26] Interestingly, two members of the department (unidentifiable because, like the others, their names are blacked out) were not interviewed because they were included on a list of individuals at Harvard not to be interviewed. A check with Stouffer's neighbors turned up nothing negative and his credit record was clean, though like Parsons and Sorokin he did have a minor traffic violation to his name.

The preliminary report from the Washington, D.C. field office was primarily concerned with providing additional information on Charles Florant and his relationship with Stouffer.[27] Florant had worked on the Myrdal study beginning in 1939, and continued to do so during the period in which Stouffer had supervised its completion. He had been a graduate student under Stouffer at Chicago from 1940 to 1941. Florant had also worked with Stouffer on the American soldier study. However, according to several former coworkers and colleagues who knew both, their relationship had never been anything but professional and there was no suggestion that Stouffer was anything but completely loyal. After Florant died, one informant suggested Stouffer had made statements giving the impression that looking back on the course of events he believed that Florant had indeed been a fellow traveler or Communist.

Based on the preliminary inquiry, in late June the Director issued a memo that the case should be immediately converted to a Full-Field Investigation, "in view of the applicant's association with alleged Communists or pro-Communists, and Communist front organizations."[28] The Atlanta, Baltimore, Boston, Chicago, Milwaukee, Mobile, New York City, Omaha, St. Louis, and Washington field offices were all mobilized. Mobile obtained Stouffer's application file from an unidentifiable official of the Civilian Personnel Branch at Maxwell Air Force Base.[29] It indicated that the base's Human Resources Research Institute had requested his appointment as a consultant for up to ninety days at $50 a day. He would be handling classified material up to and including "Secret," but would not be appointed until loyalty clearance was received from the Civil Service Commission. Stouffer listed Donald R. Young, President of the Russel Sage Foundation, Leland D. DeVinney, Assistant Director of the Rockefeller Foundation, and Parsons as his references.

Beyond a more detailed background check, Washington's report provided little additional information from its preliminary inquiry.

Milwaukee reported on Stouffer's activities during his appointment at the University of Wisconsin. Several faculty, including members of the department of sociology, were interviewed and all attested to his loyalty. St. Louis reviewed Stouffer's records with the Federal Records Center of the General Services Administration and determined that he had been intermittently employed by the military. Omaha reported on his early youth and college days.[30] He was characterized as a brilliant student who had completed his work at Morningside College, in just three years, reportedly with a B average.

Like Washington, Chicago provided little more than in its preliminary inquiry.[31] A few more colleagues were interviewed, all attesting to Stouffer's loyalty and the reputation and recognition he had earned as a major sociologist since leaving Chicago. Confidential informants in the area had no information on him. Boston's report lists several previously unmentioned organizations with Communist affiliation or influence, but since all surrounding information is blacked out it is impossible to determine what, if any, relation Stouffer had with any of them. An associate professor in the department of social relations who reported he had been acquainted with Stouffer since 1934 stated that Stouffer was "the type of individual who would associate with people of doubtful loyalty from the standpoint of expediency and that he would use any means to gain an end."[32]

New York checked out Stouffer's references, Young and DeVinney.[33] Both had worked with Stouffer in the Research Branch which he directed during the war and maintained close personal and professional relationships since then. Young considered him to be above reproach and an "extremely loyal and discreet person," while DeVinney stated Stouffer "did not have a continual reading or research interest in 'left wing' publication as did some social scientists."[34]

The Full-Field Investigation finished, Hoover sent a copy of the reports (thirty-two enclosures) to the Investigations Division of the Civil Service Commission on September 3, 1952, requesting that they advise the Bureau of the ultimate disposition made of the case.[35] Copies were also forwarded to the Records Administration Branch of the attorney general's office.

Approximately two months later, in a memo to Boston authorizing the initiation of a security-type investigation of Parsons, even though Stouffer had been alleged to be a part of Parsons's cell of Harvard professors furthering Communist Party projects and espousing its propaganda line, Director, FBI denied permission to begin a similar investigation of Stouffer.[36] "For your information the results of the loyalty investigation of Stouffer do not appear to justify the preparation of a Security Index card under current Bureau standards. . . .

However, you should be alert to submit in report form any information of a subversive derogatory nature concerning Stouffer which may be developed incidental to your investigation of [DELETED] and Parsons so that proper dissemination may be made to the Civil Service Commission."[37] The memo, however, did leave Stouffer's case open for further information pending a final decision by the Civil Service Commission.

In mid-September of the following year, Hoover requested a summary on Stouffer following a conversation in which Clifford Case, a former Congressman and new president of the Ford Foundation's Fund for the Republic had indicated that Stouffer was doing research on the Communist Party and public opinion reaction to security measures taken by the government.[38] Since neither Bureau files nor the current volume of *Who's Who in America* showed any connection between Stouffer and the Ford Foundation, no further action was taken. In fact, he was being considered by the Fund to carry out just such a study, including investigation of public perception of the activities of the FBI and J. Edgar Hoover himself, eventually to be published in his book *Communism, Conformity, and Civil Liberties.*

Bureau interest was rekindled in late October 1953, when G-2 furnished a memorandum which stated that Stouffer had been employed as a consultant by the Human Resources Research Office (HUMRRO) with security clearance up to and including "Confidential."[39] HUMRRO was located at George Washington University and under contract with the Army to do psychological studies on troop morale. According to G-2, some sixteen employees of HUMRRO, including Stouffer, had overlapping subversive connections or associates and it believed the office may have been Communist infiltrated.[40] It noted that on March 13, 1953, Stouffer's security clearance had been submitted for adjudication to the Army–Navy–Air Force Personnel Security Board with a recommendation that he be denied access to classified information.

At the request of G-2, on November 25, 1953, Director, FBI ordered a full Security Investigation on Stouffer, to include all pertinent information regarding his background and subversive activities irrespective of whether information had been included in previous reports.[41] The basis for the investigation was formally stated as "allegations that SAMUEL ANDREW STOUFFER has employed a self-admitted Communist Party member and allegedly has associated with pro-Communist individuals and been affiliated with Communist front organizations."[42]

For the most part, the reports largely rehashed already well traveled ground, with the addition of a few more pieces of background information (i.e., family, organizational affiliations, an update from the most recent *Who's Who*). However, in early January 1954, Washington office learned that Stouffer had been employed by HUMRRO only for one day, in October 1952, as a consultant to a project named "DESERT ROCK IV" and been paid $50.[43] Washington was also informed that Stouffer had later been denied access to classified information by the Eastern Industrial Personnel Security Board.

A few months later, Boston learned that the Appeal Division of the Eastern Industrial Personnel Security Board had held a hearing on March 1, 1954, in New York City, on Stouffer's appeal to its denial of his security clearance.[44] New York was instructed to consult the files of the Security Board to determine the results of the appeal. On May 13, 1954, New York sent Director, FBI a summary of the transcript from the hearing.[45] Stouffer was present at the hearing with his counsel, Arthur Sutherland. Four of the six reasons which had been given for denial of the clearance are blacked out. The two that remain make reference to his sponsorship of the Students Association for Natural and Social Sciences and his participation in the panel on atomic energy. In his testimony, Stouffer denied being a member of the Communist Party or any other suspect organization on the attorney general's list, and said that he knew of no one at Harvard who was a member of the Communist Party. Several witnesses appeared on Stouffer's behalf, including one who stated that SANSS was "an innocuous and not very effective organization to promote trust of the interrelation of natural and social sciences and the position of the scientist in society," and who denied there was anything secret or subversive about the forum on atomic energy.[46]

At the conclusion of the hearing, the Appeal Board reversed the denial of Stouffer's clearance, stating that "the granting of clearance of STOUFFER for access to classified information would be consistent with the interest of national security on the basis of all information that was available."[47] The decision was based on the excellent references of Stouffer's impressive array of witnesses as well as his own cooperative attitude. However, G-2 was not satisfied and informed the FBI that it was going to resubmit the case recommending clearance be denied. No further record of any security proceedings appears in Stouffer's file.

At the end of the year, on December 30, 1954, the FBI once again got wind of Stouffer's study on communism and civil liberties, now soon to be released.[48] L. B. Nichols reported to Clyde Tolson that George Sokolsky had advised him that on January 4 of the new year the Ford Foundation would release an announcement concerning the study for which it had granted $175 thousand, and which would be published in April by Doubleday. Sokolsky told Nichols that "it is quite obvious that these findings are designed to contradict the popular concept of public opinion."[49] Upon learning of the study, A. H. Belmont recommended that the attorney general and deputy attorney general be informed. Hoover agreed and in a handwritten addendum asked, "What do we know of him?" (see Figure 10.1).[50] A synopsis of all FBI investigations and findings on Stouffer was prepared and forwarded to the attorney general and his deputy.

Stouffer's study was commissioned by the Fund for the Republic, which received the grant from the Ford Foundation. Begun in the summer of 1954, when the McCarthy hearings were in full swing, it was not a risk-free undertaking, as Stouffer must have been well aware, and to which the FBI attention to it attests. The data were collected by the two leading American attitude survey organizations, the American Institute of Public Opinion (AIPO), better known today as Gallup, and the National Opinion Research Center (NORC), but Stouffer did all of the analysis and writing. Approximately 6 thousand people were interviewed face to face, including a randomly selected national cross section of 4,933 persons and a separate selected group of 1,500 community leaders. Stouffer split the pool between AIPO and NORC in order to test the results against each other for their internal validity. It was an unconventional survey for its time, as Stouffer employed more open-ended questions than was typical and also used scales to survey a given attitude rather than rely only on a single question.[51]

In March 1955, the FBI obtained a circular indicating that on April 5, Stouffer would be the guest speaker at a meeting to be held by the Cooperative Forum in Washington, D.C. According to the brochure he would be discussing his new book, to be released April 21, based on the "findings of the most comprehensive attitude survey of Americans ever taken on the vital subjects of Communism and civil liberties."[52] Some of the findings were said to be "startling" and others dramatically to contradict popular conceptions. According to Bureau files, the Cooperative Forum was convened once every two weeks for the purpose of "off the record" talks by governmental leaders on current public events and problems. Consisting primarily of members of the House of Representatives and Senate, other governmental officials, and leaders of private industry, attendance was by invitation only and all attendees were requested to pledge that they would not make public any information discussed at the meeting. FBI officials decided not to send an agent to infiltrate the meeting and obtain an advanced look at the book because they were afraid if uncovered that it would lead to considerable Bureau embarrassment.

Two days after the meeting, Doubleday sent Hoover an advance copy asking if he cared to be quoted on his reaction to the book.[53] As was his policy, Hoover expressed appreciation for the book, but de-

Figure 10.1

Memo to Mr. Boardman RE: SAMUEL ANDREW STOUFFER
from Mr. Belmont

<u>Communist.</u> [redacted] self-admitted former Communist Party member at Harvard University, 1947-1950, stated Stouffer not member of Communist Party to his knowledge and that Stouffer was loyal citizen.

<u>ACTION:</u>

None. For your information.

I recommend memo to AG & Rogers

yes

Yes.

Memo to AG & Deputy AG Rogers 1/7/55 b7c

<u>DETAILS:</u>

The Washington City News Service release, January 4, 1955, announced that the Fund for the Republic had announced that the Fund was publishing "the most comprehensive attitude survey of Americans ever undertaken on the subject of Communism and civil liberties." According to the release, a $125,000 nationwide poll was taken by the American Institute of Public Opinion (Gallup Poll) and the National Opinion Research Center, University of Chicago. More than 6,400 persons, 1,200 of them community leaders, answered a twelve-page questionnaire. A book reflecting the results of the survey, written by Dr. Samual A. Stouffer, Harvard University professor, is to be published in April, 1955, by Doubleday and Company, Inc. Concerning Stouffer, the Director asked "What do we know of him? H."

- 2 -

clined any comment. However, he did request a summary on Stouffer and the book was sent to the FBI's Central Research Section for review. The Central Research Section prepared a detailed review of the book, beginning with an introductory synopsis stating

Author's findings show no evidence that country is concerned either with threat of Communism or dangers to civil liberties. Average citizen's information on Communism is vague and distorted and current social, economic and technological forces are working to increase tolerance of nonconformist views. . . . Survey disclosed American public would "especially respect" opinion of Director on how to handle Communists in United States over any other public figure. Also indicated "public confidence in the F.B.I. is quite high" but author suggests that there is room for improvement.[54]

In fact, Stouffer concluded, contrary to the impression that might have been garnered from Hoover and the McCarthy hearings, "The number of people who said that they were worried either about the threat of Communism or about civil liberties was, by even the most generous interpretation of occasionally ambiguous responses, *less than 1%*."[55]

The Central Research Section paid particular attention to items about the FBI, noting, for example, that only 33 to 38 percent of the respondents were aware of the Director's opinion on the threat of communism and the danger to civil liberties and only 56 percent of the community leaders and 32 percent of the national cross section believed that the Bureau knew of most of the Communists in the United States.[56] The Research Section also reported the results of several questions of particular interest to the Bureau that Stouffer had not put forth in the summary of his interpretations and conclusions. These included that, when asked, 66 percent of the community leaders and 77 percent of the national cross section felt that admitted Communists should have their citizenship taken away; 27 percent and 51 percent, respectively, felt that they should be put in jail; 62 percent and 64 percent were in favor of using wiretapping to get evidence against Communists; 65 percent and 73 percent felt that one should report neighbors or friends suspected of being Communists; and 42 percent of community leaders and 58 percent of the national cross section felt it was more important to find out all the Communists even if some innocent people were hurt.[57]

Other than a few newspaper clippings and a photocopy of an excerpt from the book published in *Look* magazine (April 5, 1955), there is no further information in the files released on Stouffer. And finally, on April 15, 1955, the Civil Service Commission informed the FBI that it had made a favorable determination concerning Stouffer's loyalty.[58] Nonetheless, Stouffer was deeply disturbed by the questioning of his loyalty. Writes his daughter, "My father was intensely patriotic and had a great love of the American heritage. . . . It would be impossible to describe the anguish he suffered when under personal attack during the McCarthy era."[59] In the final chapter of *Communism, Conformity, and Civil Liberties*, Stouffer warned against the danger of exploiting the internal Communist threat for partisan political advantage. No doubt thinking of his own case, he noted, "It has been alleged that fear of Congressional criticism has led some agencies dealing with outside contractors, even on completely unclassified work, to apply security tests which carry guilt by association to the point of absurdity and deprive the government of valuable services. Curbing excesses in the administration of security regulations, if such excesses actually occur, is just as much a duty of responsible officials in government as is the parallel duty of making sure that the security regulations are as tight as they should be."[60]

NOTES

1. Jackson Toby, "Samuel Stouffer: Social Research as a Calling," in *Sociological Traditions from Generation to Generation*, ed. Robert Merton and Matilda White Riley (Norwood, N.J.: Ablex, 1980), 145–146.
2. James A. Davis, introduction to *Communism, Conformity and Civil Liberties*, by Samuel Stouffer (New Brunswick, N.J.: Transaction, 1992), 3.
3. As quoted in Toby, "Social Research as a Calling," 135.
4. For a detailed discussion of the relationship between Stouffer and Lazarsfeld and their respective and relative influences on the emergence of modern survey research, see Jennifer Platt, "Stouffer and Lazarsfeld: Patterns of Influence," in *Knowledge and Society: Studies in the Sociology of Culture Past and Present*, ed. Henrika Kuklik and Elizabeth Long (London: JAI, 1986).
5. Toby, "Social Research as a Calling," 146.
6. There is little information available about Stouffer's early life and what led him to the University of Chicago, and not a whole lot more afterward. With the exception of Jackson Toby's account in Merton and Riley's *Sociological Traditions from Generation to Generation*, most of it is mentioned in passing in articles, or the occasional introduction to a book commenting upon or related to his work. A major biographical treatment of his life and work remains to be done.
7. Henrika Kuklik, "Boundary Maintenance in American Sociology: Limitations to Academic 'Professionalization,'" *Journal of the History of the Behavioral Sciences* 16 (1980): 207.
8. Martin Bulmer, *The Chicago School of Sociology: Institutionalization, Diversity, and the Rise of Sociological Research* (Chicago: University of Chicago Press, 1984), 185–188. Stouffer's dissertation, completed in 1930, was titled *An Experimental Comparison of Statistical and Case History Methods of Attitude Research*.
9. Martin Bulmer, "Quantification and Chicago Social Science in the 1920s: A Neglected Tradition," *Journal of the History of Behavioral Sciences* 17 (1981): 320. See also Fred B. Lindstrom and Ronald A. Hardert, "Kimball Young on the Chicago School: Later Contacts," *Sociological Perspectives* 31 (1988): 312.
10. Toby, "Social Research as a Calling," 140.

11. Samuel Stouffer, "Some Afterthoughts of a Contributor to *The American Soldier*," in *Studies in the Scope and Method of "The American Soldier,"* ed. Robert K. Merton and Paul Lazarsfeld (Glencoe, Ill.: Free Press, 1950), 198.

12. Ibid., 200.

13. As quoted in Daniel Lerner, "*The American Soldier* and the Public," in *Studies in the Scope and Method of "The American Soldier,"* ed. Robert K. Merton and Paul F. Lazarsfeld (Glencoe, Ill.: Free Press, 1950): 217.

14. N. J. Demerath, review of *The American Soldier: Adjustment During Army Life*, by Samuel Stouffer, *Social Forces* 28 (1949): 87–90; George P. Murdoch, review of *The American Soldier: Adjustment During Army Life*, by Samuel Stouffer, *American Sociological Review* 14 (1949): 814–815; John Riley, Jr., review of *The American Soldier: Combat and Its Aftermath*, by Samuel Stouffer, *American Sociological Review* 14 (1949): 557–559.

15. Nathan Glazer, "*The American Soldier* as Science: Can Sociology Fulfill its Ambitions?" *Commentary* 8 (1949): 487–496.

16. Alfred McClung Lee, review of *The American Soldier*, by Samuel Stouffer, *Annals of the American Academy of Political and Social Science* 265 (1949): 174. See also Robert S. Lynd, "The Science of Inhuman Relations," *New Republic*, 29 August 1949, 22–25.

17. Toby, "Social Research as a Calling," 133–134.

18. Lindstrom and Hardert, "Kimball Young on the Chicago School," 313; Jens Kaalhauge Nielsen, "The Political Orientation of Talcott Parsons: The Second World War and Its Aftermath," in *Talcott Parsons: Theorist of Modernity*, ed. R. Robertson and B. Turner (London: Sage, 1991), 228.

19. Federal Bureau of Investigation, *Samuel A. Stouffer*, Bureau File 77-8728-1 (Washington, D.C.: FBI Freedom of Information–Privacy Acts Section).

20. FBI, *Stouffer*, Bufile 77-8728-2.

21. Federal Bureau of Investigation, *Samuel A. Stouffer*, Bureau File 121-38346-1 (Washington, D.C.: FBI Freedom of Information–Privacy Acts Section).

22. FBI, *Stouffer*, Bufile 121-38346-1.

23. FBI, *Stouffer*, Bufile 121-38346-5.

24. Ibid.

25. FBI, *Stouffer*, Bufile 121-38346-8.

26. Ibid.

27. FBI, *Stouffer*, Bufile 121-38346-9.

28. Ibid.

29. FBI, *Stouffer*, Bufile 121-38346-13.

30. FBI, *Stouffer*, Bufile 121-38346-14, 15, 16, 17.

31. FBI, *Stouffer*, Bufile 121-38346-20.

32. FBI, *Stouffer*, Bufile 121-38346-12.

33. FBI, *Stouffer*, Bufile 121-38346-26.

34. Ibid.

35. Ibid.

36. FBI, *Stouffer*, Bufile 121-38346-30.

37. FBI, *Stouffer*, Bufile 121-38346-29. As is common practice, Parsons's name was deleted in the copy of the memo released in Stouffer's file. However, the same memo was released in Parsons's file (Bufile 100-390459-3),

but with Stouffer's name blocked out. While one way of getting around some of the deletions would be to make an exhaustive set of requests for a given department or of friends and colleagues of a person under investigation and then to look for further cross-references, given the current pace that FOIA requests are being fulfilled such a process would take many years.

38. FBI, *Stouffer*, Bufile 121-38346-30.

39. Federal Bureau of Investigation, *Samuel A. Stouffer*, Bureau File 100-407113-1 (Washington, D.C.: FBI Freedom of Information–Privacy Acts Section).

40. FBI, *Stouffer*, Bufile 100-407113-2.

41. FBI, *Stouffer*, Bufile 100-407113-5.

42. Ibid.

43. FBI, *Stouffer*, Bufile 100-407113-7.

44. FBI, *Stouffer*, Bufile 100-407113-9.

45. FBI, *Stouffer*, Bufile 100-404113-11.

46. Ibid. The report actually gives quite a detailed summary of Stouffer's responses to the accusations as well as the testimony or affidavits of several character witnesses. Conspicuously absent from the report is any mention of Parsons, who also sent in, while he was in England, a sworn affidavit vigorously supporting Stouffer.

47. Ibid.

48. FBI, *Stouffer*, Bufile 100-407113-13.

49. Ibid.

50. FBI, *Stouffer*, Bufile 100-407113-14.

51. Samuel Stouffer, *Communism, Conformity, and Civil Liberties: A Cross-Section of the Nation Speaks Its Mind* (New Brunswick, N.J.: Transaction, 1992), 19–21.

52. FBI, *Stouffer*, Bufile 100-407113-15.

53. FBI, *Stouffer*, Bufile 100-407113-16.

54. FBI, *Stouffer*, Bufile 100-407113-18.

55. Stouffer, *Communism, Conformity, and Civil Liberties*, 59.

56. Ibid., 228–231.

57. FBI, *Stouffer*, Bufile 100-407113-18.

58. FBI, *Stouffer*, Bufile 121-38346.

59. As quoted in Toby, "Social Research as a Calling," 150.

60. Stouffer, *Communism, Conformity, and Civil Liberties*, 230.

— 11 —

Our Man in Havana: C. Wright Mills Talks, Yankee Listens

C. Wright Mills is generally recognized as one of America's foremost radical social dissenters and American sociology's most flamboyant renegade.[1] When he died in 1962, he was reported to be the most widely read sociologist in the world.[2] Mills challenged conventional wisdom in both politics and sociology. Like Thorstein Veblen, Mills felt social criticism was a prerequisite to a genuinely democratic society. His contentious intellectual style and failure to "observe the noblesse oblige of sparing his colleagues in print" led to a deep hostility directed toward him and to his marginalization from the mainstream of the discipline.[3] Asked critic Edward Shils, "What does this solitary horseman—who is in part prophet, in part a teacher, in part a rough-tongued brawler—a sort of Joe McCarthy of sociology, full of wild accusations and gross inaccuracies, bullying manners, harsh words, and shifting grounds—want of sociology?"[4] In a passage from his introduction to Veblen's *Theory of the Leisure Class*, which might just as well have been his own epitaph, Mills provides an answer for Shils: "And that is his real lasting value, he opens up our minds, he gets us 'outside the whale,' he makes us see through the official sham. Above all, he teaches us to be aware of the crackpot basis of the realism of those practical Men of Affairs who would lead us to honorific destruction."[5]

A moralist and a moral man at a time when American sociology was celebrating its value-free stance, Mills maintained a capacity for a sustained indignation directed toward the condition of American society and the sociology which examined it.[6] He understood man to be "a creature of value in a world of evaluations."[7] Mills chose sociology because he felt it was a discipline which could offer the concepts and skills to expose and respond to social injustice.[8] He became increasingly disenchanted with the profession which he felt was abdicating its responsibilities and criticized it bitterly for this, most powerfully in his classic *The Sociological Imagination*.

As every student of introductory sociology knows, Mills characterized the sociological imagination as a critical quality of mind that would help men and women "to use information and to develop reason in order to achieve lucid summations of what is going on in the world and of what may be happening within themselves."[9] He felt that the promise of the sociological imagination embodied in the classical tradition of sociology had been betrayed by many contemporary sociologists. He irreverently attacked Talcott Parsons for his "grand theory" and fetishization of the concept. He also criticized the increasingly quantitative and scientistic character of sociology and the tyranny of "the method," championed by the likes of Stouffer and Lazarsfeld, for its abstracted empiricism which resulted in a truncated view of social reality. Mills was suspicious of the aspiring scientific sociology of his day for its pseudo-objectivity, which he felt to be only a disguised legitimation of the status quo, and blasted its adherents as self-interested trivializers in the grip of a sociology of cowardice: "The self-proclaimed detached objectivity of the sociologists is not objectivity at all but a commitment to a *status quo* by people who have internalized a set of values!"[10]

Born in Waco, Texas, in 1916, as a child Mills was noted for his stubbornness and willful tenacity, qualities which would characterize him throughout his life.[11] From 1933 to 1939 Mills attended the University of Texas, where he earned a bachelor's in philosophy and master's in philosophy and sociology. He received his Ph.D. from the University of Wisconsin in 1942. Mills began his academic career at the University of Maryland, but, with the assistance of Daniel Bell, soon obtained an appointment in the Bureau of Applied Research at Columbia, directing the labor division under the supervision of Lazarsfeld. At Columbia, Mills became acquainted with Robert Merton, Robert Lynd, and several members of the emigrated Frankfurt School, including Theodor Adorno, Max Horkheimer and Herbert Marcuse.

While Mills developed an early interest in the sociology of knowledge and the role of the intellectual which influenced his sociological perspective as well as his self-image, the largest portion of his writing was concerned with the structures, stratification, and consequences of wealth and power in the United States, the underlying theme of his "trinity of power."[12] The trinity began in 1948, with *The New Men of Power,* in which Mills examines American labor and offers a critical examination of blue-collar unions and their leadership. He hoped for but was pessimistic about the prospect of an alliance between union leaders and progressive intellectuals. Mills continued with *White Collar,* a chronicle of the independent small entrepreneur and craftsmen being swallowed up by a growing corporate economy and bureaucracy and thereby relegated into a growing and increasingly alienated, relatively powerless white-collar middle class.

Mills completed the trilogy in 1959 with *The Power Elite,* the most controversial of the three. In it he described power in American society as oppressive and concentrated in the hands of an interlocking directorate of corporate executives, politicians, and military leaders which served to protect its own vested interests, leaving the rest of the population powerless, uninformed, and indifferent. The mass media played an instrumental part in this process as the new opiate of the people. When a favorable review of the book appeared on the streets of Copenhagen in the Communist publication *New Masses,* the Cultural Affairs Officer stationed there reported to the USIA that she had made arrangements with a controlled source to buy as many copies of the issue as possible to prevent its distribution.[13]

Eventually, Mills's dissatisfaction with the discipline led him to reject official sociology and turn his own sociological imagination beyond its traditional boundaries to such forbidden themes of American social science and society as imperialism, atomic war, mass society, the hungry nations, and so on.[14] No topic could be more taboo than established U.S. policy and the Cuban revolution. When invited to Cuba by Fidel Castro, Mills was "thrilled to see what man can do once he can courageously take his own life in hand and afford national self-determination and gain hope for the good life of his children."[15] For Mills, Cuba represented a third way, a hopeful alternative to the power elite in America and the totalitarian regime in the Soviet Union. However, he felt that American journalists and the state department were providing a distorted picture of the Cuban revolution in an active campaign of disinformation intended to mislead the American people, discredit the revolution, and maintain U.S. hegemony in the hemisphere. He attempted to counteract this campaign through his own account, *Listen, Yankee, The Revolution in Cuba,* published simultaneously in hardback and paper in 1960, and written in the voice of a Cuban revolutionary addressing the U.S. citizenry through a series of letters.

While U.S. reviews were generally critical of his work, Mills received widespread support and acclaim throughout Latin America, including a special letter of support from several of Mexico's most important cultural figures.[16] Placing himself in the midst of a raging hemispheric debate, Mills set himself in direct opposition to the U.S. power elite and its foreign policy. This foray into forbidden territory, paperback publication, and perhaps the popular recognition it garnered him, led to a campaign of rumors and gossip meant to discredit him within the discipline for his "journalistic" tendencies, and eventually to a full-fledged FBI investigation.[17]

Mills had first come to the formal attention of the FBI in January 1943, on the basis of a routine request for a background check when he applied for a position as Associate Organization Analyst with the Special War Policies Unit of the Department of Justice. However, the investigation was discontinued six days later.[18] Requests for a name check from the State Department and the Army, in January and December 1956, revealed that while the FBI had not yet conducted a formal investigation of Mills, his name had appeared several times in its files.[19] In a letter provided to the FBI by a confidential informant in 1949, Mills's name had been listed as a member of the Kutcher Civil Rights Committee. James Kutcher, a veteran who had lost his legs during World War II, had been fired by the Veterans Administration because of his membership in the Socialist Workers Party. The committee was set up to support Kutcher's fight as well as "strike a mortal blow" to the loyalty program.

Also in 1949, according to an article in *Labor Action*, Mills had co-hosted a May Day celebration, with his housemate Louis Coser, sponsored by the Politics Club of the University of Chicago. At the celebration, Saul Mendelson, editor of *Student Partisan*, discussed the Independent Socialist League's (ISL) position on American labor and the socialist movement. Both *Labor Action*, to which Mills reportedly subscribed, and the ISL had been designated by the attorney general under Executive Order 10450. Mills had also appeared as the signer of an open letter sent to President Eisenhower and Attorney General Herbert Brownell, Jr., asking that the Smith Act trials be ended on the basis that "the indictments and testimony point to the painful conclusion that the trials are not for 'conspiracy to teach and advocate the overthrow of the government by force and violence,' but for opinions; not for overt actions, but for political faults."[20]

In 1960, Mills came under the much closer scrutiny of the FBI. On May 16, a confidential informant and probable friend and/or colleague, NY T-1, advised the New York office that Mills was visiting the Soviet Union through a cultural exchange program and would return to the United States later that month. At the same time, Mills's wife, Gloria Olga Mills, a Polish emigre whom Mills first met in Warsaw, was herself the subject of an FBI Internal Security–R investigation. Shortly after the couple returned from their travels the FBI obtained a letter Mills had sent to Moscow addressed to Igor G. Alexandrov, head of the Union of Soviet Societies for Friendship and Cultural Relations with Foreign Countries. He thanked Alexandrov for his kindness in their recent trip to Moscow, and indicated that interviews he had conducted in Russia were on tape and that further correspondence would be forthcoming.[21] A report of the investigation of Gloria Mills, carried out between August and October, listed detailed information on both her and her husband, including note of her recent and difficult pregnancy with Nicholas Mills, born July 17, 1960, and a survey of her husband's activities.[22]

On September 9, informant NY T-1 further advised, "At the invitation of the Cuban government, C. WRIGHT MILLS visited Cuba from approximately August 7 to August 21, 1960. During this period, informant stated MILLS was visited at his hotel in Havana by FIDEL CASTRO, Premier of Cuba, who presented MILLS with a guide and jeep to tour the country, to view the economic situation in Cuba, and to see the improvements made by the revolutionary government."[23] T-1 also informed the FBI that Mills had carried out several interviews with Cuban officials and that prior to leaving for Cuba he was planning a series of five programs to be broadcast on an American or British broadcasting station under the title "Dear Yankee" or "Listen Yankee." He also indicated that Mills intended to have the interviews published.

The following month, on October 10, T-1 disclosed that Mills had visited Castro while he was in New York staying at the Theresa Hotel. The source indicated that plans had been made for Mills to conduct a seminar which would be attended by Castro and nineteen other selected Cuban leaders in Havana.[24] The seminar, which never came to fruition, was to last six to eight weeks and cover the ideological differences between Red China, Yugoslavia, and the U.S.S.R.

On October 26, SAC, New York forwarded a photostat of the manuscript of *Listen, Yankee* to Director, FBI.[25] The manuscript had been made temporarily available by a concealed source two days earlier, copied, and returned. It appears that the source had obtained his copy from Ian Ballantine, publisher of Ballantine Books, who characterized the manuscript as a great work, "destined to be a bestseller," and indicated that it would be published on November 28, 1960, with Ballantine doing a paperback edition and McGraw-Hill the hardback edition. SAC, New York further reported that, "[DELETED] after examination of the manuscript, concluded that it is such an artfully written piece of pro-CASTRO and pro-Communist propaganda, handled in a competent manner and easily readable style, it is highly likely to become a factor in disarming and confusing public opinion in this country and persuading unwary elements of the reading public to a viewpoint contrary to what he understands as the established outlook of the United States regarding the current Cuban regime."[26]

While the source could not assess Ballantine's ideological outlook, he indicated that Ballantine had a reputation as a "highly intelligent person, who in the pursuit of his business is keenly interested in timely items, including those of a possibly controversial nature, giving promise of widespread sales appeal," and that he had no reason to believe that it was Ballantine who had encouraged Mills to undertake such a work. The source also reported that, according to Ballantine, *Harper's* magazine was planning to publish a condensed version of the book in its December issue (a copy of which was placed in Mills's file on December 4, 1961), and that Mills was planning to engage in a television debate with Adolph Berle, former undersecretary of state, on the Cuban issue on December 10, 1960. The source felt that *Listen, Yankee* should be "vigorously counteracted with a suitable rebuttal" and that Ballantine had expressed interest in such a book if it could be produced immediately. He asked for the Bureau's advice and was informed of the Bureau's functions, responsibilities and limitations in matters of this sort, and was advised "neither to expect a reply nor to gage any contemplated action on his part on any such expectancy."

On October 28, SAC, Philadelphia was furnished much the same information from another confidential source, who had also been asked by an unidentifiable party to review the manuscript for its factual content and possible propaganda value. SAC, Philadelphia reported that the source is "firmly convinced it is 100 percent Cuban propaganda in favor of FIDEL CASTRO and all he stands for. [DELETED] advised that it contained a large amount of what he considered to be subtly presented Communist propaganda of the same caliber being presently issued by the CASTRO government. He stated that the book is written in a seemingly objective fashion yet is replete with distortions and lies." As further evidence of its suspect character, the source noted that among his references Mills cited such books as *The Anatomy of a Revolution* by Leo Huberman and Paul Sweezy, editors of the socialist *Monthly Review*, as well as an article from *The Nation* by Carlton Beals, whom he identified as a well-known Castro apologist. The source stated that according to his information, 600 thousand paperback copies of the book were to be printed by Ballantine. SAC, Philadelphia concluded his report with a warning that the source was from one of the wealthiest families of Havana, whose entire holdings had been appropriated by the Castro regime and who was "violently anti-Communist and anti-

CASTRO which might influence his objectivity concerning MILLS' book," but also noted that he "appears to be a sincere, serious intellectual of excellent background and education with deep religious convictions," and "continues to furnish excellent information regarding Cuban activities in the Philadelphia area."[27]

While SAC, New York made no attempt to review or analyze the manuscript, a memorandum to A. H. Belmont at the main office in Washington, D.C. reported as follows:

> Book, which is extremely well-written, makes several major arguments:
>
> 1. That Cuba and, in fact, all Latin America have up to now been suffering extreme economic privations and oppressive dictatorial governments (which have been supported by the US) despite fact that area abounds in natural wealth.
> 2. That US policies have consistently supported status quo in Cuba and Latin America and resisted needed reforms.
> 3. That US economic and political control of Cuba has been completely demolished by Castro revolution as has domination of Cuba by former military and police apparatus.
>
> At conclusion, Mills openly avows his support of Cuban revolution although he admits concern over one-man rule under Fidel Castro. In latter connection, however, Mills concludes such dictatorship is almost inevitable under revolutionary conditions now existing. He asserts that Castro regime is not communist but rather socialistic in nature; however, he declares US misunderstanding and opposition to Cuban revolution will probably result in driving Castro further in direction of Sino–Soviet camp.[28]

The memo recommends that the State Department, CIA, USIA, Internal Security Division, and military agencies be informed of Mills's activities, but without including an evaluation of the book or indication that the Bureau was in possession of a copy.

On November 8, 1960, the New York office was instructed to continue to accept any information volunteered by its informants concerning contacts between Mills and Cuban officials, but not to initiate an active investigation or make any comments indicating the Bureau's approval or disapproval of Mills's book because, "Investigation of Mills, an author and college professor, under these circumstances would appear undesirable and might well result in embarrassment to Bureau."[29]

At the end of November, SAC, New York reported additional information which it had received from NY T-1, indicating, "It is classified 'Confidential' to protect the identity of [DELETED] (NY T-2) and [DELETED] (NY T-1) who, at the present time, is one of a very few individuals having knowledge of this information, disclosure of which could compromise this informant."[30] T-1 reported that Mills had developed a close friendship with Ian Ballantine as a result of their collaboration on *Listen, Yankee*, and that Mills had spoken at a meeting of the Liberal Democratic Party faction headed by Eleanor Roosevelt on "How to Improve Relations with Cuba and South America." The television debate with Berle would be on "United States Policy Towards Cuba and South America," and be broadcast on CBS or NBC. T-1 indicated that Castro's greatest fear was that pro-Batista forces would attack the U.S. naval base at Guantanamo Bay, in disguise as Castro forces, giving the United States provocation to attack Cuba.

T-1 also informed the FBI that Mills's Cuban seminar had been canceled but that he would be visiting Cuba for several weeks in January, and that Mills had received an anonymous letter warning him that an American agent disguised as a South American would assassinate him on his next visit to Cuba. According to T-1, "Mills indicated he would not be surprised if this were true since he does not doubt that the Federal Bureau of Investigation and other similar United States organizations do not approve of his activities."[31] Another letter, with copies sent to President Eisenhower, Senator Kennedy, Allen Dulles and Hoover, playing on the title of Mills's book, begins "Listen, Communist," and accuses Mills of being a "despicable, courageous, intelligent, lying traitor" (see Figure 11.1). In response to the warning and the letters, Mills made inquiries about purchasing a gun for self-protection.

Upon the publication of *Listen, Yankee*, J. Edgar Hoover requested a summary on Mills.[32] The New York office was instructed to conduct a "discreet preliminary investigation," with special attention to the nature and extent of Mills's relationship with Cuban officials and whether or not there was any Cuban direction or financing of Mills's espousal of the Cuban propaganda line.[33] New York was also instructed to monitor the upcoming television debate, provide a complete background check, and told to "be particularly alert to report any pertinent data of a public source nature which will give an insight into his background and sympathies."

Responding to Hoover's request, on December 15, 1960, New York forwarded a detailed and comprehensive twenty-six-page report summarizing the preliminary investigation of Mills's background and activities.[34] The report lists birth data, current and former residence, marital history, educational background, employment history, and travel outside the United States. Thirteen confidential informants, many familiar with Communist Party activity in the New York area, were contacted, though no evidence of any Communist affiliation on Mills's part was discovered. Several friends, neighbors, and col-

Figure 11.1

[illegible], 1960

[C. W]right Mills
[Ba]llantine Books, Inc.
[1]01 Fifth Ave., N. Y. 3, N. Y., and
McGraw Hill Book Co., Inc.

Listen, Communist;

You are a despicable, courageous, intelligent, lying traitor to the United States of America.

Referring to page 183 of your 'Listen, Yankee'; "..Cuban..complaints about the United States, past and present, are solidly based upon historical and sociological fact. We must not believe the genteel mannerisms of U. S. spokesmen are an answer to these complaints..", I am not a U. S. spokesman but an ordinary private American citizen who sees through your masterly deceitful arguments in favor of 'peaceful co-existence' by the U. S. in the Cuban situation.

Listen, Communist, you bet your life the U. S. Marines, or the equivalent thereof, are coming to Cuba - and throw out the Castro gang - and place the government of Cuba in the hands of the Cuban people so they can have human dignity with overdue material blessings (denied them by Cubans - not the U. S.) - and without being a slave to the 'state'. And put on all the blood that is going to be spilled is on your hands; however little you and the likes of you care.

Listen, Communist, didn't you hear the MAN say, "The world cannot endure half slave and half free"?

Listen, Communist, let the Communist world tremble at the fury of free men who see their way of life threatened by a bunch of hoodlums - and in the case of Cuba, by a bunch of Judases.

Deleted Copy Sent [redacted]
by Letter Dated [illegible] [redacted] b7c
Per FOIPA Request

cc - President Eisenhower - Again, why hasn't you acted? Why hasn't the OAS acted? What about the economic calamity in agriculture about to overtake this area from Cuban imports?
Senator Kennedy
Senator Smathers
Allen Dulles
J. Edgar Hoover - Is this book legal? If the Attorney General needs a 'charge' from a private citizen, I hereby make it; C. Wright Mills is part of a conspiracy to overthrow the United States of America by force and violence.

Photostat

1cc - Miami (info) 12-7-60

VHN/st

VHN/st 12/8/60

[redacted]

[illegible] [illegible], [illegible]

REC-8 b7c 77-27024

ALL INFORMATION CONTAINED
HEREIN IS UNCLASSIFIED
DATE 3-14-94 BY 9803 [redacted]
#329,170

DEC 5 [illegible]

62DEC 14 1960

NR [illegible] 77-270

299

leagues, the passport office, and the local postmistress were also contacted, some providing intimate personal information, including that Mills made extensive demands on his wife in research and typing and that she "wished to have several children but the subject did not want to be 'tied down' rearing children."[35]

The synopsis on Mills's activities offered little more than a compilation of information already in the FBI's files, though it was noted that Mills was listed as nationally active in the New York chapter of the Fair Play for Cuba Committee (FPCC).[36] The synopsis also indicated that on the eve of the debate with Berle, broadcast on NBC, it was announced Mills had been hospitalized and his place was taken by Congressman Charles Porter, a democrat from Oregon. Mills had a history of heart problems and had suffered a heart attack a few days before the debate. Finally, the report included excerpts of several reviews of *Listen, Yankee*, as well as a transcription of an interview with Mills from the *Columbia Owl*, a student newspaper, entitled, "Our Man in Havana: C. Wright Mills Talks, Yankee Listens." Concluding that there was no evidence that Mills was being financed or directed by the Cuban government or that he was engaged in intelligence activity, the New York office indicated that no further investigation was being conducted and the case was closed. Copies of the report were sent to the CIA, the State Department, the Office of Strategic Information, G2, and the USIA.

Dissatisfied with the scope of New York's inquiries, particularly as regarded Cuban financing and support of Mills, Washington requested an additional supplemental report.[37] This investigation was carried out during the first three weeks of the new year and included FBI surveillance of Mills's residence while he was recovering from his heart attack and confined to home by orders from the doctor.[38] While Mills was convalescing, New York was informed by one of its confidential sources, T-4, that Mills was to be visited by Aleksandrov, to whom he had written the year before. The visit was confirmed by the surveillance team. Still, no evidence of Cuban direction or financing was discovered, though New York did learn that it was Robert Taber, Executive Secretary of the Fair Play for Cuba Committee, who had originally persuaded Mills to write his book. Once again New York closed its investigation and copies of this second report were forwarded to the Bureau in Washington as well as to the various intelligence agencies.

For the next few months the investigation of Mills remained relatively dormant, though Hoover received several letters from persons who had come across Mills's book and were worried about its "red" leanings. Then, on April 17, 1961, it was reignited when, as Mills had intimated, the greatest fears expressed by Cuban revolutionaries were realized and a U.S.-sponsored, CIA-trained force invaded Cuba at the Bay of Pigs, ninety miles south of Havana, with the hope of initiating a general uprising against Castro. However, as Mills had also predicted, the Castro regime was a popular one, the uprising never occurred, and the Cuban army destroyed the CIA forces, embarrassing the United States internationally and creating a foreign policy disaster for the newly inaugurated Kennedy administration. The following day, SAC, Chicago sent an urgent telegram to Washington indicating that it had been informed that Mills, in cooperation with the FPCC, had drawn up a statement opposing the invasion which was to be published as a full-page ad in the New York and Chicago papers and that the FPCC was planning to distribute more than 50 thousand leaflets in the following days as well as carry out some public demonstrations.[39]

A week later, New York reported that NY T-1 had advised that Mills was leaving for Europe and would attend a rally on the Cuban situation in London on April 25.[40] Washington asked the Passport Office and the State Department to check its records for any details of Mills's travel and informed its legal attaché in London and the other intelligence agencies. On May 1, while in London, Mills sent a telegram, published in the *National Guardian* and announced by the Tass News Agency, to a FPCC rally in San Francisco, "Kennedy and company have returned us to barbarism. Schlesinger and company have disgraced us intellectually and morally. I feel a desperate shame for my country. Sorry I cannot be with you. Were I physically able to do so, I would at this moment be fighting along side Fidel Castro."[41]

Upon receiving a copy of the telegram, Washington instructed New York to initiate a full-fledged investigation, including a mail cover. At the conclusion of the investigation, Washington was expected to submit recommendations concerning the inclusion of Mills's name in the Security Index.[42] Following a two-month investigation, New York reported that Mills and his family were out of the country obviating the need for a mail cover, though a stop was placed with the INS to notify the Bureau when they returned.[43] An informant indicated that the Mills intended to travel to England (to attend a Cuban rally) and Switzerland, then on to the Carpathian Mountain area or Black Sea region of the Soviet Union where Mills would further rest and recuperate from his heart attack. The Soviet Union had released royalties from his books sold in the country but stipulated they be spent there. Mills planned to be out of the United States from six months to one year.

The New York investigation concluded that Mills's connections with the FPCC were primarily limited to his authorship of *Listen, Yankee, The Revolution in Cuba,* and lending his name as a sponsor to pro-Cuban causes. Additional information it had obtained on the FPCC from a report of the U.S. Senate Internal Security Subcommittee indicated that the FPCC had received $3500 from the Cuban government, through the son of its foreign minister, to help pay for a full-page ad placed in support of Cuba in the *New York Times*. Several sources also advised that the Socialist Workers Party (SWP) had become active in the FPCC and was trying to remove several members of the Communist Party from its executive board. Mills was also listed as a sponsor of a rally, held just before he had left for England, to abolish the House Committee on Un-American Activities.

Based on its investigation, on July 3, 1961, New York recommended that Mills be placed on the Reserve Index of the Security Index under the heading Pro-Cuban.[44] The Bureau continued to keep tabs on Mills from the United States.[45] New York T-1 informed the FBI that Mills and his family had left their temporary residence in Switzerland in late July and were touring Europe in a microbus after having traveled to Austria and Czechoslovakia on their way to the Carpathians. The FBI also obtained a copy of an interview with Mills by *Prensa Latina*, a Cuban newswire service, in which Mills repeated his disgust with the U.S. invasion of Cuba and concluded, "I could almost write another book which would be called 'Listen Again, Yankee.'"[46]

Another informant reported that during the Socialist Workers Party National Convention in June, income from literature was up due to sales of pamphlets on the Cuban revolution and books such as Mills's. A report to the convention by Farrell Dobbs, a member of the Presidium, indicated that Mills had been commissioned to put out the selected works of Leon Trotsky in paperback form and that *Listen, Yankee* had over 500 thousand copies in circulation.[47]

In late October, the Director received a memo indicating that an unidentifiable investigator had applied for a passport to go to Cuba on behalf of Mills and Ballantine Books to gather facts and documents for defense against a suit that had been brought against them by Amadeo Barletta, Sr. and Jr., principal officers and stockholders in Ambar Motors and Elmundo and Telemundo, Cuban newspaper, radio, and television corporations mentioned in the book.[48] Referring to passages from the book, the Barlettas alleged that Mills and Ballantine "did compose and publish or cause to be published a certain book entitled, 'Listen, Yankee—The Revolution in Cuba', which contained . . . false, scandalous, malicious and libelous statements and articles concerning the plaintiffs."[49] The Barlettas were asking for a total of $25 million in settlements and a trial by jury. The investigator, listed as a Wisconsin graduate student and member of the editorial board of *Studies on the Left*, was denied a passport. It was also noted that Mills and Ballantine had received several extensions for answering the complaint.

On January 24, 1962, the INS advised that Mills had returned to the United States aboard Pan Am flight 155 from France.[50] Two months later, on March 28, SAC, New York informed the Washington office that local newspapers had announced that Mills had died of a heart attack on March 20.[51] The following day, in a memo from the Director, New York was instructed to verify his death, request removal of his name from the Security Index, and submit a closing report.[52] Included in the file are several obituaries, one with a section highlighted which indicates that a new book to be published posthumously, *The Marxists*, was due out soon. On April 4, New York confirmed that Mills had "died on 3/20/62, at his residence of arteriosteratic heart disease. The medical attendant was Dr. RICHARD S. USEN, and the place of burial at Oak Hill Cemetery, Nyack, New York."[53]

On April 16, New York submitted its closing report, but not before receiving one last bit of information from NY T-1 that, upon his return to the United States, Mills had appeared to be "disillusioned with the CASTRO regime because of the actions and statements of Prime Minister FIDEL CASTRO of Cuba concerning his Communist sympathy and Communist Party membership."[54] Mills's file was closed and copies of the final report were once more sent to all the intelligence agencies.

Mills never devoted as much of his attention to the FBI and J. Edgar Hoover as they did to him, though he once noted in passing that no witness was treated by Congress with more deference than Hoover.[55] However, there can be no doubt as to his disdain for their surveillance activities or the McCarthyist panic and ignorance that was fueling it during the early 1950s when he and his wife were under investigation. Commenting in *Listen, Yankee*, Mills suggested, "For the plain truth is that the kind of ignorant and hysterical 'anti-communism' that is now the mood, the tone and the view of many of the highest governmental officials of the United States of America *is* of the McCarthy type. And I am just as opposed to this as I am to Stalinist practice and proclamation. Surely our aim, in the U.S.A. and in the U.S.S.R., should be to go beyond both."[56]

In order to understand the McCarthy movement and the suspicions it bred, Mills subscribed to the general interpretation that it was rooted in a deep frustration caused by an unstable and ambivalent American status system in which several social constituencies, old Anglo-Saxon families, new immigrant families, the white collar and working classes were finding their positions more and more tenuous. This great strain was contributing to a status panic and bred antisubversive authoritarian ideologies and a conformist pseudoconservatism which McCarthy was able to draw upon under the guise of "anti-Communism."[57] McCarthy was attempting to harness this fear to enhance his own power and position in the struggle among the power elite between the Eastern "American aristocracy," with its liberalist leanings, Ivy League intellectual pedigrees, and command of the upper reaches of American government (especially the Executive Branch), and the "nouveau riche" recently come to wealth at the head of America's growing corporate monopolies and out of the Texas oil fields, but still excluded from genuine political power.[58] At issue was not only control of the Republican party, but also dominance among the power elite, the future direction of the country, and an end to the New Deal liberalism that had been hegemonic for the last twenty years.

Ironically, Mills's diagnosis of McCarthyism was not all that different from Parsons's, though more clearly and consciously placed within the context of the structures of stratification and power within the United States. Nor, for that matter, was his recognition of the importance of Marx for social science: "I happen never to have been what is called 'a Marxist,' but I believe Karl Marx one of the most astute students of society modern civilization has produced; his work is now essential equipment of any adequately trained social scientist as well as of any properly educated person. Those who say they hear Marxian echoes in my work are saying that I have trained myself well. That they do not intend this testifies to their own lack of proper education."[59]

The difference between Parsons and Mills was Mills's willingness to use Marx openly and without apology whenever he saw fit. Even at a time when the social climate in North America could not be less favorable, Mills refused to be cowed into silence. His courageous and outspoken stance gave a powerful, albeit controversial voice to the critical potential of the sociological imagination, even if it meant challenging rather than championing some of America's most sacred policies and ideologies.

NOTES

1. Rick Tilman, *C. Wright Mills: A Native American Radical and His American Intellectual Roots* (University Park: Pennsylvania State University Press, 1984); Barbara Chasin, "C. Wright Mills, Pessimistic Radical," *Sociological Inquiry* 60 (1990): 337–351.
2. J.E.T. Eldridge, *C. Wright Mills* (New York: Tavistock, 1983), 13.
3. Irving Louis Horowitz, *C. Wright Mills: An American Utopian* (New York: Free Press, 1983), 83. In this work, Horowitz provides a detailed critical biography of Mills.

4. Edward Shils, "Imaginary Sociology," *Encounter* 14 (1960): 78.
5. See Thorstein Veblen, *The Theory of the Leisure Class* (New York: Mentor, 1953), xix.
6. Ralph Miliband, "Mills and Politics," in *The New Sociology*, ed. Irving Louis Horowitz (New York: Oxford University Press, 1964), 81. See also Robert B. Notestein, "The Moral Commitment of C. Wright Mills," in idem, 49–53.
7. Ernest Becker, "Mills' Social Psychology and the Great Historical Consequence on the Problem of Alienation," in *The New Sociology*, ed. Irving Louis Horowitz (New York: Oxford University, 1964), 111.
8. Rose K. Goldsen, "Mills and the Profession of Sociology," in *The New Sociology*, ed. Irving Louis Horowitz (New York: Oxford University Press, 1964), 88.
9. C. Wright Mills, *The Sociological Imagination* (Oxford: Oxford University Press, 1959), 5.
10. As quoted in Anatol Rapoport, "The Scientific Relevance of C. Wright Mills," in *The New Sociology*, ed. Irving Louis Horowitz (New York: Oxford University Press, 1964), 100–101.
11. Tilman, *Native American Radical*, 5.
12. For Mills's work on the sociology of knowledge and the role of the intellectual, see C. Wright Mills, "Language, Logic and Culture," *American Sociological Review* 4 (1939), 670–680; C. Wright Mills, "Methodological Consequences of the Sociology of Knowledge," *American Journal of Sociology* 46 (1940): 316–330; and C. Wright Mills, "The Powerless People: The Role of the Intellectual in Society," *Politics* 1 (1944): 68–72.
13. Federal Bureau of Investigation, *C. Wright Mills*, Bureau File 77-27024-5 (Washington, D.C.: FBI Freedom of Information–Privacy Acts Section).
14. Pablo Gonzalez Casanova, "C. Wright Mills: An American Conscience," in *The New Sociology*, ed. Irving Louis Horowitz (New York: Oxford University Press, 1964), 69.
15. Hans H. Gerth, "On C. Wright Mills," *Society* 17 (1980): 73.
16. Horowitz, *An American Utopian*, 299.
17. Casanova, "An American Conscience," 67.
18. FBI, *Mills*, Bufile 77-27024-1, 2.
19. FBI, *Mills*, Bufile 77-27024-3, 4.
20. FBI, *Mills*, Bufile 77-27024-15.
21. FBI, *Mills*, Bufile 77-27024-6.
22. FBI, *Mills*, Bufile 77-27024-7.
23. FBI, *Mills*, Bufile 77-27024-8.
24. FBI, *Mills*, Bufile 77-27024.
25. FBI, *Mills*, Bufile 77-27024-11.
26. Ibid.
27. FBI, *Mills*, Bufile 77-27024-11x.
28. FBI, *Mills*, Bufile 77-27024-9.
29. Ibid.
30. FBI, *Mills*, Bufile 77-27024-11x1.
31. Ibid.
32. FBI, *Mills*, Bufile 77-27024-13.

33. FBI, *Mills*, Bufile 77-27024-10.
34. FBI, *Mills*, Bufile 77-27024-15.
35. Ibid.
36. A document in FBI files includes the names of several other authors associated with the FPCC, including James Baldwin, Simone de Beauvoir, Truman Capote, Norman Mailer, Jean-Paul Sartre, and I. F. Stone. The document indicates that J. Edgar Hoover requested summaries on all Fair Play for Cuba signers. Herbert Mitgang, *Dangerous Dossiers: Exposing the Secret War Against America's Greatest Authors* (New York: Ballantine, 1989), 96.
37. FBI, *Mills*, Bufile 77-27024-15.
38. FBI, *Mills*, Bufile 77-27024-18.
39. FBI, *Mills*, Bufile 77-27024-21.
40. FBI, *Mills*, Bufile 77-27024-22.
41. FBI, *Mills*, Bufile 77-27024-24.
42. Ibid.
43. FBI, *Mills*, Bufile 77-27024-28
44. FBI, *Mills*, Bufile 77-27024-29.
45. FBI, *Mills*, Bufile 77-27024-31.
46. Ibid.
47. Ibid.
48. FBI, *Mills*, Bufile 77-27024-33.
49. See C. Wright Mills, *Listen, Yankee: The Revolution in Cuba* (New York: Ballantine, 1960), 139–140.
50. FBI, *Mills*, Bufile 77-27024-40.
51. FBI, *Mills*, Bufile 77-27024-37.
52. FBI, *Mills*, Bufile 77-27024-36.
53. FBI, *Mills*, Bufile 77-27024-38.
54. FBI, *Mills*, Bufile 77-27024-77. While several commentators have suggested that Mills was backing away from some of his statements in *Listen, Yankee: The Revolution in Cuba*, sociologist and Mills's biographer Irving Louis Horowitz has argued that no evidence of such a retreat exists. While T-1's report appears to support the formers' claims, given the questionable reliability of information in FBI files the issue remains open. See Horowitz, *An American Utopian*, 302.
55. C. Wright Mills, *White Collar* (Oxford: Oxford University Press, 1956), 205.
56. Mills, *Listen, Yankee,* 180.
57. C. Wright Mills, *The Power Elite* (Oxford: Oxford University Press, 1956), 325–342. See also Richard Hofstadter, "The Pseudo-Conservative Revolt," *The American Scholar* 24 (1954–1955), 9–27.
58. See Paul Sweezy and Leo Huberman, "The Roots and Prospects of McCarthyism," *Monthly Review* 5 (1954): 417–434.
59. C. Wright Mills, "Letter to the Editor," *Commentary* 23: 580–581.

— 12 —

The Crimefighter and the Criminologist: The Case of Edwin H. Sutherland and J. Edgar Hoover

Though he took only one course in the field as a student, Edwin H. Sutherland has come to be recognized as America's most prominent and influential criminologist. Prior to Sutherland, American criminology was mired in a multiplicity of biological determinist and psychiatric individualist explanations of crime. Criminals and criminal behavior were looked for and assumed to be concentrated only among the lower classes. Through his development of the theory of differential association, which placed emphasis on the social origins of crime and argued that criminal behavior was learned not inherited, Sutherland displaced biological and psychological approaches and led American sociology in the establishment of a disciplinary hegemony over criminology which has survived to the end of the twentieth century.[1]

Through his work on white-collar crime, Sutherland challenged fellow criminologists to discard their ideological blinders and the attendant class-based sampling and bias which had resulted, "quite as certain as it would be if the scholars selected only red-haired criminals for study and reached the conclusion that redness of hair was the cause of crime."[2] Urging criminologists to look up as well as down the American class structure in their analyses of crime and search for a general theory of criminal behavior, he argued that "the causal factor is not poverty, in the sense of economic need, but the social and interpersonal relations which are associated sometimes with poverty and sometimes with wealth, and sometimes with both."[3]

Sutherland was born in 1883 and grew up on the plains in a fundamentalist household where card playing and dancing were not allowed and alcohol was considered the "great corruptor of mankind."[4] The third of three boys and four girls, he was said to be the family favorite, always eager to please his authoritarian father, George Sutherland, a stern and austere member of the Baptist clergy.[5] As an undergraduate Edwin attended Grand Island College in Nebraska, a small Baptist institution with one building where his father served as president. Though he would eventually break with the church and as an adult enjoyed the forbidden pleasures of his childhood, bridge, cigarettes, magazines, and movies, throughout his life he remained under the influence of his father's ethic. Even when returning home as an adult, he would childishly sneak out behind the barn to have a smoke with his brother, safely hidden from the censuring gaze of their father. Like his father, Sutherland was known to be intellectually demanding, sharply critical of the shortcomings of the work of colleagues, and unstintingly self-critical.[6]

An outstanding student with a broad background in the humanities, science, and religion, after receiving his B.A. in 1904, Sutherland taught Latin, Greek, history, and shorthand at Sioux Falls College, another small Baptist institution in South Dakota. Two years later he entered the University of Chicago with the intent of pursuing a Ph.D. in history, but through a correspondence course developed an interest in sociology and came under the influence of Charles Henderson and W. I. Thomas. However, he became disillusioned with sociology and returned to Grand Island in 1908 to teach at his father's college. After a three-year break, in 1911, Sutherland went back to Chicago, but soon decided not to take any more courses in sociology "unless I am absolutely held to it."[7] He turned instead to political economy and Robert Hoxie, a protege of Thorstein Veblen, in a search for a value-free and objective social science through which human behavior could be studied and controlled, and graduated in 1913 with a Ph.D. in both sociology and political economy.

Upon graduation, Sutherland took a position at William Jewell College in Liberty, Missouri. It was the poorest job among his graduating cohort, with a heavy teaching load and little time or facilities for research. After six unsatisfying years at William Jewell, and even though he had published only one article, Chicago's old-boy network came through and Sutherland was offered a position in the budding two-person sociology department at the University of Illinois, chaired by Edward C. Hayes. Hayes asked Sutherland to write a criminology text for the Lippincott Series in Sociology, which he was editing, thereby rather serendipitously launching Sutherland's career into the area for which he would become renowned but in which he had previously shown little interest.[8] After an exhaustive review of the existing literature, Sutherland produced a relatively conventional text, albeit one with a sociological perspective which avoided the pitfalls of biological determinism and other abnormalist explanations of the causes of crime. He offered no systematic theoretical alternative and continued to adopt the eclectic multiple-factor approach of the day, more by default than conviction. Published in 1924, *Criminology* quickly became the dominant text in the field. Through its many editions, Sutherland would eventually discard the multiple-factor approach and develop his own general sociological theory of differential association.

Along with being catapulted into recognition as one of the leading criminologists in the country, in 1926, Sutherland was offered a position as full professor at Minnesota. No doubt he looked forward with anticipation to joining the likes of Stuart Chapin (chair), Manuel Elmer, and Pitirim Sorokin in the prestigious department, then ranked fourth in the nation. What he encountered was a faculty at war among itself and quickly slipping into the twilight of its golden age.[9] In 1928, Chapin left and Sutherland was appointed acting chair. Things continued to worsen under his leadership and in 1929 he took leave in frustration to spend a year at the Bureau of Social Hygiene in New York City.

In 1930, Sutherland was given the opportunity to return to Chicago through a non-tenure-track research professorship made possible with the support from the Laura Spellman Rockefeller Foundation. The appointment, however, was not as fruitful as anticipated.[10] During his five years at Chicago, Sutherland received ten grants from the Social Science Research Council, but, overcommitted, only completed seven of them. And while he conducted a wide variety of research, relatively little made it into publication at the time. In 1935, Sutherland was determined not to be of Chicago quality and departmental chair Ellsworth Faris recommended he not be reappointed. Deeply embarrassed, he quietly took the helm of the newly independent sociology department at Indiana University (IU), not telling even his closest friends and colleagues the real reason for his move.[11]

Perhaps somewhat shell-shocked by his termination, Sutherland wasted no time in capitalizing on the work he had done at Chicago. In 1937, he published *The Professional Thief*, one of the few criminological studies which involved the collaboration of a criminal himself. The book was coauthored with Broadway Jones, an unusually observant and articulate professional thief whom Sutherland had met at Chicago.[12] Jones and Sutherland brought to light an insider's view of the hidden world of the professional thief, including the considerable corruption on the part of the police and politicians that made it possible. Challenging social pathology and poverty theories of crime and moving Sutherland yet another step forward in the formulation of his own theory, they presented the professional thief as a highly intelligent expert whose panoply of skills could only be obtained through learning and apprenticeship within the company of other adepts.

At Indiana, Sutherland attracted a small cadre of loyal graduate students who sensed something special was occurring: "It was not only that we felt *Sutherland* was at the frontier, we felt that *we* were at the frontier . . . that we were partners in a quest."[13] In 1939, he presented the initial fruits of that quest, a first rendition of his theory of differential association that criminal behavior is learned in the same manner as is lawful behavior (i.e., through a process of social interaction in association with others).[14] He published his theory with considerable trepidation and only after strong encouragement by colleagues, as he considered the theory to be "in progress," and was worried because, "I knew that every criminological theory which had lifted its head had been cracked down by everyone except its author."[15] As he anticipated, his work was met with considerable controversy and has been the subject of research and debate ever since.[16] Yet half a century later it still remains influential. Sutherland himself was one of the theory's most demanding critics and during the next decade he continued to work on it and presented his last version in 1947.[17]

Sutherland argued that any theory of crime must account for the incidence of criminal behavior in all of its manifestations. He was also skeptical of official crime statistics, which tended to be biased in their focus on the crimes of the lower classes. Consequently, throughout his career he pursued an interest in illegal practices typically ignored by the traditional criminology of his day, including lynching, Indian land frauds, circus grafting, kidnapping, smuggling, and piracy.[18] However, none caught his attention more than the crimes of the upper classes and the powerful corporate and political organizations they controlled, which he exposed in his arguably most famous work, *White Collar Crime*. Rated as the most influential book of the decade, prior to its release in 1949, Dryden Press and a skittish Indiana University administration, acting as censors, forced Sutherland to expunge the names of all corporations and individuals mentioned within it.[19]

While Sutherland seemed to have admired and ennobled the professional thief of the ilk of Broadway Jones as "wayward Puritans of the underworld,"[20] he exhibited a powerful disdain for the white-collar criminal whose activities he felt to be much more pernicious and damaging to society. He used the term "white collar" to focus not only on the criminal activity, but also on the social position of its business, professional, and political perpetrators.[21] As he had intended, the book contributed to a reformation of criminological theory and helped to lay the groundwork for the acceptance of his own theory of differential association by making it no longer possible to pursue overtly class-biased explanations of criminal behavior.

When Sutherland died in 1950, taken by a stroke as he was walking across the IU campus on his way to class, he was arguably America's most prominent criminologist, influential and respected among academics and practitioners alike, with the exception of J. Edgar Hoover, generally reputed to be America's number-one crimefighter. The relationship between the two began with a cordial exchange in December 1931, when Hoover invited him to attend a conference being held at the Bureau. Sutherland accepted the invitation, indicating, "I am very much interested in the conference on classification of crimes and I shall be glad to attend, as I expect to be in Washington for the conference of the American Sociological Society."[22] Hoover replied, "I am pleased to note from your letter of December 15th, that it will be possible for you to attend the conference on crime statistics which will be held in the offices of the Bureau of Investigation during the holidays."[23]

During the same period, Sutherland was serving as vice president of the National Institute on Mercenary Crime (NIMC) Board of Trustees which had invited J. Edgar Hoover to speak at its first annual meeting to be held at the Congressional Hotel in Chicago, December 7 and 8, 1931.[24] A leaflet attached to the letter indicated that NIMC was incorporated as a nonsectarian and nonpartisan organization "to learn what we can, from every possible source, of the social and economic causes of mercenary crime."[25] The term "mercenary crime" referred to crimes committed for pecuniary profit, and no doubt Sutherland was interested in the organization since its focus roughly paralleled his own lifetime interest in the white-collar criminal which he regarded with such disdain.

Hoover was also interested in the organization, though not likely for the same reasons, and requested information on it from W. A. McSwain, Special Agent in Charge of the Chicago office.[26] McSwain dispatched an agent to visit the offices of the Institute and also conducted an inquiry, under a pretext, with the American Bar Association (ABA). He reported to Hoover that the Institute's president, Ernest D. MacDougall, was a Chicago lawyer and member of the ABA and its Committee on Mercenary Crime, but that the Institute itself was a freestanding organization with no relationship to the Bar Association. McSwain also noted that the Institute's board of trustees consisted of men who were highly respected and prominent in Chicago, but qualified his remarks by noting, "It would appear, however, that most of them are educators and sociologists."[27]

Following McSwain's report, Hoover politely declined the invitation, indicating, "I find that it will be impossible for me to leave Washington during that period, a number of engagements in connection with current cases before the Bureau accruing at that time in such a manner as to render my absence from the city impossible."[28] After the meeting, the executive committee of NIMC extended an invitation to Hoover to join its advisory council, but once again he declined the invitation.[29]

Sutherland came to the more critical attention of the Director when Albert G. McCord, a reporter for the *Indianapolis Times*, provided the Indianapolis field office with copies of excerpts from a transcript of a talk Sutherland had delivered in support of the parole system at a district meeting of county welfare directors and parole officers in Anderson, Indiana on April 19, 1938.[30] SAC Herold H. Reinecke forwarded the transcripts to Hoover, indicating that Sutherland was a professor of sociology at Indiana University, "with whom, I believe, you are familiar, as he is considerably publicized as a 'criminologist.'"[31] Of particular interest was a rather extended paragraph from the transcript in which Sutherland critiqued statements made by Hoover himself:

> Some of the arguments that are made sound quite impressive until we stop to think of them. For instance, J. Edgar Hoover writes with much vehemence that they have in the Federal Bureau of Investigation a list of 13,477 of the most dangerous murderers, robbers, thugs, hoodlums, kidnappers, hold-up and confidence men, extortionists, rapists, arsonists and thieves. "A den of rattlesnakes could be no more dangerous. And of this list, 30% have been freed one or more times as the result of benevolent or silly action by some parole board." That sounds like a rather bad indictment of parole, doesn't it? But let's think about it. Unfortunately we do not have the same access to records that he has and cannot speak with the same assurance. But what about the other 70%? If this group is as dangerous as he states they must all have served time in penal institutions, and if so 70% were released by order of the court on completion of a fixed penalty. Then more than twice as many of these mad dogs were released from prison without parole as were released from prison by parole. He should have brought his indictment against the court which was benevolent or silly rather than against the parole board, if these statistics can be accepted.[32]

A week later, Hoover acknowledged having received the transcripts from Reinecke, indicating, "For your information, Professor Sutherland is on the Editorial Board of the Journal of Criminal Law and Criminology and utterances such as he made are to be expected."[33] In retaliation for his remarks, Hoover ordered Sutherland's name be stricken from the Bureau's mailing list for copies of the Uniform Crime Reports, which he had been receiving since September 1936.[34] Perplexed and unaware that he had been officially purged, a year later, on February 27, 1939, Sutherland sent Hoover a letter requesting to be replaced on the list: "I wish you would see that my name is restored to the mailing list of the Uniform Crime Reports, and that the four numbers in Volume IX are sent to me. I have a complete file of the reports, including the first ones . . . until for some reason they ceased to come to me after the completion of Volume VIII. I make continuous use of these reports and should like very much to receive them."[35]

In April, when his letter was not answered, Sutherland contacted Indiana Senator Sherman Minton's office for assistance in obtaining the reports. The senator's secretary contacted the Bureau and obtained the two most recent volumes but was informed that the prior volumes were exhausted. In June, the senator's secretary once again requested Sutherland's name be placed on the mailing list, but was told that this would not be possible "in view of the necessity of restricting the distribution of the publication and also in view of the fact that the University of Indiana [*sic*] Library already was on the mailing list."[36] Finally, on August 2, 1940, Sutherland again appealed directly to Hoover, indicating, "I have written to the Bureau three times previously during the last two or three years and did not receive the Reports or a reply to my request." He further explained, "I teach the course in criminology at Indiana University and am preparing several graduate students each year for work in this field. I am using the Uniform Crime Reports frequently for information on trends in crime rates. I doubt if anyone in the United States makes more continuous use of them than I do. Consequently it would be a great convenience to me to have them readily available in my own office.[37]

As a result of his last letter, R. C. Hendon prepared a memorandum for Hoover's second in command, Clyde Tolson, summarizing the Bureau's contacts with Sutherland. After reading the memo, Tolson wrote at the bottom of the second page, "I suggest we now give him Uniform Crime Statistics only. His old parole cohorts have been pretty well licked." Hoover grudgingly agreed, scrawling beneath Tolson's note, "Place him on list for crime reports from now on. Need not send back issues. Need not acknowledge his letters. H."[38] Hoover's denial to Sutherland was particularly ironic given that Sutherland had been a member of the staff of the Bureau of Social Hygiene in 1930, when the Uniform Crime Statistics system was taken over by the Bureau, and that he had actually assisted in the transfer.

Sutherland's treatment does not appear to be atypical. Not only were suspected subversives the target of FBI surveillance, but so was anyone making critical remarks about Hoover and the Bureau. With the assistance of his agents and their national network of informants, he kept a vigilant eye out for any criticisms of himself, the Bureau, or its policies. He seems to have held a special disdain for sociologists and "criminologists." Another criminologist who crossed Hoover's path and was caught up in this net was Norman Hayner, a professor at the University of Washington. On December 28, 1939, the FBI was informed that Hayner was planning to present a paper "The Prison as a Community" to the American Sociological Society meetings in Philadelphia.[39] Coauthored with a graduate student, Ellis Ash, the paper was extremely critical of the director of the FBI and would be characterized by the *Philadelphia Ledger* as "a scathing denunciation of J. Edgar Hoover's vigorous defense of the machine-gun school of criminology." On instruction from E. A. Tamm, a top Hoover aid, Special Agent T. J. Scott from the Philadelphia office was sent to the meeting undercover.[40] He was instructed to obtain a copy of the paper from the session chair under the pretext that he was a representative of Trans-Radio Press. Both a copy of the meeting program and the paper were forwarded to the Washington office and eventually found their way to Hoover's desk. Hoover read the paper carefully, marking special attention to a passage toward the end: "Generally speaking a country gets the kind of prison that it deserves. As long as fraud, corruption and disorganization continue to pervade American life, it cannot be expected that prisons will be much better. The prison is a part of a given social structure and tends to reflect that culture. Russia has challenged the world by providing correctional labor colonies that are self-governing, pay union wages, encourage normal family life and produce graduates who voluntarily return to their 'alma mater' to live. But that is Russia and this is America."[41]

Hoover felt that this passage indicated the source of his critics' remarks. On a handwritten memo attached to the paper, he scrawled, "The answer to this diatribe is found on page 6 of the effusion. The writers are apparently 'Soviet lovers.' Just a couple of 'fellow travelers' who have gotten off of the main highway into a morass of cow dung" (see Figure 12.1).[42]

Several FBI offices from around the nation sent copies of additional newspaper articles or editorials concerning the paper. To the correspondence from R. C. Suran, Special Agent in Charge of the Seattle office, Hoover replied with a personal and confidential memo, enclosing a copy of the paper and noting, "Several newspaper items appeared in the press in the East mentioning Professor Hayner's ref-

Figure 12.1

F 1 DO-7

OFFICE OF DIRECTOR, FEDERAL BUREAU OF INVESTIGATION

TO

OFFICIAL INDICATED BELOW BY CHECK MARK

Mr. Tolson ( )
Mr. Nathan ( )
Mr. E. A. Tamm ( )
Mr. Clegg ( )
Mr. Ladd ( )
Mr. Coffey ( )
Mr. Egan ( )
Mr. Glavin ( )
Mr. Harbo ( )
Mr. Hendon ( )
Mr. Lester ( )
Mr. McIntire ( )
Mr. Nichols ( )
Mr. Rosen ( )
Mr. Quinn Tamm ( )
Mr. Tracy ( )
Secretary ( )
( )

See Me ( )
Note and Return ( )
Remarks:

The answer to this diatribe is found on page 6 of the effusion. The writers are apparently "Soviet lovers". Just a couple of "fellow travelers" who have gotten off of the main highway into a morass of cow dung.

N.

Send Cooper a copy of the speech. He ought to get a kick out of it.

H.

1-6

erence to me, which of course is characteristic of the effusion of so many sociologists and so-called reformers. . . . I would like very much to have you discretely advise me of the background of Professor Hayner and Professor Ash at an early date."[43]

Following two weeks of inquiries among students, staff, and perhaps faculty, Suran reported back to Hoover, "[NAME DELETED] stated he had understood that Professor HAYNER was probably radical and he would endeavor to obtain further information concerning this. . . . It was learned recently that the Sociology Department of the University has the reputation of being a 'nest' for those individuals of 'pinkish' complexion; however neither [NAME DELETED] or [NAME DELETED] were able to state definitely that Professor HAYNER was a 'red' but he has the reputation of being a 'leftist.'"[44]

Suran concluded the memo by assuring Hoover that "if I have occasion to meet either Professor HAYNER or Mr. Ash I will inform them in no uncertain terms as to how misinformed they are with reference to your views on the handling of prisoners."[45]

It is not surprising that Hoover had declined the invitation that Sutherland and NIMC offered him in 1931 to join the movement against mercenary crime. For while Sutherland was outraged at the threat such crimes posed to the political and economic order, this was not a view shared by Hoover and the FBI. If anything, the chilly academic climate created by FBI and McCarthy activities suppressed interest in the investigation of white-collar crime, which would only really take off in the late 1970s and early 1980s in the aftermath of Watergate.[46] And while Hoover retaliated against Sutherland for his criticisms of the FBI, one might speculate that had he known of the full scope of Hoover's and the FBI's activities, Sutherland might well have considered Hoover himself to be a white-collar criminal. In fact, Sutherland's theory of differential association and analysis of white-collar crime might well provide a sociological model for understanding the widespread abuse of authority and disregard for the law, civil rights, freedom of speech, and the right to privacy which developed under the Hoover regime.

In propounding his theory of white-collar crime, Sutherland argued that the crime of corporate executives had its roots in the same general processes of differential association and social isolation as other crimes: "As a part of the process of learning practical business, a young man with idealism and thoughtfulness for others is inducted into white collar crime. In many cases he is ordered by the manager to do things which he regards as unethical or illegal, while in other cases he learns from those who have the same rank as his own how they make a success. He learns specific techniques of violating the law, together with definitions of situations in which those techniques may be used."[47] In addition to learning illegal techniques and practices through his association with others, Sutherland further argued that the young businessman develops a general ideology which helps to make acceptable and justify his behavior within the organization.[48]

Sutherland also suggests that a process of social isolation contributes to the development of criminal behavior and argues that "the essential reason why persons become criminals is that they have been isolated from the culture of the law abiding group."[49] This shelters them from any negative feedback which would likely occur were their activities to be more generally known and their associations more broadly dispersed: "The persons who define business practices as undesirable and illegal are customarily called 'communists' or 'socialists' and their definitions carry little weight."[50]

However, Sutherland just as easily might have been talking about Hoover and the FBI. As he rose to Director and then consolidated his position, Hoover established covert liaisons with selected congressmen and when possible the president, and created an internal security bureaucracy to maintain his influence as well as isolate and insulate himself and his Bureau from the scrutiny and authority of both his superiors and the public. In the process, he developed a complex set of record-keeping practices for handling information which shielded the more questionable and sometimes outright criminal activities from being uncovered (i.e., illegal and unauthorized wiretaps, and "black bag" breaking and entry jobs). Hoover also used his highly secret files full of potentially compromising information to blackmail those individuals, up to and including the president, who might threaten either his position of influence or fiefdom of secrecy.

In a fashion similar to that of the young businessman, the attitudes and practices built into the culture of the Bureau were passed on to its agents and, through recruitment, training, and evaluation and promotion procedures, all protected from scrutiny, criticism, or self-doubt under the cover of an anti-Communist ideology. Agents were drawn from selected colleges and universities. At the training academy they were carefully inducted into the Bureau, informed of its strict dress and grooming codes, and taught its practices and procedures, including unquestioned obedience to the absolute authority of the Director. They formed a homogenous grouping with similar backgrounds and a common ideology, and were easily recognizable with their short haircuts and white-collar shirts; no colored shirts or red ties were allowed.[51] No female agents were allowed under Hoover's tenure, and the first African-American agent was not admitted into the academy until after then Attorney General Robert

Kennedy remarked on the lack of diversity within the Bureau.[52] Once in the field, newly graduated agents would complete their education through association with other agents and were carefully scrutinized both on and off the job. Any breach of protocol or questioning of authority provided grounds for immediate dismissal or reassignment to one of the Bureau's most remote field offices.

Once agents left the Bureau, they continued to be "kept in the family" through its Society of Former Agents of the Federal Bureau of Investigation. The result of this carefully organized and orchestrated process of indoctrination, association, and isolation was the creation of a large white-collar cadre of Special Agents ready to carry out the bidding of the Bureau and convinced, like "the Boss," of the righteousness of their endeavors, legal or not.[53] No doubt many also shared his suspicion of academics and would not think twice when ordered to surveil a prominent sociologist and criminologist such as Sutherland.

While Hoover was consumed with the threat of subversives, Sutherland warned that white-collar crime threatened to subvert the legitimacy of the nation's most basic institutions because of its potential to "tear at the core of a society and render citizens cynical and selfish."[54] He argued, "The large corporations, through restraint of trade and other illegal behavior, have been the principal subversives in the sense that their behavior, regardless of their intentions, has undermined and fundamentally changed the economic and political institutions of the United States."[55] Through their illegal activities, businessmen had conspired to create a system of "private collectivism" that "is very similar to socialism in its departure from free enterprise and free competition, but differs from socialism in that it does not include representation and consideration of the public."[56] He added that "we may adopt one of the collectivistic systems in which the public has some representation: socialism, communism, fascism, or large-scale cooperative enterprises. In any case, we are in a transition from free competition and free enterprise toward some other system, and the violations of the antitrust laws by large corporations are an important factor in producing this transition."[57]

In retrospect, it would appear that Sutherland was much more farsighted than Hoover and the FBI in recognizing the threat of white-collar crime. Since he first brought national attention to the white-collar crime of corporations and politicians, such activities have continued unabated. Hardly a week passes by without yet another revelation hitting the headlines. The result, just as Sutherland predicted, has been an increasingly cynical and apathetic population. Public trust in government has sunk even lower than it was during Watergate.[58] The consequent erosion in the legitimacy of many of our most basic institutions, no doubt fueled in some part by revelations of abuses of Hoover and the FBI, has turned out to be a much more serious menace to the social fabric than any which were posed by the Communist threat.

NOTES

1. Mark S. Gaylord and John F. Galliher, *The Criminology of Edwin Sutherland* (New Brunswick, N.J.: Transaction, 1988), 1.
2. Edwin H. Sutherland, *White Collar Crime* (New York: Dryden Press, 1949), 9.
3. Edwin H. Sutherland, *White Collar Crime: The Uncut Version* (New Haven: Yale University Press, 1983), 6. Tony G. Poveda, *Rethinking White-Collar Crime* (Westport, Conn.: Praeger, 1994), 32–37, argues that Sutherland's work represented a paradigmatic challenge to the discipline which threatened to expose the ideological underpinnings of the field by pointing out the role of power and privilege in the shaping of the law as well as its differential application to upper- and lower-class offenders.
4. Gaylord and Galliher, *Criminology of Edwin Sutherland*, 7.
5. Jon Snodgrass, "A Biographical Sketch and Review of the Work of Edwin H. Sutherland (1889–1950)," *History of Sociology* 6 (1985): 58–59.
6. Gilbert Geis and Colin Goff, introduction to Sutherland *Uncut Version*, xviii.
7. Gaylord and Galliher, *Criminology of Edwin Sutherland*, 36.
8. Hayes had received his Ph.D. from Chicago in 1902. A charter member of the American Sociological Society, he was elected its president in 1921. He served for many years on the editorial board of the *American Journal of Sociology*, and his book, *Introduction to the Study of Sociology*, served as a major text in the field from its publication in 1915 into the mid-1920s. Sutherland felt Hayes was a poor departmental chair and had mislead him in quoting a salary considerably higher than what he was actually paid once he arrived at Illinois. He was also upset that Hayes pressured him to use his *Introduction* in Sutherland's intro classes. Gaylord and Galliher, *Criminology of Edwin Sutherland*, 94–95.
9. To a large extent, the departmental woes were fueled by Sorokin's embitterment at having been taken advantage of when desperate for a position in the United States, having just emigrated from Russia and been offered only $2,000 a year as full professor, half of that typically paid to others of the same rank. However, all of the members of the department were known to have strong egos and to be intense competitors. For a detailed account of its rise and fall see Don Martindale, "The Golden Age of Minnesota Sociology 1921–1930," *Journal of the History of Sociology* 2 (1980): 35–60.
10. Martin Bulmer, *The Chicago School of Sociology: Institutionalization, Diversity, and the Rise of Sociological Research* (Chicago: University of Chicago Press, 1984), 146. Research professors were not required to teach, though some did. Sutherland offered a seminar held in his own home.
11. Snodgrass, "Biographical Sketch," 61–62.

12. Jones actually wrote the main body of the text which Sutherland then edited, annotated, and interpreted. Jones's account was so compelling that the author of the screenplay for *The Sting* used its description of the "con game" as the foundation for the movie's plot. Jones and Sutherland became lifelong friends and Jones would often travel to Bloomington to lecture in Sutherland's classes. See Jon Snodgrass, "The Criminologist and His Criminal: The Case of Edwin H. Sutherland and Broadway Jones," *Issues in Criminology* 8 (1973): 1–17.

13. As quoted in Snodgrass, "Biographical Sketch," 56. This opinion was not unanimously shared by all of the students in the sociology department. Sutherland was also said to play favorites and not be particularly open to those not in his inside circle. See Randy Martin, Robert J. Mutchnick, and W. Timothy Austin, *Criminological Thought: Pioneers Past and Present* (New York: MacMillan, 1990), 143.

14. Edwin H. Sutherland, *Principles of Criminology* 3d ed. (Chicago: J. B. Lippincott, 1939), 1–9.

15. Sutherland first made this remark in an account of the development of the theory delivered in his 1942 Presidential Address to the Ohio Valley Sociological Association, which can be found in Edwin H. Sutherland, *On Analyzing Crime* ed. Karl Schuessler (Chicago: University of Chicago Press, 1973), 13–29.

16. Sutherland's student and protege provides a survey of the most common critiques of the theory and responds to them in Donald R. Cressey, "The Development of a Theory: Differential Association," in *The Sociology of Crime and Delinquency*, ed. M. E. Wolfgang, L. Savitz, and N. Johnston (New York: Wiley, 1962), 81–90. One of the most caustic critiques was that of Sheldon Glueck, "Theory and Fact in Criminology," *British Journal of Criminology* 7 (1956): 92–109, who argued that in comparing the contribution to the advance of science of Sutherland's theory to those of Copernicus, Newton, Darwin, and Einstein, "One only has to put the question to see how absurdly deficient is the elaborately adumbrated theory of differential association and its accompanying definitions of the situation." Sutherland had been engaged in a debate over the causes of crime with Sheldon and Eleanor Glueck, proponents of an interdisciplinary and multiple-factor approach, for several years. See John H. Laub and Robert J. Sampson, "The Sutherland–Glueck Debate: On the Sociology of Criminological Knowledge," *American Journal of Sociology* 96 (1991): 1402–1440.

17. Anticipating many of the comments his critics would make, Sutherland presented his own outline of the weaknesses of the theory in an unpublished paper written in 1944, under the title "The Swan Song of Differential Association." See Sutherland, *On Analyzing Crime*, 30–41. Theodore G. Chiricos, "The Concept of Cause: A Developmental Analysis of the Theory of Differential Association," *Issues in Criminology* 3 (1967): 91–99, discusses the development of the theory, with particular attention to the major transformations it underwent over time. For a final rendition of the theory, see Edwin H. Sutherland, *Principles of Criminology*, 4th ed. (Chicago: J. B. Lippincott, 1947).

18. Snodgrass, "Biographical Sketch," 62.

19. Dryden's legal counsel was worried about potential lawsuits and the IU administration about alienating its wealthy corporate donors. From the beginning, Sutherland was planning a second uncensored edition to be published in 1953 when the statute of limitations for any legal action would have passed. However, his premature death left these plans unfulfilled and an uncensored edition was not published until 1983. Based on a survey of the crimes of seventy manufacturing, mining, and mercantile corporations and fifteen public utilities, the list of corporate criminals reads like a listing of the Fortune 500 and includes the likes of American Can, American Tobacco, Armour, Bethlehem Steel, Chrysler, DuPont, General Electric, Swift, U.S. Steel, and Woolworth. See Sutherland, *Uncut Version*.
20. Snodgrass, "Criminologist and His Criminal," 6.
21. Geis and Gilbert, "Introduction," xviii.
22. Federal Bureau of Investigation, *American Sociological Association*, Bureau File 62-26505-55 (Washington D.C.: FBI Freedom of Information–Privacy Acts Section).
23. Ibid.
24. Federal Bureau of Investigation, *Edwin Hardin Sutherland*, Bureau File 62-26249-1 (Washington, D.C.: FBI Freedom of Information–Privacy Acts Section).
25. Ibid.
26. FBI, *Sutherland*, Bufile 62-26249-3.
27. Ibid.
28. FBI, *Sutherland*, Bufile 62-26249-1.
29. FBI, *Sutherland*, Bufile 62-26249-4.
30. FBI, *Sutherland*, Bufile 62-26249-5. The scare quotes are Reinecke's.
31. Ibid.
32. Ibid.
33. Ibid.
34. FBI, *Sutherland*, Bufile 62-26249-6.
35. Ibid.
36. FBI, *Sutherland*, Bufile 62-26249-7.
37. Ibid.
38. Ibid.
39. Federal Bureau of Investigation, *American Sociological Association*, Bureau File 94-1-14882-2 (Washington, D.C.: FBI Freedom of Information–Privacy Acts Section). Coincidently, this happened to be the same year that Sutherland presided over the meetings as president of the ASA.
40. Ibid.
41. FBI, *American Sociological Association*, Bufile 94-1-14882-1.
42. Ibid.
43. FBI, *American Sociological Association*, Bufile 94-1-14882-4.
44. FBI, *American Sociological Association*, Bufile 94-1-14882-5.
45. Ibid.
46. Gilbert Geis and Colin Goff, "Edwin H. Sutherland: A Biographical and Analytical Commentary," in *White-Collar and Economic Crime*, ed. Peter Wickman and Timothy Dailey (Lexington, Mass.: Lexington Books, 1982), 17. See also Poveda, *Rethinking White-Collar Crime*, 37–39.

47. Sutherland, *White Collar Crime*, 240.
48. Ibid.
49. Sutherland, *Principles of Criminology*, 4th ed., 595.
50. Sutherland, *White Collar Crime*, 247.
51. Athan G. Theoharis and John Stuart Cox, *The Boss: J. Edgar Hoover and the Great American Inquisition*, (New York: Bantam, 1990), 119.
52. Ibid., 98.
53. Not all agents succumbed to the indoctrination of the Bureau. There were some notable exceptions, such as dissident agent William Turner, who was branded a traitor by Hoover for his disloyalty and attempts to expose the illegal and authoritarian practices of the Director. See William W. Turner, *Hoover's F.B.I.* (New York: Thunder's Mouth Press, 1993).
54. As quoted in Geis and Goff, "Introduction," x.
55. Sutherland, *Uncut Version*, 90.
56. Sutherland, *White Collar Crime*, 84–85.
57. Ibid., 88.
58. Poveda, *Rethinking White-Collar Crime*, x.

— 13 —

Conclusion

Robert Merton warns us that we must always keep in mind that historical documents, in the strictest sense, are "writings generated by occasion and circumstance, designed for their designated recipients and not, surely, for some inquisitive sociologist or historian of the future."[1] No doubt this is true, especially in the case of FOIA documents with the extensive withholdings and deletions to which they are subject prior to being released. Nonetheless, the historian of sociology has no choice but to work with them, though advisedly and with caution. These documents reveal previously unknown details of the biographies of several of American sociology's most prominent contributors, and through them an important and little-documented hidden chapter in the history of American sociology that has been influential in defining its distinctive character. As Barbara Laslett has recognized, biography enables us to "examine the social process *through* the individual's experience of it, an approach that makes it possible to observe how actions construct social structures and, in turn, how such structures support some kinds of actions while constraining others."[2]

The picture that emerges from these documents is that of a national law enforcement agency, ostensibly a crime-fighting organization, taking on the role of a secret police under the tutelage of a J. Edgar Hoover driven by racist and anti-Communist ideologies.[3] As Helen Lynd feared, the anti-Communist hysteria that Hoover was propagating, even though, as Stouffer's study indicated, less than 1 percent of the public actively shared his concerns, constituted an attack on independent thought and action.[4] Sorokin shared her fears, warning that the pervasive attempts to suppress the Communist Party and subversive activity threatened to destroy the freedoms they were ideologically claimed to protect by adopting the very repressive and undemocratic methods for which the Communist countries were being publically deplored. Ogburn added an additional sociological dimension to this critique, pointing out the danger of the abuses that could result from the growing centralization and concentration of power resulting from the increasing bureaucratization of American society and its most important social institutions.

Clearly, the domestic surveillance and national security apparatus created within the FBI by Hoover reflected just such a development. Even the normal research activities of sociologists were suspect and surveilled by the FBI. Ogburn was suspected of espionage for a simple survey on industrial dispersion, Frazier for requesting a few blueprints of buildings. Any interest in Russian society was taboo. Burgess's comparative sociological interest in the Russian family was suspect, especially since he had taken the trouble to learn to speak some Russian, no doubt to carry out his participant observation, and because he had a collection of Russian books, the kind of materials any competent qualitative sociologist would assemble. No one was above suspicion. Even Talcott Parsons could be subject to a major investigation based only on the unlikely accusations of a disgruntled colleague.

Stouffer's sociological survey of Americans' attitudes toward communism made him a target of surveillance. In addition, his questions concerning attitudes about the FBI and its Director brought further attention. Hoover was very sensitive to any criticisms, potential or actual, of the Bureau or himself. This was surely the reason he almost childishly denied Sutherland access to the Uniform Crime Report, and had such a negative attitude regarding criminologists, such as Hayner, who might criticize his policies or develop research that contradicted them. However, it was those sociologists who were most outspoken and critical of the status quo, the likes of Mills, the Lynds, Du Bois, and Frazier, who were subject to the most extensive scrutiny. The latter two were doubly suspect, for being both Black and red. Whether it be the nature of the economic system and the class structure, race relations, or international foreign policy, any sustained sociological critique of American society was regarded as subversive and potentially disloyal.

Hoover seems to have held a general disdain for sociologists, so it is no wonder that the sociological imagination was placed under surveillance. As Robert Lynd has suggested, "It's precisely the role of the social scientist to be troublesome."[5] Hoover had little tolerance for such dissenters and felt them to be subversive and disloyal. However, as Helen Lynd further recognized, the possibility for creativity and discovery, the requisite of a vibrant sociology, is a social climate which tolerates rebellion to accepted ideas. Certainly this has been the assumption shared by all of those Western scholars who have routinely discounted Eastern European sociology under Communist influence as ideologically suspect orthodoxy, intellectually shackled by the political authorities and state functionaries of the Communist Party.[6] What is now clear is that American sociology was subject to similar, though less overt and certainly not as extreme, pressures.

In an ironic parallel, in the Cold War era following World War II, at the same time that sociology was being politically suppressed in Eastern Europe and the Soviet Union on the grounds that it was a "bourgeois pseudo-science," in the United States it was being regarded as a hotbed of subversives and potentially "pinkish" fellow travelers. In both cases, sociology was felt to be ideologically threatening, politically suspect, and in need of careful monitoring for the threat it posed to the legitimacy of the norms of the dominating status quo. At the same time that the KGB and other intelligence agencies throughout the Soviet Union and Eastern Europe were keeping close track of the activities and registering the contacts of their sociologists, J. Edgar Hoover and the FBI, in close cooperation with the rest of the intelligence community and the House and Senate investigating committees, were carrying out a similar and extensive surveillance of American sociologists. Those professors identified as "subversive," on either side, were often marginalized within or pushed out of the discipline.

While it is difficult to determine the precise impact this has had on the character of American sociology, a few suggestions might be ventured. Perhaps the most obvious is the lack of a serious tradition of Marxist scholarship in the United States, at least until the 1960s, and then only at the margins of the discipline.[7] As indicated earlier, there was a notable lack of attention to Marx in the works of American sociology's most prominent theorist, Parsons, even though he agreed with his vociferous critic, C. W. Mills, that no adequately educated sociologist could ignore the Marxist tradition. This absence, even today, is virtually unique to American sociology, especially when compared to its European and Latin American counterparts.

It might also be suggested that the climate of fear and repression fostered by Hoover and the FBI contributed to the growing hegemony of quantitative methodologies and statistical analyses that were championed within the discipline by Ogburn, Stouffer, and Lundberg.

Young Soviet sociologists in the 1950s attempted to import methodologies from the natural sciences as a protective shield with which to avoid running afoul of the reigning orthodoxy of historical materialism.[8] Members of the American sociological community may well have adopted similar strategies. Coincidently, the earliest movements in the United States toward a more empirical and scientific sociology, purged of the reformist elements represented by the likes of Jane Addams and the women of Hull House, were being carried out at Chicago during the time of America's first red scare. Hoover already was responsible for the Department of Justice's antiradical excesses.[9]

An unexpected revelation which emerges from the FBI's files is the glimpse they afford of the terrific amount and diversity of resistance that was mobilized in opposition to the anti-Communist hysteria being fostered by Hoover. This is a story that usually gets overshadowed by the focus on the activities of the FBI, and the Senate and House investigating committees. Yet what is clear from the few cases examined here is that there were literally hundreds if not thousands of petitions, committees, letters, and other actions protesting the climate of suspicion and the pervasive surveillance being carried out under the anti-Communist umbrella. What is also clear is that many sociologists were playing an active role in this resistance movement, though not without risk to themselves and the standing of the profession.

The participation of sociologists, from Parsons's opposition to the California Loyalty Oath to Sorokin's and Du Bois's willingness to sign virtually any petition protesting encroachments on political discourse or in support of international peace and disarmament, may well have played a factor in the elimination of any reference to the social sciences in the original bill which established the National Science Foundation. It was only after concerted lobbying by social scientists, including the enlistment of sociology and the behavioral sciences in the confrontation with international communism, that the social sciences were eventually deemed worthy of NSF support and, by the end of 1960, a Division of Social Sciences was established.[10]

Those sociologists most critical of American society and sociology, Du Bois, the Lynds, Frazier, Mills, and many others not treated here, such as members of the Frankfurt School and Scott Nearing, were also those most suspect by J. Edgar Hoover and the FBI.[11] Ironically, at the same time they were the sociologists most marginalized within the mainstream of American sociology. While there is no reason to suggest any kind of conscious and conspiratorial collaboration between the two communities, there is a provocative parallel here that cannot be easily ignored.

Finally, it must be recognized that this story is incomplete, for included herein are only the accounts of a few of the sociologists who were subject to FBI surveillance, and in some cases harassment. And, having risen to the ranks of those recognized as most prominent in the discipline, they were also the survivors. Perhaps the most important story remains untold, if not untellable. That is of the uncountable numbers of relatively unknown and anonymous sociologists at institutions small and large across the nation who either did not survive or quietly censored themselves out of fear of the consequences, stunting the growth and development and blunting the critical edge of the sociological imagination.

The FBI's activities, including its widespread surveillance of American sociologists, served to silence dissent, inhibit democratic discourse, and push the mainstream of the discipline toward an uncritical support of the status quo. If there is a lesson to be learned from this, it is that sociologists must always remain vigilant, for while the FBI has been reigned in and McCarthyism long discredited, new threats have appeared on the horizon. Recent efforts to bolster the canons of various disciplines and undermine movements toward more diversity and inclusiveness, often conducted under the guise of rooting out "political correctness," smack of a kind of neo-McCarthyist resurrection attempting to eradicate any remaining critical elements of the discipline that were able to survive the great purges of the 1940s and 1950s, and roll back the gains made since the 1960s. Additional pressures have come in the form of the politics of research funding and the increasing need to attract private and corporate support for research.[12] Lest we forget our history, it is not an overstatement to suggest that the struggle for democracy, tolerance, and the freedom of speech and dissent, necessary for the creative discovery of a vibrant sociological imagination, is a never-ending one which cannot be left untended.

NOTES

1. Robert K. Merton, "The Sorokin–Merton Correspondence on 'Puritanism, Pietism, and Science,' 1933–1934," in *Sorokin and Civilization: A Centennial Assessment*, ed. Joseph B. Ford, Michel P. Richard, and Palmer C. Talbutt (New Brunswick, N.J.: Transaction, 1996), 22.
2. Barbara Laslett, "Biography as Historical Sociology: The Case of William Fielding Ogburn," *Theory and Society* 2 (1991): 518.
3. Herbert Mitgang, *Dangerous Dossiers: Exposing the Secret War Against America's Greatest Authors* (New York: Ballantine, 1989), 6–7, makes a similar observation based on his examination of Hoover's record and the FBI's files on America's writers. See also Athan G. Theoharis and

John Stuart Cox, *The Boss: J. Edgar Hoover and the Great American Inquisition* (New York: Bantam, 1990), 6.

4. As Ellen Schrecker notes, the anti-Communist movement was primarily a top-down phenomenon and might have more accurately been given the moniker "Hooverism," and not McCarthyism, because of the indispensable role Hoover and the FBI played as the designer and bureaucratic heart of repressive machinery of the movement. See Ellen Schrecker, *Many Are the Crimes: McCarthyism in America* (New York: Little, Brown, 1998), xiii, 203.

5. As quoted in Barry Johnston, *Pitirim A. Sorokin: An Intellectual Biography* (Lawrence: University of Kansas Press, 1995), 126.

6. In fact, the story of sociology in Eastern Europe and the Soviet Union under communism is not such a simple one. The ideological restrictions and climate of repression, especially after World War II, notwithstanding, sociologists in these countries, both those under the Communist umbrella as well as those purged from the academy and/or forced underground, created a tremendously rich body of social scientific scholarship addressing the most crucial issues, questions, and challenges facing their societies (e.g., ethnicity and identity, industrialization, modernization, family, work, healthcare, deviance, and even stratification and inequality). This work represents a broad and sophisticated body of social scientific research which should not be ignored and which offers an until recently unavailable and ignored resource for American sociologists. For an overview of the recent history of Eastern European sociology and its various national traditions, including extensive bibliographic references, see Mike Forrest Keen and Janusz Mucha, ed., *Eastern Europe in Transformation: The Impact on Sociology* (Westport, Conn.: Greenwood, 1994).

7. As soon as some of the more critical and radical elements of American sociology, as well as a fledgling Marxist tradition, began to become more visible and make significant inroads within American sociology in the 1960s, they too came under FBI scrutiny, as evidenced by its surveillance of the ASA meetings and counterconvention held in San Francisco in 1968. However, the full scope and details of this story remain to be determined as the files which chronicle it are not yet fully available. Since many of the principals are still alive, these files cannot be released unless they request them.

8. Gennady S. Batygin and Inna F. Deviatko, "The Metamorphoses of Russian Sociology," in Keen and Mucha, *Eastern Europe in Transformation,* 18. Similar strategies were adopted in Poland and Hungary. See Wladyslaw Kwasniewicz, "Dialectics of Systemic Constraint and Academic Freedom: Polish Sociology under Socialist Regime," and Attila Bechkehazi and Tibor Kuczi, "The Sociology of Reformist Socialism: The Hungarian Model," in idem.

9. Theoharis and Cox, *The Boss*, 16–17.

10. In 1958, Robert Merton and Samuel Stouffer joined thirteen other behavioral scientists in presenting a pamphlet, "National Support for Behavior Science," which outlined the place of behavioral science in national defense and discussed how it might contribute to national strength and spirit. Robert Friedrichs, *A Sociology of Sociology* (New York: Free Press, 1970), 86–89.

11. For example, Herbert Marcuse's file consists of more than 500 pages, beginning with instructions that he be investigated following a speech he delivered at the University of Notre Dame in April 1966 during which he identified himself as a Marxist. In addition to a file on the Institute of Social Research in general, the FBI also has files on Theodore Adorno, Ernst Bloch, Eric Fromm, Max Horkheimer, and Karl Wittfogel. Scott Nearing was not one of the survivors. After holding positions at the University of Pennsylvania and the University of Toledo, he was eventually forced out of the academy and retreated to his homestead in Vermont, where he and his wife Helen became popular figures in the simplicity and self-sufficiency movement. See Scott Nearing, *Making of a Radical: A Political Autobiography* (New York: Harper & Row, 1972), and Helen Nearing and Scott Nearing, *Living the Good Life* (New York: Schocken, 1970).

12. David Dickson, *The New Politics of Science* (New York: Pantheon, 1984), provides an excellent account of how some of these forces are influencing the contemporary production of scientific knowledge. While his account is primarily geared to the natural sciences, the major issues he raises are also applicable to sociology and the social sciences.

Bibliography

Adler, Robert Allan. 1990. *Using the Freedom of Information Act: A Step by Step Guide*. Washington, D.C.: American Civil Liberties Union.

Allen, Phillip J., ed. 1963. *Pitirim A. Sorokin in Review*. Durham: Duke University Press.

Batygin, Gennady S., and Inna F. Deviatko. 1994. The Metamorphoses of Russian Sociology. In *Eastern Europe in Transformation: The Impact on Sociology*, edited by Mike Forrest Keen and Janusz Mucha, 11–23. Westport, Conn.: Greenwood.

Bechkehazi, Attila, and Tibor Kuczi. 1994. The Sociology of Reformist Socialism: The Hungarian Model. In *Eastern Europe in Transformation: The Impact on Sociology*, edited by Mike Forrest Keen and Janusz Mucha, 39–52. Westport, Conn.: Greenwood.

Becker, Ernest. 1964. Mills' Social Psychology and the Great Historical Consequence on the Problem of Alienation. In *The New Sociology*, edited by Irving Horowitz, 108–133. New York: Oxford University Press.

Becker, Howard. 1988. Herbert Blumer's Conceptual Impact. *Symbolic Interaction* 11: 13–21.

Blumer, Herbert. 1933. *Movies and Conduct*. New York: Macmillan.

———. 1943. On Morale. In *American Society in Wartime*, edited by William F. Ogburn, 207–231. Chicago: University of Chicago Press.

———. 1956. Sociological Analysis and the Variable. *American Sociological Review* 21: 685–691.

———. 1967. Ernest W. Burgess. *American Sociologist* 2: 103–104.

———. 1969. Collective Behavior. In *Principles of Sociology*. 3d ed. edited by Alfred McClung Lee, 65–121. New York: Barnes and Noble.

———. 1969. *Symbolic Interactionism: Perspective and Method.* Englewood Cliffs, N.J.: Prentice-Hall.
Bogue, Donald J., ed. 1974. *The Basic Writings of Ernest W. Burgess.* Chicago: Community and Family Study Center.
Bowser, Benjamin, and Deborah Whittle. 1996. Personal Reflections on W.E.B. Du Bois: The Person, Scholar and Activist by Herbert and Fay Aptheker. In *Research in Race and Ethnic Relations.* Vol. 9, edited by Rutledge M. Dennis, 29–63. Greenwich, Conn.: JAI.
Boyer, Paul. 1985. Social Scientists and the Bomb. *Bulletin of the Atomic Scientists* 41(1985): 31–37.
Bracey, John H., August Meier, and Elliot Rudwick, eds. 1971. *The Black Sociologists: The First Half Century.* Belmont, Calif.: Wadsworth.
Broderick, Francis L. 1974. W.E.B. Du Bois: History of an Intellectual. In *Black Sociologists: Historical and Contemporary Perspectives,* edited by James E. Blackwell and Morris Janowitz, 3–24. Chicago: University of Chicago Press.
Bulmer, Martin. 1980. The Early Institutional Establishment of Social Science Research: The Local Community Research Committee at the University of Chicago, 1923–1930. *Minerva* 18: 51–110.
———. 1981. Quantification and Chicago Social Science in the 1920s: A Neglected Tradition. *Journal of the History of Behavioral Sciences* 17: 312–331.
———. 1983. The Society for Social Research: An Institutional Underpinning to the Chicago School of Sociology in the 1920's. *Urban Life* 11: 421–439.
———. 1984. *The Chicago School of Sociology: Institutionalization, Diversity, and the Rise of Sociological Research.* Chicago: University of Chicago Press.
Burgess, Ernest W. 1916. *The Function of Socialization in Social Evolution.* Chicago: University of Chicago Press.
———. 1974a. The Family as a Unity of Interacting Personalities. In *The Basic Writings of Ernest W. Burgess,* edited by Donald J. Bogue, 142–150. Chicago: Community and Family Study Center.
———. 1974b. The Growth of the City: An Introduction to a Research Project. In *The Basic Writings of Ernest W. Burgess,* edited by Donald T. Bogue, 95–106. Chicago: Community and Family Research Center.
———. 1974c. Statistics and Case Studies as Methods of Sociological Research. In *The Basic Writings of Ernest W. Burgess,* edited by Donald J. Bogue, 367–373. Chicago: Community and Family Study Center.
Burgess, Ernest W., and Harvey J. Locke. 1945. *The Family: From Institution to Companionship.* New York: American Book Company.
Camp, Walter, ed. 1922. *Official Intercollegiate Football Guide.* New York: American Sports Publishing.
Casanova, Pablo Gonzalez. 1964. C. Wright Mills: An American Conscience. In *The New Sociology,* edited by Irving Louis Horowitz, 66–75. New York: Oxford University Press.
Cavan, Ruth Shonle. 1983. The Chicago School of Sociology, 1918–1933. *Urban Life* 14: 407–420.

Chasin, Barbara. 1990. C. Wright Mills, Pessimistic Radical. *Sociological Inquiry* 60: 337–351.

Chiricos, Theodore G. 1967. The Concept of Cause: A Developmental Analysis of the Theory of Differential Association. *Issues in Criminology* 3: 91–99.

Churchill, Ward, and Jim Vander Wall, ed. 1990. *The COINTELPRO Papers: Documents from the FBI's Secret Wars against Domestic Dissent.* Boston: South End.

Coser, Louis. 1978. American Trends. In *A History of Sociological Analysis*, edited by Thomas Bottomore and Robert Nisbet, 287–320. New York: Basic.

Cressey, Donald R. 1962. The Development of a Theory: Differential Association. In *The Sociology of Crime and Deliquency*, edited by M. E. Wolfgang, L. Savitz, and N. Johnson, 81–90. New York: Wiley.

Criley, Richard. 1990. *The FBI v. the First Amendment.* Los Angeles: First Amendment Foundation.

Cumming, Ruiz Dorothy Smith, and Robert G. Cumming. 1993. Cultural Ideology and the Moynihan Report. *The Western Journal of Black Studies* 17(2): 65–72.

Daugherty, Rebecca. 1987. *How to Use the Federal Freedom of Information Act.* Washington, D.C.: FOI Service Center.

Davis, Arthur P. 1962. E. Franklin Frazier (1894–1962): A Profile. *The Journal of Negro Education* 31: 429–435.

Davis, James A. 1992. Introduction to *Communism, Conformity and Civil Liberties*, by Samuel Stouffer. New Brunswick, N.J.: Transaction.

Davis, James Kirkpatrick. 1992. *Spying on America: The FBI's Domestic Counterintelligence Program.* New York: Praeger.

Deegan, Mary Jo. 1988. *Jane Addams and the Men of the Chicago School, 1892–1918.* New Brunswick, N.J.: Transaction.

———. 1988. W.E.B. Du Bois and the Women of Hull-House, 1895–1899. *American Sociologist* 19 (Winter): 301–311.

———. 1991. Helen Merrell Lynd (1896–1982). In *Women in Sociology: A Bio-Bibliographical Sourcebook.* Westport, Conn.: Greenwood.

Demerath, N. J. 1949. Review of *The American Soldier: Adjustment During Army Life*, by Samuel Stouffer. *Social Forces* 28: 87–90.

Dennis, Rutledge M. 1996. Continuities and Discontinuities in the Social and Political Thought of W.E.B. Du Bois. In *Research in Race and Ethnic Relations.* Vol. 9, 3–23. Greenwich, Conn.: JAI.

———. 1996. Du Bois's Concept of Double-Consciousness: Myth and Reality. In *Research in Race and Ethnic Relations.* Vol. 9, 69–90. Greenwich, Conn.: JAI.

Denniston, Lyle. 1989. FOIA Ruling Helpful to Media. *Washington Journalism Review* 11 (October): 61.

Diamond, Sigmund. 1992. *Compromised Campus: The Collaboration of Universities with the Intelligence Community, 1945–1955.* New York: Oxford University Press.

Dickson, David. 1984. *The New Politics of Science.* New York: Pantheon.

Du Bois, W.E.B. 1899. *The Philadelphia Negro: A Social Study.* Philadelphia: University of Philadelphia Press.

———. 1908. Symposium on Race Friction. *American Journal of Sociology* 13: 836.
———. 1968. *Dusk of Dawn: An Essay Toward an Autobiography of a Race Concept*. New York: Schocken Books.
———. 1968. *The Autobiography of W.E.B. Du Bois*. New York: International Publishers.
———. 1990. *The Souls of Black Folk*. New York: Vintage Books.
Duncan, Otis Dudley, ed. 1964. *On Culture and Social Change*. Chicago: University of Chicago Press.
Dupree, Sherry Sherod, and Herbert C. Dupree. 1993. *EXPOSED! The FBI's Unclassified Reports on Churches and Church Leaders*. Washington D.C.: Middle Atlantic Regional Press.
Edwards, G. Franklin. 1974. E. Franklin Frazier. In *Black Sociologists: Historical and Contemporary Perspectives*, edited by James E. Blackwell and Morris Janowitz, 85–117. Chicago: University of Chicago Press.
———. 1980. E. Franklin Frazier: Race, Education, and Community. In *Sociological Traditions from Generation to Generation*, edited by Robert K. Merton and Matilda White Riley, 109–130. Norwood, N.J.: Ablex.
Eldridge, J.E.T. 1983. *C. Wright Mills*. New York: Tavistock.
Engler, Robert. 1979–1980. Knowledge for What? Indeed. *Journal of the History of Sociology* 2: 121–126.
Etzioni, Amitai. 1978. FBI and the Scientific Community. *Science News* 114(20): 334.
Faris, Robert E. L. 1967. *Chicago Sociology, 1920–1932*. Chicago: University of Chicago Press.
Federal Bureau of Investigation. *American Sociological Association*. Bureau Files 100-455276; 94-1-14882. Washington, D.C.: FBI Freedom of Information–Privacy Acts Section.
———. *Herbert George Blumer*. Bureau File 138-3450. Washington, D.C.: FBI Freedom of Information–Privacy Acts Section.
———. *Ernest Watson Burgess*. Bureau Files 77-28993; 100-28732; 121-22014. Washington, D.C.: FBI Freedom of Information–Privacy Acts Section.
———. *William E. B. Du Bois*. Bureau File 100-99729. Washington, D.C.: FBI Freedom of Information–Privacy Acts Section.
———. *Edward Franklin Frazier*. Bureau Files 101-1603; 138-825. Washington, D.C.: FBI Freedom of Information–Privacy Acts Section.
———. *Helen Merrell Lynd*. Bureau File 100-357382. Washington, D.C.: FBI Freedom of Information–Privacy Acts Section.
———. *Robert S. Lynd*. Bureau File 77-15837. Washington, D.C.: FBI Freedom of Information–Privacy Acts Section.
———. *C. Wright Mills*. Bureau File 77-27024. Washington, D.C.: FBI Freedom of Information–Privacy Acts Section.
———. *William F. Ogburn*. Bureau Files 100-148350; 100-29013, 100-35330; 100-430091. Washington, D.C.: FBI Freedom of Information–Privacy Acts Section.
———. *Talcott Parsons*. Bureau Files 100-390459; 138-2572. Washington, D.C.: FBI Freedom of Information–Privacy Acts Section.

———. *Russian Research Center*. Bureau File 100-360557. Washington, D.C.: FBI Freedom of Information–Privacy Acts Section.
———. *Pitirim Alexandrovich Sorokin*. Bureau File 100-409199. Washington, D.C.: FBI Freedom of Information–Privacy Acts Section.
———. *Samuel A. Stouffer*. Bureau Files 77-8728; 100-407113; 121-38346. Washington, D.C.: FBI Freedom of Information–Privacy Acts Section.
———. *Edwin Hardin Sutherland*. Bureau File 62-26249. Washington, D.C.: FBI Freedom of Information–Privacy Acts Section.
———. *Thorstein Veblen*. Bureau File 62-30348. Washington, D.C.: FBI Freedom of Information–Privacy Acts Section.
———. *Women's International League for Peace and Freedom*. Bureau File 61-1538. Washington, D.C.: FBI Freedom of Information–Privacy Acts Section.
Fine, Gary Allan. 1988. Editor's Introduction. *Symbolic Interaction* 11: i–ii.
Ford, Joseph B., Michel P. Richard, and Palmer C. Talbutt. 1996. *Sorokin and Civilization: A Centennial Assessment*. New Brunswick, N.J.: Transaction.
Franklin, John Hope. 1963. The Dilemma of the American Negro Scholar. In *Soon One Morning: New Writings by American Negroes, 1940–1962*, edited by Herbert Hill, 62–76. New York: Knopf.
Frazier, E. Franklin. 1922. Scandinavian vs. American Universities. *The Nation* 114: 597.
———. 1927. The Pathology of Race Predjudice. *Forum* 70: 856–862.
———. 1932. *The Negro Family in Chicago*. Chicago: University of Chicago Press.
———. 1939. *The Negro Family in the United States*. Chicago: University of Chicago Press.
———. 1947. Sociological Theory and Race Relations. *American Sociological Review* 12: 265–271.
———. 1949. Race Contacts and Social Structure. *American Sociological Review* 14: 1–11.
———. 1957. *The Black Bourgeoisie*. New York: Free Press.
———. 1957. *Race and Culture Contacts in the Modern World*. New York: Knopf.
Fried, Albert. 1997. *McCarthyism: The Great American Red Scare*. New York: Oxford University Press.
Friedrichs, Robert. 1970. *A Sociology of Sociology*. New York: Free Press.
Gallen, David, ed. 1991. *Malcolm X: The FBI Files*. New York: Carroll and Graf.
Garrow, David J. 1981. *The FBI and Martin Luther King, Jr.: From "Solo" to Memphis*. New York: W. W. Norton.
Gaylord, Mark S., and John F. Galliher. 1988. *The Criminology of Edwin Sutherland*. New Brunswick, N.J.: Transaction.
Geis, Gilbert, and Colin Goff. 1982. Edwin H. Sutherland: A Biographical and Analytical Commentary. In *White-Collar and Economic Crime*, edited by Peter Wickman and Timothy Dailey, 3–21. Lexington, Mass.: Lexington Books.
———.1983. Introduction to *White Collar Crime: The Uncut Version*, by Edwin H. Sutherland. New Haven: Yale University Press.

Gelbspan, Ross. 1991. *Break-ins, Death Threats and the FBI: The Covert War against the Central American Anti-War Movement.* Boston: South End.

Gentry, Curt. 1991. *J. Edgar Hoover: The Man and the Secrets.* New York: W. W. Norton.

Gerhardt, Uta, ed. 1993. *Talcott Parsons on National Socialism.* New York: Aldine de Gruyter.

Gerth, Hans H. 1980. On C. Wright Mills. *Society* 17: 71–73.

Glazer, Nathan. 1949. *The American Soldier* as Science: Can Sociology Fulfill its Ambitions? *Commentary* 8: 487–496.

Glueck, Sheldon. 1956. Theory and Fact in Criminology. *British Journal of Criminology* 7: 92–109.

Goldsen, Rose K. 1964. Mills and the Profession of Sociology. In *The New Sociology*, edited by Irving Louis Horowitz, 82–93. New York: Oxford University Press.

Gould, Mark. 1981. Parsons versus Marx: "An Earnest Warning . . ." *Sociological Inquiry* 51: 197–218.

Gouldner, Alvin W. 1970. *The Coming Crisis of Western Sociology.* New York: Basic.

Green, Dan S., and Edwin E. Driver. 1976. W.E.B. Du Bois: A Case in the Sociology of Sociological Negation. *Phylon* 37: 308–333.

Hamilton, Peter. 1983. *Talcott Parsons.* New York: Tavistock and Horwood.

Hammersley, Martyn. 1989. *The Dilemma of Qualitative Method: Herbert Blumer and the Chicago Tradition.* London: Routledge.

Henry, Charles P. 1995. Abram Harris, E. Franklin Frazier, and Ralph Bunche: The Howard School of Thought on the Problem of Race. *National Political Science Review* 5: 36–56.

Hernon, Peter. 1979. *Uses of Government Publications by Social Scientists.* Norwood, N.J.: Ablex.

Hernon, Peter, and Charles R. McClure. 1987. *Federal Information Policies in the 1980's.* Norwood, N.J.: Ablex.

Hinkle, Roscoe C., and Gisela J. Hinkle. 1954. *The Development of Modern Sociology: Its Nature and Growth in the United States.* New York: Random House.

Hofstadter, Richard. 1954–1955. The Pseudo-Conservative Revolt. *The American Scholar* 24: 9–27.

Horne, Gerald. 1986. *Black and Red: W.E.B. Du Bois and the Afro-American Response to the Cold War, 1944–1963.* Albany: State University of New York Press.

Horowitz, Irving Louis. 1979. Lynd, Robert S. and Helen Merrell. In *International Encyclopedia of the Social Sciences: Biographical Supplement.* Vol. 18, edited by David L. Sills, 471–477. New York: Free Press.

———. 1983. *C. Wright Mills: An American Utopian.* New York: Free Press.

House, Floyd Nelson. 1936. *The Development of Sociology.* New York: McGraw-Hill.

Huff, Toby E. 1973. Theoretical Innovation in Science: The Case of William F. Ogburn. *American Journal of Sociology* 79: 261–277.

Jefferson, Paul. 1996. Present at the Creation: Rethinking Du Bois's "Practice Theory." In *Research in Race and Ethnic Relations*. Vol 9, edited by Rutledge M. Dennis, 127–169. Greenwich, Conn.: JAI.

Johnston, Barry. 1986. Sorokin and Parsons at Harvard: Institutional Conflict and the Rise of a Hegemonic Tradition. *Journal of the History of Behavioral Sciences* 22: 107–127.

———. 1995. *Pitirim A. Sorokin: An Intellectual Biography*. Lawrence: University of Kansas Press.

Jones, Atlas Jack. 1976. The Sociology of W.E.B. Du Bois. *The Black Sociologist* 6 (December): 4–15.

Keen, Mike Forrest. 1992. The Freedom of Information Act and Sociological Research. *American Sociologist* 23(2): 43–51.

Keen, Mike Forrest, and Janusz Mucha, ed. 1994. *Eastern Europe in Transformation: The Impact on Sociology*. Westport, Conn.: Greenwood.

Keller, William W. 1989. *The Liberals and J. Edgar Hoover: Rise and Fall of a Domestic Intelligence State*. Princeton: Princeton University Press.

Kilson, Martin. 1983. The Black Bourgeoisie Revisited. *Dissent* 30: 85–96.

Kuklik, Henrika. 1980. Boundary Maintenance in American Sociology: Limitations to Academic "Professionalization." *Journal of the History of the Behavioral Sciences* 16: 201–219.

Kurtz, Lester. 1984. *Evaluating Chicago Sociology: A Guide to Literature*. Chicago: University of Chicago Press.

Kwasniewicz, Wladyslaw. 1994. Dialectics of Systemic Constraint and Academic Freedom: Polish Sociology under Socialist Regime. In *Eastern Europe in Transformation: The Impact on Sociology*, edited by Mike Forrest Keen and Janusz Mucha, 25–38. Westport, Conn.: Greenwood.

Lackey, Pat N. 1987. *Invitation to Talcott Parsons' Theory*. Houston: Cap and Gown.

Landry, Bart. 1978. A Reinterpretation of the Writings of Frazier on the Black Middle Class. *Social Problems* 26: 211-222.

Laslett, Barbara. 1990. Unfeeling Knowledge: Emotion and Objectivity in the History of Sociology. *Sociological Forum* 5: 413–433.

———. 1991. Biography as Historical Sociology: The Case of William Fielding Ogburn. *Theory and Society* 2: 511–537.

Laub, John H., and Robert J. Sampson. 1991. The Sutherland–Glueck Debate: On the Sociology of Criminological Knowledge. *American Journal of Sociology* 96: 1402–1440.

Lee, Alfred McClung. 1949. Review of *The American Soldier*, by Samuel Stouffer. *Annals of the American Academy of Political and Social Science* 265: 173–175.

Lemert, Charles. 1994. A Classic from the Other Side of the Veil: Du Bois's *The Souls of Black Folk*. *Sociological Quarterly* 35: 383–396.

Lerner, Daniel. 1950. *The American Soldier* and the Public. In *Studies in the Scope and Method of "The American Soldier,"* edited by Robert K. Merton and Paul F. Lazarsfeld, 215–245. Glencoe, Ill.: Free Press.

Lindstrom, Fred B., and Ronald A. Hardert. 1988. Kimball Young on the Chicago School: Later Contacts. *Sociological Perspectives* 31: 298–314.

Lindt, Gillian. 1979–1980. Introduction—Robert S. Lynd: American Scholar-Activist. *Journal of the History of Sociology* 2: 1–12.

Lipset, Seymour Martin. 1955. "The Department of Sociology." In *A History of the Faculty of Political Science, Columbia University*, edited by Robert G. Hoxie. New York: Columbia University Press.

Lucal, Betsy. 1996. Race, Class, and Gender in the Work of W.E.B. Du Bois: An Exploratory Study. In *Research in Race and Ethnic Relations*. Vol. 9, edited by Rutledge M. Dennis, 191–210. Greenwich, Conn.: JAI.

Lyman, Stanford M., and Arthur J. Vidich. 1988. *Social Order and the Public Philosophy: An Analysis and Interpretation of the Work of Herbert Blumer*. Fayetteville: University of Arkansas Press.

Lynd, Helen Merrell. 1945. *England in the Eighteen-eighties: Toward a Social Basis for Freedom*. New York: Oxford University Press.

———. 1949. Truth at the University of Washington. *The American Scholar* 18: 346–353.

———. 1951–1952. Realism and the Intellectual in a Time of Crisis. *The American Scholar* 21: 21–32.

———. 1958. *On Shame and the Search for Identity*. New York: Harcourt, Brace.

———. 1965. What is Democratic Loyalty? In *Toward Discovery*. New York: Hobbs, Dorman.

———. 1983. *Possibilities*. rev. ed. Youngstown, Ohio: Inkwell Press.

Lynd, Robert S. 1922. Done in Oil. *The Survey Graphic* 49(3): 137–146.

———. 1939. *Knowledge for What? The Place of Social Science in American Culture*. Princeton: Princeton University Press.

———. 1949. The Science of Inhuman Relations. *New Republic*, 29 August, 22–25.

———. 1956. Power in the United States. *The Nation* 182: 408–411.

Lynd, Robert S., and Helen Merrell Lynd. 1931. *Middletown: A Study in Contemporary American Culture*. New York: Harcourt, Brace.

———. 1937. *Middletown in Transition: A Study in Cultural Conflicts*. New York: Harcourt, Brace.

Lynd, Straughton. 1979–1980. Robert S. Lynd: The Elk Basin Experience. *Journal of the History of Sociology* 2: 14–22.

———. 1993. Father and Son: Intellectual Work Outside the University. *Social Policy* 23(3): 4–11.

Maines, David R. 1988. Myth, Text, and Interactionist Complicity in the Neglect of Blumer's Macrosociology. *Symbolic Interaction* 11: 43–57.

Martel, Martin. 1979. Talcott Parsons. In *International Encyclopedia of Social Sciences*. Vol. 18, edited by David L. Sills, 609–630. New York: Free Press.

Martin, Randy, Robert J. Mutchnick, and W. Timothy Austin. 1990. *Criminological Thought: Pioneers Past and Present*. New York: MacMillan.

Martindale, Don. 1980. The Golden Age of Minnesota Sociology 1921–1930. *Journal of the History of Sociology* 2(2): 35–60.

Mathis, Arthur. 1978. Contrasting Approaches to the Study of the Black Family. *Journal of Marriage and Family* 40: 667–676.

Mencken, H. L. 1929. A City in Moronia. *American Mercury* 16: 379–381.

Merton, Robert. 1949. *Social Theory and Social Structure: Toward the Codification of Theory and Research*. Glencoe, Ill.: Free Press.
———. 1970. *Science, Technology, and Society in Seventeenth Century England*. New York: Harper and Row.
———. 1996. The Sorokin–Merton Correspondence on "Puritanism, Pietism, and Science," 1933–1934. In *Sorokin and Civilization: A Centennial Assessment*, edited by Joseph B. Ford, Michel P. Richard, and Palmer C. Talbutt, 21–28. New Brunswick, N.J.: Transaction.
Miley, James D. 1980. Critical Dimensions in Human Ecology: Ideology in American Sociology. *Urban Life* 9: 163–185.
Miliband, Ralph. 1964. Mills and Politics. In *The New Sociology*, edited by Irving Louis Horowitz, 76–87. New York: Oxford University Press.
Mills, C. Wright. 1939. Language, Logic and Culture. *American Sociological Review* 4: 670–680.
———. 1940. Methodological Consequences of the Sociology of Knowledge. *American Journal of Sociology* 46: 316–330.
———. 1944. The Powerless People: The Role of the Intellectual in Society. *Politics* 1: 68–72.
———. 1948. *The New Men of Power*. New York: Harcourt Brace.
———. 1956. *The Power Elite*. Oxford: Oxford University Press.
———. 1956. *White Collar*. Oxford: Oxford University Press.
———. 1957. Letter to the Editor. *Commentary* 23: 580–581.
———. 1959. *The Sociological Imagination*. Oxford: Oxford University Press.
———. 1960. *Listen, Yankee: The Revolution in Cuba*. New York: Ballantine.
Mitgang, Herbert. 1989. *Dangerous Dossiers: Exposing the Secret War Against America's Greatest Authors*. New York: Ballantine.
Morrione, Thomas J. 1988. Herbert G. Blumer (1900–1987): A Legacy of Concepts, Criticisms and Contributions. *Symbolic Interaction* 11: 1–12.
Murdock, George P. 1949. Review of *The American Soldier: Adjustment During Army Life*, by Samuel Stouffer. *American Sociological Review* 14: 814–815.
Myrdal, Gunnar. 1944. *An American Dilemma: The Negro Problem and Modern Democracy*. New York: Harper & Brothers.
Nearing, Helen, and Scott Nearing. 1970. *Living the Good Life*. New York: Schocken.
Nearing, Scott. 1972. *Making of a Radical: A Political Autobiography*. New York: Harper & Row.
Nelson, Benjamin, and Jerome Gittleman. 1973. Max Weber, Dr. Alfred Plaetz, and W.E.B. Du Bois: Max Weber on Race and Society. *Sociological Analysis* 34: 308–312.
Nichols, Lawrence T. 1996. Sorokin and American Sociology: The Dynamics of a Moral Career in Science. In *Sorokin and Civilization: A Centennial Assessment*, edited by Joseph B. Ford, Michel P. Richard, and Palmer C. Talbutt, 45–64. New Brunswick, N.J.: Transaction.
Nielsen, Jens Kaalhauge. 1991. The Political Orientation of Talcott Parsons: The Second World War and Its Aftermath. In *Talcott Parsons: Theorist of Modernity*, edited by R. Robertson and B. Turner, 215–233. London: Sage.

North, Mark. 1991. *Act of Treason: The Role of J. Edgar Hoover in the Assassination of President Kennedy.* New York: Carroll and Graf.

Notestein, Robert B. 1964. The Moral Commitment of C. Wright Mills. In *The New Sociology,* edited by Irving Horowitz 49–53. New York: Oxford University Press.

Ogburn, William Fielding. 1922. Bias, Psychoanalysis and the Subjective in Relation to the Social Sciences. *Publication of the American Sociological Society* 17: 62–74.

———. 1930. The Folkways of a Scientific Sociology. In *Studies in Quantitative and Cultural Sociology,* 1–11. Chicago: University of Chicago Press.

———. 1930. Three Obstacles to the Development of a Scientific Sociology. *Social Forces* 8: 347–350.

———. 1934. Studies in Prediction and the Distortion of Reality. *Social Forces* 13: 224–229.

———. 1946. Aviation and Society. *Air Affairs* 1: 10–20.

———. 1946. Sociology and the Atom. *American Journal of Sociology* 51: 267–275.

———. 1948. Thoughts on Freedom and Organization. *Ethics* 58: 256–261.

———. 1966. *Social Change: With Respect to Culture and Original Nature.* New York: Dell.

Ogburn, William F., Jean L. Adams and S. C. Gilfillan. 1946. *The Social Effects of Aviation.* Boston: Houghton Mifflin.

O'Reilly, Kenneth. 1983. *Hoover and the Un-Americans: The FBI, HUAC and the Red Menace.* Philadelphia: Temple University Press.

———. 1989. *"Racial Matters": The FBI's Secret File on Black America, 1960–1972.* New York: Free Press.

Park, Robert E. and Ernest W. Burgess. 1921. *Introduction to the Science of Sociology.* Chicago: University of Chicago Press.

Park, Robert E., Ernest W. Burgess, and Roderick D. McKenzie. 1925. *The City.* Chicago: University of Chicago Press.

Parsons, Talcott. 1937. *The Structure of Social Action.* New York: McGraw Hill.

———. 1951. *The Social System.* Glencoe, Ill: Free Press.

———. 1954. "McCarthyism" and American Social Tension: A Sociologist's View. *Yale Review* 44: 226–245.

———. 1977. On Building Social System Theory: A Personal History. In *Social Systems and the Evolution of Action Theory,* 22–76. New York: Free Press.

Perkus, Cathy, ed. 1975. *COINTELPRO: The FBI's Secret War on Political Freedom.* New York: Monad Press.

Pitts, Jesse R. 1980. Talcott Parsons: The Sociologist as the Last Puritan. *The American Sociologist* 15: 62–64.

Platt, Anthony, 1987. E. Franklin Frazier and Daniel Patrick Moynihan: Setting the Record Straight. *Contemporary Crises* 11: 265–277.

———. 1991. *E. Franklin Frazier Reconsidered.* New Brunswick, N.J.: Rutgers University Press.

Platt, Jennifer. 1986. Stouffer and Lazarsfeld: Patterns of Influence. In *Knowledge and Society: Studies in the Sociology of Culture Past and Present,* edited by Henrika Kuklik and Elizabeth Long, 99–117. London: JAI.

Poveda, Tony G. 1994. *Rethinking White Collar Crime*. Westport, Conn.: Praeger.
President's Research Committee on Social Trends. 1932. *Recent Social Trends in the United States*. New York: McGraw-Hill.
Rapoport, Anatol. 1964. The Scientific Relevance of C. Wright Mills. In *The New Sociology*, edited by Irving Louis Horowitz, 94–107. New York: Oxford University Press.
Raushenbush, Winfred. 1979. *Robert E. Park: Biography of a Sociologist*. Durham, N.C.: Duke University Press.
Riley, John, Jr. 1949. Review of *The American Soldier: Combat and Its Aftermath*, by Samuel A. Stouffer. *American Sociological Review* 14: 557–559.
Robertson, Roland, and Bryan S. Turner. 1991. *Talcott Parsons: Theorist of Modernity*. London: Sage.
Robins, Natalie S. 1992. *Alien Ink: The FBI's War on Freedom of Expression*. New York: William and Morrow.
Rockefeller, John D., Jr. 1922. A Promise of Better Days. *The Survey Graphic* 49(3): 147–148.
Rosten, Leo C. 1941. *Hollywood: The Movie Colony, the Movie Makers*. New York: Harcourt Brace.
Rudwick, Elliott. 1974. W.E.B. Du Bois as a Sociologist. In *Black Sociologists: Historical and Contemporary Perspectives*, edited by James. E. Blackwell and Morris Janowitz, 25–53. Chicago: University of Chicago Press.
Ryan, William. 1976. *Blaming the Victim*. New York: Vintage.
Schrecker, Ellen. 1986. *No Ivory Tower: McCarthyism and the Universities*. New York: Oxford University Press.
———. 1998. *Many Are the Crimes: McCarthyism in America*. New York: Little, Brown.
Schwendinger, Julia, and Herman Schwendinger. 1973. Sociologists of the Chair and the Natural Law Tradition. *Insurgent Sociologist* 3(2): 3–18.
Semmes, Clovis E. 1986. The Sociological Tradition of E. Franklin Frazier: Implications for Black Studies. *The Journal of Negro Education* 55: 484–494.
Shibutani, Tamotsu. 1988. Herbert Blumer's Contribution to Twentieth Century Sociology. *Symbolic Interaction* 11: 23–31.
Shils, Edward. 1960. Imaginary Sociology. *Encounter* 14: 78–81.
Smith, Dennis. 1988. *The Chicago School: A Liberal Critique of Capitalism*. New York: St. Martin's.
Smith, Mark C. 1979–1980. Robert Lynd and Consumerism in the 1930's. *Journal of the History of Sociology* 2: 99–120.
Snodgrass, Jon. 1973. The Criminologist and His Criminal: The Case of Edwin H. Sutherland and Broadway Jones. *Issues in Criminology* 8: 1–17.
———. 1985. A Biographical Sketch and Review of the Work of Edwin H. Sutherland (1889–1950). *History of Sociology* 6: 55–67.
Sorokin, Pitirim A. 1927. *Social Mobility*. New York: Harper & Brothers.
———. 1928. *Contemporary Sociological Theories*. New York: Harper & Brothers.
———. 1941. Declaration of Independence of the Social Sciences. *Social Science* (16): 221–229.

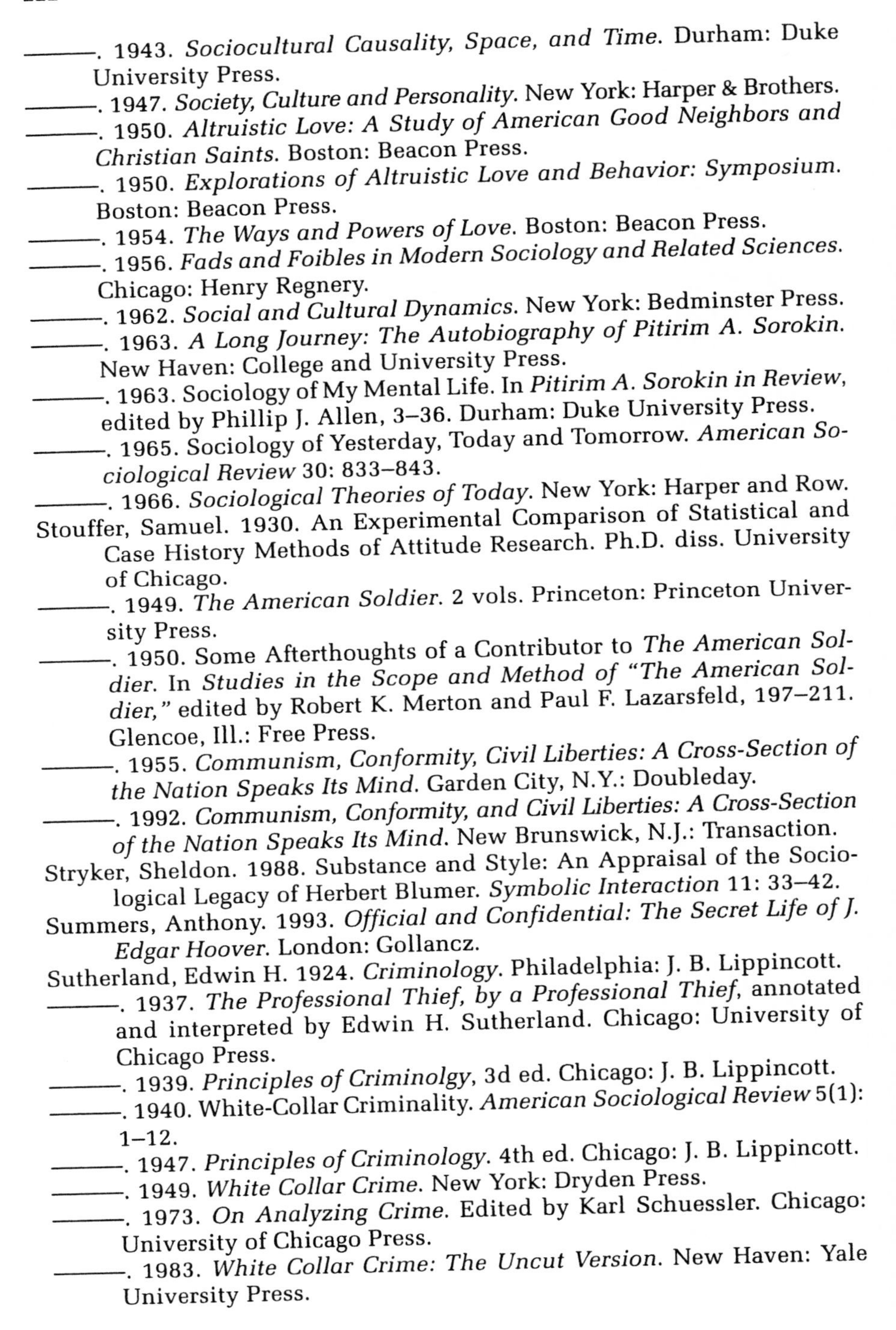

———. 1943. *Sociocultural Causality, Space, and Time*. Durham: Duke University Press.

———. 1947. *Society, Culture and Personality*. New York: Harper & Brothers.

———. 1950. *Altruistic Love: A Study of American Good Neighbors and Christian Saints*. Boston: Beacon Press.

———. 1950. *Explorations of Altruistic Love and Behavior: Symposium*. Boston: Beacon Press.

———. 1954. *The Ways and Powers of Love*. Boston: Beacon Press.

———. 1956. *Fads and Foibles in Modern Sociology and Related Sciences*. Chicago: Henry Regnery.

———. 1962. *Social and Cultural Dynamics*. New York: Bedminster Press.

———. 1963. *A Long Journey: The Autobiography of Pitirim A. Sorokin*. New Haven: College and University Press.

———. 1963. Sociology of My Mental Life. In *Pitirim A. Sorokin in Review*, edited by Phillip J. Allen, 3–36. Durham: Duke University Press.

———. 1965. Sociology of Yesterday, Today and Tomorrow. *American Sociological Review* 30: 833–843.

———. 1966. *Sociological Theories of Today*. New York: Harper and Row.

Stouffer, Samuel. 1930. An Experimental Comparison of Statistical and Case History Methods of Attitude Research. Ph.D. diss. University of Chicago.

———. 1949. *The American Soldier*. 2 vols. Princeton: Princeton University Press.

———. 1950. Some Afterthoughts of a Contributor to *The American Soldier*. In *Studies in the Scope and Method of "The American Soldier,"* edited by Robert K. Merton and Paul F. Lazarsfeld, 197–211. Glencoe, Ill.: Free Press.

———. 1955. *Communism, Conformity, Civil Liberties: A Cross-Section of the Nation Speaks Its Mind*. Garden City, N.Y.: Doubleday.

———. 1992. *Communism, Conformity, and Civil Liberties: A Cross-Section of the Nation Speaks Its Mind*. New Brunswick, N.J.: Transaction.

Stryker, Sheldon. 1988. Substance and Style: An Appraisal of the Sociological Legacy of Herbert Blumer. *Symbolic Interaction* 11: 33–42.

Summers, Anthony. 1993. *Official and Confidential: The Secret Life of J. Edgar Hoover*. London: Gollancz.

Sutherland, Edwin H. 1924. *Criminology*. Philadelphia: J. B. Lippincott.

———. 1937. *The Professional Thief, by a Professional Thief*, annotated and interpreted by Edwin H. Sutherland. Chicago: University of Chicago Press.

———. 1939. *Principles of Criminolgy*, 3d ed. Chicago: J. B. Lippincott.

———. 1940. White-Collar Criminality. *American Sociological Review* 5(1): 1–12.

———. 1947. *Principles of Criminology*. 4th ed. Chicago: J. B. Lippincott.

———. 1949. *White Collar Crime*. New York: Dryden Press.

———. 1973. *On Analyzing Crime*. Edited by Karl Schuessler. Chicago: University of Chicago Press.

———. 1983. *White Collar Crime: The Uncut Version*. New Haven: Yale University Press.

Sweezy, Paul, and Leo Huberman. 1954. The Roots and Prospects of McCarthyism. *Monthly Review* 5: 417–434.

Theoharis, Athan G. 1978. *Spying on Americans: Political Surveillance from Hoover to the Huston Plan*. Philadelphia: Temple University Press.

Theoharis, Athan G., and John Stuart Cox. 1990. *The Boss: J. Edgar Hoover and the Great American Inquisition*. New York: Bantam

Tilman, Rick. 1984. *C. Wright Mills: A Native American Radical and His American Intellectual Roots*. University Park: Pennsylvania State University Press.

Tiryakian, Edward A., ed. 1963. *Sociological Theory, Values, and Sociocultural Change: Essays in Honor of Pitirim A. Sorokin*. New York: Harper Torchbooks.

———. 1988. Sociology's Dostoyevski: Pitirim A. Sorokin. *The World and I* 3: 569–581.

Toby, Jackson. 1980. Samuel Stouffer: Social Research as a Calling. In *Sociological Traditions from Generation to Generation*, edited by Robert Merton and Matilda White Riley, 131–151. Norwood, N.J.: Ablex.

Toynbee, Arnold J. 1963. Sorokin's Philosophy of History. In *Pitirim A. Sorokin in Review*, edited by Phillip J. Allen, 67–94. Durham: Duke University Press.

Trask, David F. 1984. *User's Guide to the FOIA*. Bloomington, Ind.: Organization of American Historians.

Trent, James W. 1987. A Decade of Declining Involvement: American Sociology in the Field of Child Development, the 1920s. *Sociological Studies of Child* Development 2: 11–37.

Tucker, Charles W. 1988. Herbert Blumer: A Pilgrimage with Pragmatism. *Symbolic Interaction* 11: 99–124.

Turner, William, W. 1993. *Hoover's F.B.I.* New York: Thunder's Mouth Press.

Veblen, Thorstein. 1953. *The Theory of the Leisure Class*. New York: Mentor.

Weber, Max. 1930. *The Protestant Ethic and the Spirit of Capitalism*, translated by Talcott Parsons. London: Allen and Unwin.

Wellman, David. 1988. The Politics of Herbert Blumer's Sociological Method. *Symbolic Interaction* 11: 59–68.

Wiener, Jon. 1989. Bringing Nazis to the U.S.: Talcott Parsons's Role. *The Nation* 248: 289, 306–309.

Williams, Robin M. Jr. 1980. Pitirim A. Sorokin: Master Sociologist and Prophet. In *Sociological Traditions from Generation to Generation*, edited by Robert K. Merton and Matilda White Riley, 93–107. Norwood, N.J.: Ablex.

———. 1980. Talcott Parsons: The Stereotypes and the Realities. *American Sociologist* 15: 64–66.

Wiseman, Jacqueline P. 1987. In Memoriam: Herbert Blumer (1900–1987). *Journal of Contemporary Ethnography* 16: 243–249.

Zimmerman, Carle C. 1968. *Sorokin: The World's Greatest Sociologist*. Saskatoon: University of Saskatchewan Press.

Bibliography (2004)

Aftergood, Steven. 2002. Making Sense of Government Information Restrictions. *Issues in Science and Technology* 18(4) Summer: 25–26.

American Civil Liberties Union. 2002. Urge Congress to Protect Against Domestic Spying! *ACLU Website* 3 October: http://www.aclu.org/NationalSecurity/NationalSecurity.cfm?ID=9950&c=110.

Benner, Jeffrey. 2002. Closing the Books. *Reason* 34(5): 33–35.

Berlet, Chip. 1991. Hunting the "Green Menace." *The Humanist* July/August: 24–32.

Bilsker, Richard. 2000. Stalking the Sociological Imagination. *Humanity and Society* 24(3): 318–19.

Blackstock, Nelson. 1988. Cointelpro: The FBI's Secret War on Political Freedom. New York: Pathfinder.

David Brin. 1998. *The Transparent Society: Will Technology Force Us to Choose Between Privacy and Freedom?* Reading, Pa.: Perseus Books.

Cate, Fred H. 1997. *Privacy in the Information Age*. Washington, D.C.: The Brookings Institute.

Chang, Nancy. 2002. *Silencing Political Dissent: How Post-September 11 Anti-Terrorism Measures Threaten Our Civil Liberties*. New York: Seven Stories.

Clymer, Adam. 2003. Government Openness at Issue as Bush Holds on to Records. *New York Times* 3 January: A1, A16.

Christensen, John O. 1990. *The FBI, Libraries, and the Library Awareness Program Controversy: Selected References*. Monticello, Ill.: Vance Bibliographies.

Coben, Stanely. 2001. Review Essay: J. Edgar Hoover. *Journal of Social History* 34(3) Spring: 703–706.

Croog, Charles F. 1992. FBI Political Surveillance and the Isolationist-Interventionist Debate. *Historian* 54(3) Spring: 441–59.

Cunningham, David. 2001. Stalking the Sociological Imagination. *Contemporary Sociology* 30(5): 525–26.

Davis, James Kirkpatrick. 1997. *Assault on the Left: The FBI and the Sixties Antiwar Movement*. Westport, Conn.: Praeger.

Dempsey, Jack X. and David Cole. 2002. *Terrorism and the Constitution: Sacrificing Civil Liberties in the Name of National Security*. Washington, D.C.: First Amendment Foundation.

Donner, Frank J. 1980. *The Age of Surveillance: The Aims and Methods of America's Political Intelligence System*. New York: Alfred A. Knopf.

Douglas, Charles M. 1999. Franklin D. Roosevelt, J. Edgar Hoover, and FBI Political Surveillance. *USA Today Magazine* 128(2652): 74–77.

Etzioni, Amitai. 1999. *The Limits of Privacy*. New York: Basis Books.

Fagan, Laureen. 2003. Toying With Spying. *South Bend Tribune* 21 January: C1–2.

Foerstel, Herbert N. 1991. *Surveillance in the Stacks: The FBI's Library Awareness Program*. Westport, Conn.: Greenwood.

Foucault, Michel. 1995. *Discipline and Punish: The Birth of the Prison*. Translated by Alan Sheridan. New York: Vintage.

Frank, Michael. 2001. Stalking the Sociological Imagination. *Science & Society* 65(3): 409–11.

Fried, Richard M. 1990. *Nightmare in Red: The McCarthy Era in Perspective*. New York: Oxford University Press.

Geis, Gilbert and Colin Goff. 1992. Lifting the Cover from Undercover Operations: J. Edgar Hoover and Some of the Other Criminologists. *Crime, Law and Social Change* 18: 91–104.

Giddens, Anthony A. 1987. *The Nation-State and Violence*. Berkeley: University of California.

Gotham, Kevin. 1992. A Study in American Agitation: J. Edgar Hoover's Symbolic Construction of the Communist Menace. *Mid-American Review of Sociology* 16(2): 57–70.

Graham, Mary. 2002. *Democracy by Disclosure: The Rise of Technopopulism*. Washington, D.C.: The Brookings Institution.

Haines, Gerald K. and David A. Langbart. 1993. *Unlocking the Files of the FBI: A Guide to its Record and Classification System*. Wilmington, Del.: Scholarly Resources.

Halstuk, Martin E. 2002. In Review: The Threat to Freedom of Information. *Columbia Journalism Review* 40(5) Jan/Feb: 8.

Holt, Pat M. 1995. *Secret Intelligence and Public Policy: A Dilemma of Democracy*. Washington, D.C.: Congressional Quarterly Press.

Horowitz, Irving Louis. 1970. Reactionary Immortality: The Private Life in Public Testimony of John Edgar Hoover. *Catalyst* 5 (Summer): 64–75.

Hunter, Richard. 2002. *World Without Secrets: Business, Crime and Privacy in the Age of Ubiquitous Computing*. New York: John Wiley & Sons.

Jerome, Fred. 2002. *The Einstein Files: J. Edgar Hoover's Secret War Against the World's Most Famous Scientist*. New York: St. Martin's Press.

Kessler, Ronald. 2002. *The Bureau: The Secret History of the FBI*. New York: St. Martin's.

Lazarsfeld, Paul F. and Wagner Thielens, Jr. 1958. *The Academic Mind: Social Scientists in a Time of Crisis*. Glencoe, Ill.: The Free Press.

Lyotard, Jean-Francois. 1984. *The Postmodern Condition: A Report on Knowledge*. Translated by Geoff Bennington and Brian Massumi.

Marx, Gary T. 1990. *Undercover Police Surveillance in America*. Berkeley: University of California Press.

Murray, Robert K. 1964. *Red Scare: A Study of National Hysteria, 1919–1920*. New York: McGraw-Hill.

Nash, Jay Robert. 1972. *Citizen Hoover: A Critical Study of the Life and Times of J. Edgar Hoover and His FBI*. Chicago: Welson Hall.

Noakes, John A. 1994. A "New Breed of Detective": The Rise of the FBI Special Agent. *Studies in Law, Politics and Society* 14: 25–42.

———. 1995. Using FBI Files for Historical Sociology. *Qualitative Sociology* 18(2): 271–86.

O'Driscoll, Patrick. 2003. Big-time Security to Accompany Big Game. *USA Today* 21 January: 9C.

Olmstead, Kathryn S. 1996. *Challenging the Secret Government: The Post-Watergate Investigations of the CIA and FBI*. Chapel Hill: University of North Carolina.

Poveda, Tony G. 1982. The FBI and Domestic Intelligence: Technocratic or Public Relations Triumph. *Crime and Delinquency* 28(2) April: 194–210.

———. 1990. *Lawlessness and Reform: The FBI in Transition*. Pacific Grove: Brooks/Cole.

Powers, Richard Gid. 1987. *Secrecy and Power: The Life of J. Edgar Hoover*. New York: Free Press.

Price, David. 1997. Anthropological Research and the Freedom of Information Act. *CAM: Cultural Anthroplogy Methods* 9(1): 12–15.

———. 2000. Anthropologists as Spies. *The Nation* 271(16) 20 November: 24–27.

———. 2001. Spying on Radicals. *Radical History Review* 79(Winter): 169–72.

Rosen, Jeffrey. 2001. *The Unwanted Gaze: The Destruction of Privacy in America*. New York: Vintage.

Rutherford Institute. 2002. *Forfeiting "Enduring Freedom" for "Homeland Security": A Constitutional Analysis of the USA PATRIOT Act of 2001 and the Justice Department's Anti-Terrorism Initiatives*. Charlottesville, VA: The Rutherford Institute.

Schmidt, Regin. 2000. *Red Scare: FBI and the Origins of Anticommunism in the United States, 1919–1943*. Copenhagen: Museum Tusculanum Press.

Schneier, Bruce and David Banisar, eds. 1997. *The Electronic Privacy Papers: Documents on the Battle for Privacy in the Age of Surveillance*. New York: John Wiley & Sons.

Stanley, Jay and Barry Steinhardt. 2003. *Bigger Monster, Weaker Chains: The Growth of the American Surveillance Society*. New York: American Civil Liberties Union.

Theoharis, Athan. 1990. Dissent and the State: Unleashing the FBI, 1917–1985. *The History Teacher* 24(1): 42–52.

———, ed. 1991. *From the Secret Files of J. Edgar Hoover*. Chicago: Ivan R. Dee.

———. 1995. *J. Edgar Hoover, Sex, and Crimes: An Historical Antidote*. Chicago: Ivan R. Dee.

———. 1999. "Stalking the Sociological Imagination." *CHOICE* 37(2): 1205.

———. 2002. *Chasing Spies: How the FBI Failed in Counterintelligence But Promoted the Politics of McCarthyism in the Cold War Years*. Chicago: Ivan R. Dee.

Theoharis, Athan G., Tony G. Poveda, Susan Rosenfeld and Richard Gid Powers. 2000. *The FBI: A Comprehensive Reference*. New York: Checkmark Books.

Thomas, Douglas and Brian Loader, eds. 2002. *Cybercrime: Law Enforcement, Security and Surveillance in the Information Age*. New York: Routledge.

Whitaker, Reg. 1999. *The End of Privacy: How Total Surveillance is Becoming a Reality*. New York: Free Press.

Index